# THE STRATEGIC CAREER

# THE STRATEGIC CAREER

## Let Business Principles Guide You

**Bill Barnett**

**STANFORD BUSINESS BOOKS**

An Imprint of Stanford University Press • Stanford, California

Stanford University Press
Stanford, California



Special discounts for bulk quantities of Stanford Business Books are available to corporations, professional associations, and other organizations. For details and discount information, contact the special sales department of Stanford University Press. Tel: (650) 736-1782, Fax: (650) 736-1784

Printed in the United States of America on acid-free, archival-quality paper

Library of Congress Cataloging-in-Publication Data

Barnett, Bill, 1947– author.
The strategic career : let business principles guide you / Bill Barnett.
pages cm
Includes bibliographical references and index.
ISBN 978-0-8047-9358-2 (cloth : alk. paper)
1. Career development. 2. Strategic planning. I. Title.
HF5381.B318 2015
650.1—dc23

2014042502

ISBN 978-0-8047-9556-2 (electronic)

# CONTENTS

# ACKNOWLEDGMENTS

**I GOT THE IDEA** to tie business strategy concepts to careers while at Yale, so that's where I'll begin. Barry Nalebuff arranged my invitation to teach business strategy there; he's provided wise counsel on many topics over the years, including on this book. Stan Gartska gave me the green light to offer my first career course. Once I started preparing the course, I discovered Amy Wrzesniewski's research into jobs, careers, and callings; that became a core concept in my course and now in this book. And Sharon Oster first suggested that I turn the course into a book.

I'm not sure I'd have been able to complete the research into careers without the opportunity to teach it repeatedly and learn from that experience. Rice provided an ideal platform for that, while also feeding my desire to add value to students just when they needed it. Two people helped me get started at Rice: Bob Clarke and Jeff Fleming; K. Ramesh has supported my program since then.

The core idea behind this book is the connection between career strategizing and the business strategy principles that guided much of my consulting career. I can't possibly mention everyone who contributed to that, but here's one. The late Ali Hanna led the Microeconomics Center when I first got involved. He then paved the way for me to assume that leadership role when he shifted to other McKinsey responsibilities. It was from there that I became Strategy Practice leader. That led to different things in my life, including this book. Ali was a very special person in general, and he left some prized fingerprints on me.

I've had a lot of helpers on the substance of the career/business connection.

Most important are the people I've counseled and the students I've taught. I hope I helped you set the right course and that you're now on the way to callings. What you might not have realized is how much I learned from our discussions. Stories about thirty-three of you are here in the book, and the many others who aren't mentioned in the book also shaped my thinking in important ways. There also were search consultants who provided advice on how to network with people like them and on some of the other topics here, together with career counselors who commented on my blog and shared ideas in live conversations. I'd like to mention all these names, or at least the top forty or fifty, but all those discussions were confidential. Please know how much I appreciate your role in this.

One thing I noticed after I left McKinsey was how much I missed colleagues and the natural way they can both critique work and stimulate thinking. I've especially appreciated those people who read draft materials and gave me their reactions. Several read an entire draft. A few (to whom I guess I owe an apology) read an early draft before I'd worked out the main ideas. I hope I haven't omitted anyone from this list: Jim Balloun, Karen Blumenthal, Nina Cortell, Kevin Coyne, Brian Fisher, Bruce Frankel, Rik Kirkland, Lee Koffler, Suzanne Nimocks, JJ Richards, Scott Sonenshein, Chris Turner, Patrick Viguerie, and Dave Wenner.

The book reflects the first-class editing advice I've received, advice that included both substantive reactions to my ideas and diplomatically put comments on style. Courtney Cashman from Harvard reviews my blog posts. She's helped me simplify, clarify, and fit into the blog's seven- to eight-hundred-word format. Margo Fleming is my Stanford editor for this book. She not only envisioned the opportunity for the book to contribute to people's lives but also taught me more than a few things about how to present these ideas. I've been going to school with some great teachers. I'll also mention the book's graphics. That's a long way from my signature skill, and Morag Everill made them happen.

I'll conclude with my family. Alice is a valued discussion partner on most everything. She's listened to countless stories about my stories. She's become a career strategist too. I got lucky the day I met her at the bus stop in Arlington, Virginia. And there are my children and sons-in-law, Sandy and Zak, Lauren and Ross, and Kate. You too have helped me think about the book. I hope there's a payback if these ideas help you plan your futures.

# THE STRATEGIC CAREER

# INTRODUCTION

**FIND THE WORK YOU'RE MEANT FOR** and you'll be better at it, your accomplishments will expand, you'll be happier, and you'll find personal satisfaction. You have the freedom to seek this work, but with this freedom comes the need to choose wisely and the risk of disappointment. The twin challenges of globalization and IT-driven productivity increase the pressure.

How to set your course? First, pick a field of work where you'll meet your values, pursue your interests, and make good use of your strengths. That field is your target "market." Know why you're the best solution to your target employer's needs. Then pursue a portfolio of initiatives to make your "product" highly competitive in that market and to grow your "marketing" muscle to uncover opportunities there. Execute that strategy with productive searches for opportunities that can get you started toward reaching those long-term aspirations. Make sound decisions about which opportunity to accept. Finally, follow good practices to check progress and stay on track.

This book shows how to chart your course through these activities. It presents a distinctive approach, drawing on business strategy principles for career strategy ideas. It shows you how to develop winning strategies and in the process build skill at career strategy. Much is at stake.

The starting point for this book was my experience as a business strategy consultant. In my twenty-three years at McKinsey & Company, I helped clients assess big strategy decisions like mergers, capital investments, and new product introductions. I not only served clients but also led the firm's Strategy Practice. We pioneered new ways to help develop strategy—for example, game theory and uncertainty management, two concepts that now help people develop winning career strategies.

Even though I was a strategy consultant, my strategy career didn't begin there. It goes back to my work on public policy issues in the State Department and the Office of the Secretary of Defense. It goes back to my strategy and policy courses at Harvard Business School and at West Point. It may even trace to my interest in chess and board games in high school.

This book also reflects my experience on the people side. I directed McKinsey's recruiting on several MBA campuses. I ran the process to determine which associates my office would recommend for partnership. I led personnel committee discussions to determine the evaluations of partners in three other offices and then did the follow-up coaching. I helped others think through their personal strategies to have the most impact within McKinsey.

I regularly found myself in the role of career counselor. Junior consultants sought my advice when wondering whether to stay in McKinsey or leave. Friends and clients asked about their careers. Some asked me to talk to their children. Students in the business strategy courses I taught at Yale sought career advice. I would apply to their career choices the same business strategy principles I was teaching. I now know that that approach makes good sense, and I believe I provided constructive ideas, but looking back on that now, I see I was winging it. I was using the strategic approach without a career-centered body of knowledge behind it.

The field of business strategy is well researched and proven. Business school professors, consultants, and others have built careers based on their expertise in business strategy. I did.

What I've discovered is that although the specifics are different, business strategy and career strategy are conceptually identical. When people deploy business concepts to plan their careers, they come up with more ideas, better assessments of those ideas, better decisions, and stronger conviction. Applying business strategy concepts to careers is a fundamental innovation.

Executives who are involved with these business concepts in their day-to-day work know the concepts and easily relate them to career choices. So do the leaders of public institutions and charities. MBA students who are studying these concepts find the career connection a natural extension of their other classes. And people in professions, such as attorneys, physicians, engineers, and teachers, recognize and use these concepts. These people are this book's target audience. The strategy tools work well for them.

I took this linkage between business and careers and established a new career strategy course, which I taught at Yale and now teach at Rice. I've used the same approach in many other counseling situations. I drew on those experiences to write this book.

Let's go back a few years to the time when I created that first career strategy course. I was confident this was a big idea, but I needed to prove it. I needed to show that it actually would lead to better career decisions. I had nine months before the first day of class.

I led with my own expertise. I listed the strategy approaches I knew worked well in business settings—for example, enterprise visioning, development of a value proposition, market research, game theory, and scenario planning. I'd emphasized these topics at McKinsey and in the business strategy class I was teaching at Yale.

They were the natural place to begin. I imagined how they might apply to careers.

Armed with these hypotheses, I looked for connections to my own career decisions. I interviewed people about their past strategy choices. Most important, I tried out my ideas. I sought opportunities to help people make career decisions by explicitly applying these concepts with them. I learned a lot from all these people. They were the most important part of my investigation. They became the sources for the first cases in the course and some of the stories in this book.

Rigor was critical to success in business consulting, so I also hunted for ways to approach career choices rigorously, with facts and logical discipline. The benefits of rigor in career choice quickly became evident. In both business strategy and career strategy, people who fully understand what's going on do better than those who don't.

I read into the topic. I explored the literature on careers and on related topics, such as the research of economists and psychologists into the sources of happiness, satisfaction, and personal resilience.

When I put all this together, I had the content for my first career strategy class. It went reasonably well, though it fell short of what I hoped to be able to do. I learned from that experience and from the students, learned from my ongoing career counseling, spoke to professionals in the area (executive search consultants and career counselors), revised the course, began writing this book, and taught the course again. Then I did all that for another year and then another and another. This book now embodies that collective experience and learning.

So how can business strategy concepts drive career strategy? I'll illustrate that connection with previews of two of the stories you'll see later in the book.

How many people get the chance to consider taking a COO or CEO position three or four times a year? Steve, fifty-four, does just that. The calls come from his professional network. And the biggest surprise about his network is its size—a grand total of three people. Can this be possible?

Steve knows that successful business strategies result from winning value propositions—the benefits a product offers to a target segment of the market, along with actions that deliver those benefits. He also knows that a narrowly constructed value proposition almost always is best, as long as the market for it isn't too small.

With this strategic concept in mind, Steve framed a very tight value proposition for himself—what I call a personal value proposition (PVP). In his words, he targets leadership positions in privately held industrials—"operations-intensive companies who can benefit from significant performance improvement."

Steve's PVP is narrow, but clear. Three people know Steve well, understand his skills, and know where he'd fit. Two are leaders of firms who invest in companies like Steve's targets, and one is a search consultant who focuses on similar companies. Beyond viewing him as a potential candidate to fill a job, they value their relationship with him. Seldom interested in the job they call about, Steve always tries to provide useful insights about the position they're filling. Calling Steve is time well spent.

Here's another situation where business concepts are guiding a career. Imagine you're a management consultant with a top-tier firm who expects to be elected a partner within the next year. Out of the blue, you get an appealing offer to join a highly regarded company. You make the startling decision not only to decline that offer but also to resign from the consulting firm and look for something else. What could make you do that?

That's what happened to Isabel, thirty-three, who discovered some surprises when she applied her strategy skills to her own career. One tool she regularly used with clients was to construct a matrix to rate alternatives against objectives in a rigorous way. When she applied this tool to herself, she realized that the consulting life that had been a perfect fit a few years before no longer matched her needs. She still valued colleagues, client relationships, interesting problems, and the professional culture, but she was troubled by her difficulty tamping down the intensity of her job and by the time spent away from her children. These issues may have been in the back of her mind already, but until she consciously evaluated her current situation, she hadn't recognized how much she'd changed.

Isabel wanted the new position only if there was a plausible path to the top. As she would when conducting business scenario planning, she tested that path by looking ahead five and ten years and imagining how things might develop. Once she realized that advancement would require transfers to different cities, she knew she had to turn down the offer. Moves like that were unacceptable. They'd torpedo her husband's career.

No one can know what Isabel would have done without this rigorous assessment, but few people quit when near partner election. Her assessment gave her the strong conviction needed to act. She says it best: "Call me crazy, but in a year when jobs were scarce, I decided to quit and look for a job! Putting it on paper made everything transparent and easy. . . . The assessment took the emotions out." Isabel then adopted a similar approach to look into alternative fields of work, to identify specific opportunities, and then to decide to accept an offer.

Isabel conducted a career strategy study. Steve was intuitive. Those assessment processes are very different, but both of them use business strategy concepts to plot careers. Both people are highly capable. That's essential to success. Strategic thinking allows them to make the most of their talents.

This book fleshes out Isabel's and Steve's stories more completely, and tells what happened to thirty-one others. All these people care about their work lives and hope to accomplish a lot. They're ambitious. Most used sound concepts to guide their strategies and now enjoy the results. A few failed to do that and suffered the consequences.

The surprising job offer was the trigger that led Isabel to reassess her career, but you don't have to wait for something like that to get you started. Let this book be your trigger! Let this book become the stimulus that leads you to a fresh career strategy.

There's another way this book draws on my management consulting experience. The success of an idea is defined not just by its intellectual accomplishment but, more important, by its impact. No one retains a consultant without expecting to do things differently and to benefit from that change. And no one picks up a career book without looking forward to better decisions and enhanced prospects.

I hope you'll use these concepts to develop your winning career strategy. Many people who've seen these concepts did just that. They took the ball and ran with it.

I've also seen people who liked these ideas fail to take advantage of them. Some assumed they could benefit without going through the rigorous process. They skimmed the surface and got little back. Others couldn't imagine how to begin. When I was with them in the role of counselor or professor, I could push for good applications. But I won't be with you when you read this book. Explaining the concepts isn't enough.

I know from consulting that people are most likely to reap the benefits from a new idea if it meets three tough tests: the idea must be comprehensive to build confidence and understanding, the way to execute the idea must be clear, and the presentation must be interesting and memorable. I resolved to write this book so that it would pass all three tests.

First, the book touches all the bases. You can go more deeply into some of these topics if you choose to (the academic research behind callings or how to use social media in careers, for example), but this book's structure is comprehensive. If you apply these concepts to your career, you'll be taking a highly strategic approach.

Second, the book demonstrates how to implement each career strategy concept. The fifteen chapters are—at a high level—the fifteen steps to a strategic career. Within each chapter, moreover, you'll find step-by-step exercises or other activities to apply that chapter's overall concept. The chapters and their associated activities put you in position to develop a competitive career strategy. This is a "how-to" book.

Third, stories of real people in real situations making real decisions show these concepts in action. Each of these stories reports on how the concepts worked for an individual, but names have been changed to ensure anonymity. In a few cases, I also altered nonmaterial facts when individuals asked me to. I hope that you find the stories interesting, that they stimulate your thinking and imagination, and that you naturally begin applying the concepts to yourself.

Notice this last point: you'll need to apply the concepts to yourself. This book helps build career strategy skill. It doesn't provide the answer that's right for you. Craig, whom you'll meet later, summed up what he'd gotten from our discussion this way: "I sort of hoped you'd say, 'Here's the deal; here's how to hit it big.' But no. What we've done is think about how we got here and where we are. I got a perspective on the future. I thought it through and discovered conclusions." There was no way for me to give Craig his answer. I couldn't know what was best for him. I did provide ways to help him structure his thinking and ensure that it was complete. That's where his conviction and confidence came from. And that's exactly what I hope you'll get out of this book.

•

This suggests a question that may already have occurred to you: "If I read this book and seriously engage in the exercises, will that help my career?" It's a fair question, but also a hard question.

Different people experience different outcomes, and there are good reasons for that. Some people must confront pressing decisions, unlike others who have the luxury of time. Differences in urgency naturally lead to different decisions.

What people bring to the party also differs, sometimes by a lot. Some people already know themselves reasonably well and are familiar with their field of interest. They lack strategies, but when they apply the exercises you'll see in this book, they understand their choices, make commitments to that field, and draw up concrete plans. They can't be absolutely sure that's where they'll find the happiness and meaning they want, but those plans both increase their chance for success in that field and put them in a good position to adjust plans and perhaps to shift direction as they learn from the experience.

Others start out behind. They aren't close to being able to commit to one field or another. They first must reflect on their strengths and aspirations and explore different possibilities. They usually select a field to investigate in depth or to actually try out, without making a full commitment to it. Different starting points naturally lead to different results.

I have some data on results from a group of people who've used this approach in a comprehensive way—the MBA students in my Career Strategy class. That half-semester elective engages students in most of the material in this book. Some register for the course to help land a great job offer before graduation. Others have that job, but want a long-term plan.

On the first day of class, their career strategy skills may not be much different than yours. They're bright, they've had good work experiences, and they've completed most of their MBA courses. Most would make a good first impression on a potential employer, but few have thought strategically about their career or have imagined job search as a skill they can cultivate. Some were conducting their searches haphazardly.

My two most recent classes had a total of forty-three students. Here's an overview of the outcomes.

First, the short-term: By the end of the course, almost all the students (forty-one of the forty-three) committed to short-term career objectives (a field of work, a role, or a specific position to target). The other two continued exploring possibilities. Of the forty-one who set short-term objectives, nine were in fields that were different or at least somewhat different from those they'd considered before. Thirty-five completed plans to achieve their short-term objectives.

Now to the long-term: Twenty-seven of the forty-three students adopted long-term aspirations. Of those twenty-seven, eleven set new directions. The others already had the ideas in the back of their mind, but had never gotten serious about pursuing them. Twenty students prepared plans to move toward their long-term objectives.

These are good outcomes. I can't promise you a career epiphany, but if you apply these concepts, you can expect results similar to the results these students found: deeper insight and the prospect of making commitments and setting plans to get there.

Even if you've never thought much about career strategy, you have one. Your strategy is the net result of your experiences, your skills, and your knowledge, together with the future options and limitations they imply. If your current strategy feels incomplete or wrong or if changes are coming, you need a new strategy. Deploy the same strategic concepts you would if you were developing your institution's strategy. Use at least the same level of rigor. Be your own consultant. Think of Yourself, Inc. as the client.

This book is your step-by-step guide to that assessment. As you see in Figure I-1, the first four parts of the book show you how to develop a winning career strategy, and the last part shows how

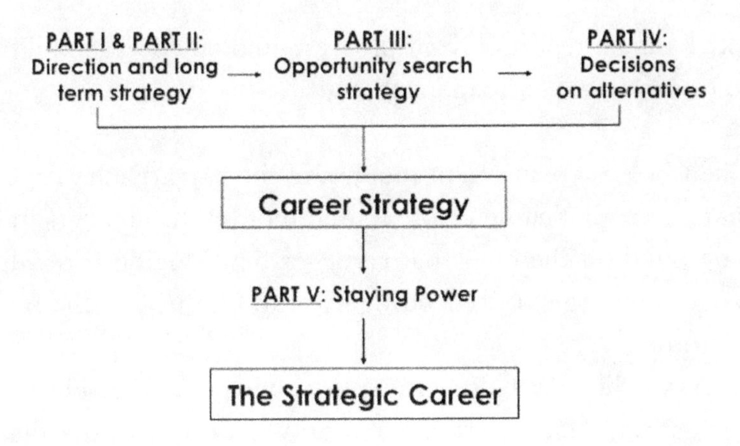


**FIGURE I-1** Architecture of the Book

to pursue that strategy over time or how to adjust when things change.

Part I shows you how to set long-term direction. You'll see how to recognize your fundamental values, spot distinctive strengths, identify and evaluate fields of work, and integrate all that into the personal value proposition you hope to build over time.

Fundamental strategy is more than a direction. Part II shows how to set the long-term plan of initiatives to reach that long-term target aspiration.

The first step in this long-term plan often is a search for the right opportunity to get started. Or there may be other reasons to seek a new opportunity. How to identify opportunities and how to get offers is the topic of Part III.

Next comes the decision whether to accept an offer or keep looking. Part IV shows you how to evaluate alternatives against objectives, manage the associated uncertainty, and decide what's best.

You'll like some of the things that happen in your life, others will disappoint, and all those events can take your eye off the ball. You'll benefit from tools to keep yourself on track as you deal with these challenges—the subject of Part V. These tools include a personal annual report on your progress, and practices to build resilience in the face of disappointment.

The whole is greater than the sum of the parts. Each part builds on the one that came before it, and most of the chapters in each part build on the ones that came earlier. Moving through this sequence is logical. I encourage you to go through the book in this order.

As you do that, I also encourage you to be flexible. The insights you gain in a later section may lead you to revisit work that you did earlier. Learning leading to more learning is natural. Strategic thinkers engage in this style of iterative learning all the time. I'll elaborate on this at several points in the book.

Although following this sequence makes the material most powerful, people will be in different situations when they pick up this book. Some will feel urgency; others won't. Some will be evaluating an offer; others won't have started a search. With that in mind, here are suggestions about how to proceed if you're in one of two situations.

If your job search is urgent, begin with most of Part I to help you get clear on your values, strengths, fields of interest, and long-term personal value proposition. Then turn to Part III on how to conduct a winning job search.

If you're reading this book to help you decide whether to accept an offer, begin with Part I on your values and strengths, and familiarize yourself with the learning tactics described there. That will give you a solid foundation from which to deploy the evaluation methodologies from Part IV to help you make a wise decision.

One other tip: if you're going to follow an alternative path, you'll do best if you read the book through without doing the exercises, before focusing on one part or another. That way, you'll be approaching your immediate challenge with a full appreciation of the strategic approach.

In the first sentence of this introduction, I pointed to a bold and hard-to-attain goal for career strategy: to find the work you're meant for. Some people doubt that anyone can do that at his or her desk; they emphasize learning from experience and are skeptical about the benefits of rigorous career strategizing. Although I fully agree that experience can be a great teacher, the more important question is this: How to be a great student of experience? That's where the strategic mind-set is most powerful. You'll learn more from your experience if you target, pursue, and secure the right opportunities, periodically reassess how your work life is developing, and then make well-reasoned decisions about what to do next. No aimless trials, but no bullheaded insistence that you got everything right at the outset. Do this well, and you'll be assembling The Strategic Career.

I'll offer one final suggestion here in the introduction. Reading this book and doing the exercises will give you an excellent prospect of finding fresh insights and making better decisions. That will be a fine result, but you can do better.

My suggestion is this: Work together with someone else who is developing career strategy. Better yet, do it with several others. Read the book in parallel, do the exercises on your own, meet (or conference-call) after each chapter (or after a few chapters), share the ways everyone conducted the exercises, and critique one another's work. You'll encourage one another to do the exercises, you'll learn from seeing how your colleagues implement the concepts, and you'll benefit from their reactions to your work. You'll be developing strategies together while building skill at career strategizing. Your experience will be something like sitting in my classroom. In fact, you'll have created your own "class."

## Part I

# CAREER DIRECTION

Choose a job you love, and you will never
have to work a day in your life.
**CONFUCIUS**

Your work is going to fill a large part of your life,
and the only way to be truly satisfied is to do
what you believe is great work. And the only
way to do great work is to love what you do.
**STEVE JOBS**

There are three things extremely hard,
Steel, a Diamond, and to know oneself.
**BENJAMIN FRANKLIN**

**YOUR STARTING POINT** is to determine which field of work or which role to pursue, or at least to determine where to start. This fundamental direction setting is critical. It's also difficult. Answers can be elusive.

To do this well, you'll need to blend diverse styles of inquiry. Direction setting is a deeply personal endeavor. Intuitively seek insight and revelation. Look within yourself, identify your intrinsic strengths, sense where you might find passion, and learn from what happens to you. Imagine where your interests and values may lead. Direction setting also requires an external perspective. Conduct a structured and rational search. Investigate interesting fields, learn

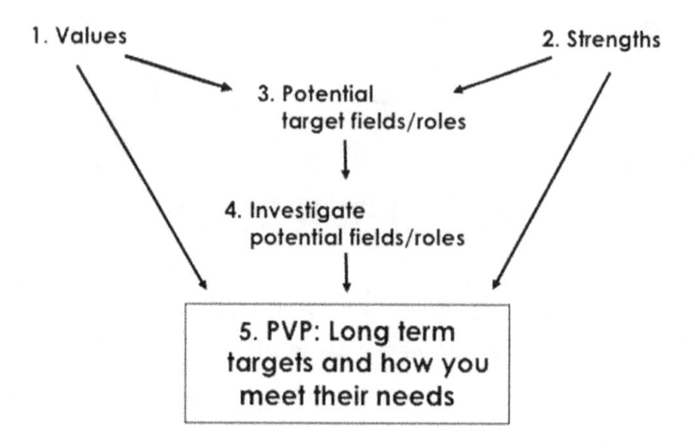


**FIGURE PI-1** Part I: Develop Your Aspirational Personal Value Proposition

what people do there, and evaluate how you'd fit. And direction setting requires experimentation. Try out your ideas and then judge where to place your bets.

The five chapters of Part I present the progression of activities that incorporate these diverse ways of learning. Follow them to set your long-term career direction, as you see in Figure PI-1. I express that direction in terms of the aspirational personal value proposition (PVP)—your target field or role for the long term, what's required to succeed there, and why you match those requirements.

Chapter 1 shows how to identify the fundamental values you derive from your work. Much like a founder setting a vision for the new company, you'll begin your career strategy journey with values and aspirations.

Knowing your strengths is critical. You should seek to work in an area where you can use your strengths every day. You'll enjoy it and accomplish a great deal. Chapter 2 demonstrates how to assess your strengths, parallel to the way strategists and marketers evaluate products before bringing them to market.

Potential fields and roles come next. How to imagine fields and roles that reflect your fundamental values and strengths is presented in Chapter 3.

On the other side of the ledger are the characteristics of different fields and roles and what's required to thrive in them. Chapter 4 shows how to investigate them, following study processes like the ones business strategists use to assess industries and companies.

Everything comes together when you set your aspirational PVP for the long term, a concept like the value propositions that executives hope to deliver when kicking off new product development. That's the subject of Chapter 5.

Moving through these five steps is a proven process. Everyone I've known who developed career strategy in this way uncovered valuable insights. Most set aspirations and plans for their futures.

Chapter 1

# FUNDAMENTAL VALUES LEADING TO A CALLING

**A BUSINESS FOUNDER STARTS** with his or her interests, ideas, and skills and determines how to meet the needs of the market. The founder designs products to fit the market and establishes the capabilities to manufacture and sell them. In established companies, fundamental aspirations guide decisions big and small. When contemplating a big strategy shift, corporate leaders test that shift against those aspirations. If the shift doesn't fit, that raises questions about whether it's a good idea.

Just as they do in business, uplifting aspirations can guide your work life. They motivate: the word *aspiration* suggests hope and opportunity. They lead to action: aspirations you believe in will target personal growth, stimulate initiatives to position yourself to be competitive, and guide your search for opportunities. Before your strategy can take you to your desired destination, you need to know where you wish to go.

Determining what you want from work, however, can be a tall order. Work is a financial necessity for almost everyone, and that work sometimes will require sacrifice. Work can be drudgery, but it also can be fun and exciting. The competition can be energizing. There's no perfect scorecard to consult for answers. Digging into aspirations is a big part of career strategizing.

My goal in this chapter is to show you how to structure thinking about your own values related to work. I'll begin by describing the job/career/calling framework. I'll take a deep dive into the factors that underpin this framework and then describe how to use it to guide your own thinking.

## Jobs, Careers, and Callings

What matters most to you at work? Most people must wrestle with this question to get to bedrock values. This inside-out thinking is highly personal, but you don't have to do it without guidance. The experiences of others offer lessons into which aspirations provide the greatest prospect of happiness and satisfaction.

The best framework I've seen of attitudes toward work is the *job/career/calling* model, introduced to me by Amy Wrzesniewski from Yale:[1]

- *Job*—People focus "on the material benefits of work to the relative exclusion of other kinds of meaning and fulfillment." They may contain time at work, spend some work time thinking about what they'll do after work, and resent occasions when work requirements expand.
- *Career*—"The increased pay, prestige, and status that come with promotion and advancement are the dominant focus of their work."
- *Calling*—People "work not for financial rewards or for advancement, but for the fulfillment that doing the work brings. . . . The work is an end in itself, and is usually associated with the belief that the work contributes to the greater good and makes the world a better place."

Investigating people from different walks of life, Wrzesniewski found that roughly a third fall into each category. (Throughout the book, I use the words *job* and *career* in a conventional way. In this part of Chapter 1, however, I use those words in the particular way defined in the preceding list.)

When I first saw this model, I smiled to myself and nodded. The job/career/calling model captured much of what I'd experienced in my own work life and what I'd observed in others. I knew that if I could use this idea to help people find callings or at least begin their journeys, I'd have something big.

When I began the research that led to this book, therefore, a principal goal was to classify people among these categories and learn what causes them to end up in one category or another. I did that by talking to executives, managers, and professionals, most in their thirties and forties. As I deployed this emerging thinking into the classroom, I added MBA students to the mix, most of whom were in their late twenties and early thirties. I asked about motivations and values, along with accomplishments and how they felt about their work lives. I'll describe what I've learned about these differences in a moment, but first let's get some misconceptions about callings out of the way.

Some people hear the word *calling* and assume that a calling requires a great deal of self-sacrifice and denial. They imagine people working with charities or religious institutions—an extreme version being Mother Theresa in Calcutta's slums. They imagine people in lower-paid positions than they otherwise could have. I'm sure some calling people are like that, but that level of sacrifice and denial isn't what I've found. Some highly paid corporate leaders have callings; others don't. Some Legal Aid attorneys have callings; others are there because it was the only position they found. Some people in public service roles bring career or job mentalities to their work. Some physicians are healers; others are in it for the money.

None of the calling people I've known live in conditions anywhere close to those of Mother Teresa's life. Although they work hard, most of these people find their lives appealing—with average to above-average incomes and not much difference in hours at work.

Many assume that once you find a calling, it's with you for the rest of your life. In the stories in this book, you'll see some people who, so far at least, are pursuing the calling they first found. But you'll also see others who find callings, lose them, and then move on to something else.

People may suppose that only the young without family obligations can sacrifice in the way required to pursue a calling, especially a calling that comes with a modest paycheck. Callings, however, are far more prevalent among experienced people. Few young adults really know what they want from work. They're experimenting with possibilities, largely bringing a career mentality to decisions about which field of work to pursue and which positions to accept.

Some assume that callings arrive in a visionary way, perhaps coming down from on high, and feel like a command. I'm sure that's possible, and it certainly would clarify things. However, only one person I've worked with on careers had anything close to that experience. Callings, at least in the way I'll be using the term in this book, are far more likely to result from a multiyear journey that includes some trials and some errors than from a single astonishing flash of insight.

At first glance then, calling people don't look much different than everyone else. They have good-looking resumes, but so do many others. Their occupations largely overlap the occupations of career or job people. Their academic preparation is similar. On paper, it's hard to see who's who. So what causes the differences among people with jobs, careers, and callings?

•

One result of this classification exercise is no surprise. Just as what business strategists find when they analyze market segmentation, some people fit squarely at the center of one of the categories, and others sit at the borders between categories. That said, the patterns are clear.

Although people with callings are different, it's not their occupation, work hours, level of sacrifice, or field of work that distinguishes them. *Calling people are different because they see their work as a positive end in itself.* They emphasize service to others, achieving excellence at their craft, and/or strengthening their institution. They accept and may like the things they take out of work, such as pay and prestige, but they don't emphasize them. They're ambitious and accept sacrifice to meet goals in the work. They enjoy work most of the time and take personal satisfaction from it. Although they encounter disappointments, those frustrating moments seldom take center stage. More than a third of the people I've spoken with have callings or are close.

The majority of people in my research take career mentalities to work. *For career people, advancement, pay, prestige, and power are front of mind.* These careerists are ambitious and will sacrifice to succeed. They have widely different levels of happiness and satisfaction. Some see themselves as winning; they're happy and optimistic. Others are uneasy and insecure. They worry that they're not advancing at the right pace or that they're not in the role they merit. They wonder whether they might find something better. If this feeling continues for some time, they may find that their work has dropped into the next category—jobs.

Only a few of the people I've known see their work as jobs. *Job people find little meaning in what they do. They hope to contain sacrifice while earning acceptable pay.* Much of their energy goes to activities outside work. Many are looking for something new. (I assume that the small proportion of job people I've encountered relative to Wrzesniewski's research reflects my focus on managers, professionals, and students whom I met because they were committed to developing personal strategies, rather than on a more general population.)

I'll explore all this in depth in the rest of this chapter. I'll begin with values in the work itself (service, craftsmanship, institution, and ambition), then review what's taken from work (money, prestige, and power), and finish with the conditions of work (organization culture and sacrifice). You'll see how calling people view these values and how career and job people diverge.

## The Work Itself

People with callings put a high priority on the work itself. They are ambitious and hope for big accomplishments in one, two, or all three of these areas: serving others, attaining excellence in the work, and strengthening their institution and the people there.

### Service

Many people with callings emphasize serving others. That service can be hands-on. They also can serve through their role at an institution. Those institutions can be direct service providers, such as charities or public service organizations. They can be businesses or professional firms whose better products or lower prices improve customers' lives.

Career and job people are different. When making career choices, few put service high on the list. Career people may put energy into their work at service-driven institutions, but for them it's mostly with the expectation that their contributions will be rewarded. I'm not suggesting that they don't care about other people, but in their work, other things come first. Job people do what's required to meet standards and little else. If that includes service, fine; but they don't seek service.

### Craftsmanship

When I use the term *craftsman,* I mean someone who strives toward excellence at what he or she does, who believes that quality is intrinsically worthwhile, and who seeks opportunities to improve whether or not that excellence comes with rewards. Craftsmen want to be world class in their fields. This kind of excellence can motivate university professors who hope to reshape thinking in their fields. It can motivate factory managers striving to achieve zero defects. Craftsmen can be found doing most anything—from the operating room to the court room to a cubicle without windows several floors below the corner office.

Craftsmanship is the leading motivation for some calling people, and most calling people pay attention to it because it can help them meet other high-priority goals.

Career people also can value craft, because skills can lead to advancement. But their priority is advancement, not excellence. Few job people take satisfaction from their craft and seldom select a position with that in mind.

### Institution and Colleagues

Most calling people like their employer, believe in what it does, and want it to succeed. For some, achieving that success becomes the top priority. They're part of a team, the team is important, and they hope the team will win. Calling people also may like their colleagues and hope they win. Career people often emphasize their institution as a way to get ahead, but few would turn down, out of loyalty to their institution or colleagues, an opportunity to advance somewhere else. Job people seldom see their institution this way, though they may value their job and hope the institution does well.

### Ambition

Calling people have high ambitions. For some, it's to change the world by building a new business, remaking politics, or curing cancer. Other calling people operate on a smaller playing field, but set big goals on that field—for example, bringing a first-class education to a third-grade class in an impoverished neighborhood school or providing the best midpriced restaurant meal in town. Those accomplishments would be good things, perhaps very good things. That conviction builds confidence. Although achieving their goal is sure to be difficult, people with callings see themselves as having a good shot.

Career people also pursue big accomplishments within their competitive space, because those accomplishments are required to get ahead and to realize the rewards that success can bring. If career people are winning, their ambitions can grow. If not, their ambitions can flag.

Job people are different. They may have been motivated when they started out, but they have lost interest in their work. Longing for a career or a calling, some hope to find something new. Others look for personal fulfillment outside work.

As I noted, service, craftsmanship, institution building, and ambition often overlap with calling people. I'm an example. First in government and then as a management consultant, I was enthusiastic about the intellectual side of my work. I wanted to solve the most challenging problems and to establish new problem-solving methodologies. I was a craftsman. As my skills developed and my perspective broadened, this craftsmanship led to better results for my clients. I liked seeing that happen, those clients became a second source of inspiration, and I became service driven. Throughout this time, commitments to my institutions and the people there added to my energy and the feeling that what I did was important. I received a degree of pay and status. I also put up with an intense work environment and a great deal of business travel. I was lucky to find a calling. I can't say I loved every day, but I enjoyed most of it; and as I look back, I feel a good measure of satisfaction.

Now, I'm excited about connecting business strategy concepts to work. It's both craft and service—a fresh intellectual connection that has helped most people I've worked with. My calling today is to use this book to help people seek their calling.

Let's now examine three people with callings. Entrepreneur Brian, educator Nathan, and Fortune 500 officer Charlie are in quite different fields of work. Yet all three share the critical in-the-work motivations. We'll start with Brian, who demonstrates the twin goals of service and institution building in action.

### Brian's Good-for-You Start-Up

Working for a mutual fund, Brian called on brokers and prospective investors who wanted good returns from socially responsible companies. He liked the fund's purpose. He enjoyed his colleagues and clients. At thirty-four, he was happy and had started a family.

Despite that, Brian felt too little connection between what he did and his desire to improve others' lives. The more he thought about it, the more incomplete he felt. What was the right path forward?

Brian had long been interested in new ventures. He'd won the business plan competition while getting his MBA. Although funding offers came at the time, he didn't follow up. As he told me years later, "It was a good business idea, but not one I was passionate about. If I were to start a company, I knew it'd have to be something I'd be fired up about."

He contacted a friend from school and asked whether they might join forces. His friend had a specific idea to create a new category of branded food products that improved diets. Although Brian's only experience in the industry was his childhood lemonade stand, he was interested. The two of them talked frequently over the next six months. Brian upgraded his market knowledge. On weekly business trips, he found time to visit grocery stores and other retail outlets. He talked to friends with food experience. At the end of this period, he and his partner decided to create the new business together. Brian resigned from his job.

Why take the leap? Brian was highly motivated by the twin goals of creating better products and building a new institution with committed people. As he said:

> I had an entrepreneurial itch. I wasn't wanting to make a lot of money. I wanted to create something. For me, I get up every day and think we're making a change. Building a brand is 50 percent of it, but it's also creating change. At a mutual fund, you're dealing with people who are connected to the status quo. I wanted to be around people who were taking more risk. In the start-up, I had a lot of impact on who I was working with.

Brian recognized he'd have to work long hours and do a great deal of business travel to start the company, but that was no obstacle. He also knew he'd have to live off his savings for a year or longer, but the prospect of creating the new business was worth it.

Ten years in, the business was on retail shelves throughout the country and growing nicely. The product was substituting for higher-calorie and less nutritious products—just as he'd hoped. He'd built a capable organization. Brian's infectious enthusiasm not only was personally rewarding but also helped with the business. It motivated people. It provided the energy he needed to deal with the inevitable disappointments that every start-up encounters and to solve problems rather than feeling unlucky.

Brian and his partner sold the company to a large consumer goods company at an attractive price. He still runs the business and remains excited about what he's doing, how he spends his days, and how it benefits people. It's a calling.

## How Nathan's Service Drive Guided Decisions

I'll now describe a second person who's all about values in the work—educator Nathan.

Nathan is confident. His confidence comes from success at a highly competitive college and on athletic fields. It's also the product of a noble purpose. He shows how a calling can both guide choices and create opportunity.

Nathan's interest in education goes back to childhood. Both of his parents were educators. Here's how he described the origin of his calling:

> I was committed to education going into my first year of college. What struck me was the inequity. I hadn't entered college on a level playing field. People had received better preparation, because they could afford a good private school. Looking around at graduation and hearing about the jobs a lot of people were choosing reinforced this. People receiving the best education money could buy were taking the high-paying jobs and continuing the cycle.

Nathan graduated, entered a streamlined onboarding program for new teachers, and began teaching at an urban school. It wasn't easy. As he recalled, "I didn't have great control of my classroom. My lessons never came off quite the way I planned them. My first couple of years, I used to stay till six or seven every night, observe our best teachers, and get coaches to model lessons." He set objectives for each student at the start of the school year, and recalled his excitement when several of the weaker students passed the year's final exams, some by a healthy margin. It was hard to become a real teacher. Nathan was a craftsman and was proud of it.

When Nathan's two-year teaching commitment came to an end, his decision was simple. There was no need to assess pros and cons. He re-upped.

In the middle of Nathan's third year, his principal needed to name a special education (special ed) coordinator. Most people in that role had been teaching for at least a decade, but the principal picked twenty-five-year-old Nathan. In the new job, Nathan tested students, placed them in the right mix of special learning and regular classes, evaluated progress, determined placement for the next year, and coached teachers to make all that happen. He focused on impact and regularly measured progress. Over the next three years, his school's advancement rate for special ed students more than doubled. He felt close to and responsible for those students and, in a different way, for their parents.

Nathan was a member of the school's five-person leadership team. He became the principal's main confidant "like the House whip in Congress" and led school system initiatives across the organization, whether or not special ed.

Although Nathan hadn't consciously tried to network, he'd built a strong set of professional acquaintances through his active involvement in the school system's special ed meetings. That's how he got to know one of the headquarters group heads. She invited Nathan to apply for a new position coordinating special ed across her thirty-three schools. The job spec called for someone with ten years of experience, but Nathan got the offer.

This wasn't the first time a promotion had come up, but he'd declined two earlier moves into headquarters desk jobs. Here's why he liked this one: "What it comes down to is where I can have the most effect. The job description is my ideal. Most decisions aren't made on data, but on anecdotal evidence. My job would be to help all the schools, to push a set of systematic structures that really work."

If he took the new job, it also would have what for him were secondary benefits: recognition, a consequential pay increase, and personal growth. Despite all that, he was conflicted and took several weeks to decide.

Nathan was uncomfortable leaving his principal. One of the school's other leadership team members would be taking maternity leave in a couple of months, and another one was facing health issues. He also hated the idea of leaving his students and their parents. "These are kids and families I know and I've worked with for the last four years. I'm not sure they'll get the support needed to make choices. It'll feel like I'm walking out on them and on my school."

When the administrator responsible for Nathan's school recommended the move, however, Nathan and his principal began working to minimize the disruption. Nathan recalls: "It turned from 'all the work will stop if you leave" to 'OK, this is manageable.' It also cleared my thinking. Knowing what I would need to do before I left and choosing competent people to take over certain things made me feel less like I was abandoning the place." Nathan took on the new role, did well at it, and became a principal two years later.

Nathan shows the simplicity and the power that can come from a commitment to a high purpose. He follows that compass to make career choices. Other factors are secondary. If he'd accepted some of the earlier headquarters promotions, today he might be pushing papers rather than leading his own school. By focusing on his mission, Nathan secured the opportunity to make things happen at the front line.

I asked Nathan how he traded off objectives. He was puzzled. It was hard for him to imagine how someone could make decisions for any reason other than what was best for his or her purpose. Some might say Nathan's approach to career choice is naive. I think it's wise and the ticket to great success.

### How Institutional Commitment Kept Charlie on Board

The third values-in-the-work story is about corporate officer Charlie. His top motivator was institution building, which in turn led him to emphasize developing excellence at the craft of marketing and sales—both in himself and in the people who reported to him.

Charlie got an engineering degree in the late 1960s, became a jet pilot, and flew missions over Vietnam. Leaving the service, he saw himself more as an implementer of technology-rich products than an inventor. He found an ideal position to do that: a company that hired engineers for the sales force. Starting in the United States, he learned how to sell the company's products. He moved overseas and received several other international assignments before returning to America. Charlie didn't plan these moves. He largely trusted the system to provide the right opportunities. As Charlie moved through positions in sales and then in marketing, the system was preparing him for bigger things.

He eventually was promoted to lead worldwide sales and marketing. He loved that role, but got frustrated seeing the technical side make all product and strategy decisions with little input from his team. He felt that the decisions would be better and the company would be stronger if the right marketing or sales people had a seat at the table. Making that happen became Charlie's cause. As he began to achieve successes, his commitment grew.

By the time he was fifty, Charlie still hadn't worked in product development. He knew that meant he was unlikely to get another promotion in this technology-driven company. That might have been grounds to leave.

He'd certainly had good opportunities. New ventures were hot during most of Charlie's career, and he'd been asked to run several. He usually declined without much discussion. Without product development expertise, he didn't think he was right for those positions.

Only twice did Charlie flirt with leaving. At one point, he was unhappy with his boss, and a large customer whom he knew well offered him a senior position. He considered it seriously and spoke to his CEO. Charlie had assumed no one was aware of the problem, but the CEO asked him to stay and said there was a plan to solve the problem. Two weeks later, Charlie's boss was gone and Charlie had the job.

Another customer Charlie knew and liked tried to hire him, this time to be CEO. The critical functions at this company were right up Charlie's alley—sales and marketing rather than product development. He was tempted, but declined. He was attached to his company and didn't want another move. He also had unfinished business to advance marketing and sales capabilities and roles in strategy decisions. He didn't win all these internal battles, but he won some. He was in a groove.

I'll describe how calling people view money in a moment, but here I'll share Charlie's view. He told me this: "I take the long-term view of money. I was more promotion oriented than most and less money oriented. I never got bored or felt unchallenged. I never had to ask for a raise. I was compensated fairly, although I wasn't working for money."

That's how he ran his life and how he advised people who worked for him. "I've counseled people, 'Don't go for a little deal. Go for a big deal.' That's especially important in sales, where people hop around for another $25,000."

Not many people today will spend their work lives at the same institution or even at two or three. The calling people I interviewed, however, frequently decided to stay where they were rather than leave. Charlie had attractive opportunities outside, but his calling was building institutional capability in sales and marketing and supporting his people. When Charlie retired, his work left him feeling good about what he'd accomplished. We all should be so lucky.

Who could argue with putting a premium on the work itself? Things become complicated, though, when we shift attention to what's taken from work. That's when trade-offs appear.

## What's Taken from Work

Work provides benefits—money, prestige, and power—to everyone. Those values matter most to people with career and job mentalities.

### Money

The purpose of career strategy is to generate greater and then greater income. Or is it? Although almost everyone seeks money, the role of money is complicated. For some people, money is the main thing in careers, or at least that's what they think. Others wonder about the roles of money and other objectives. Some MBA students have been surprised when I kick off the first class by asking them how important the role of money is in their careers.

How money affects happiness and personal satisfaction has been the subject of a great deal of research by psychologists and economists.[2] Although there are differences from study to study, in the aggregate it's clear that money contributes significantly to happiness (sometimes called "emotional well-being") as people move up from poverty, contributes in a more modest way as income rises up to an average level (a level that varies across communities), and doesn't add or doesn't add much to happiness beyond that point.

People react positively or negatively to changes in income, that's for sure. Over time, however, most people's level of happiness returns to something like it was before the change. Researchers call this "adaptation."

Using US data from 2008, one study concluded that this basic income level where happiness flattens out was $75,000, near the mean income of $71,500 and well above the $52,000 median.[3] This study also investigated whether money adds to the long-term satisfaction people have when they think about their lives (called "life evaluation" in the survey data). Beyond that $75,000 point, the researchers found that money continues adding to satisfaction, though the rate of increase may be flattening out as incomes rise.

Some are skeptical when they see these data. They don't question the statistics or the analysis, but they wonder whether the conclusions really are true and whether they'd be happy at average income levels. After some reflection, however, some of the skeptics begin to wonder what they really need.

"I've been rich and I've been poor. Rich is better." So said Sophie Tucker or Mae West or one of the others to whom that statement is attributed. I can't disagree, but it's not very helpful to the career strategizing discussed in this book. Consider this version of that famous remark: "I've been average income and I've been poor. Average is better." Not catchy, but more meaningful to our purpose here.

What matters for this book is not the importance of money in general. What matters is how money affects career decisions. Almost everyone whom I've interviewed about work put a lot of effort into their education and early work experiences. They were ambitious. They selected demanding fields, fields that often come with above-average pay. They worked hard to be successful. That's true for calling people, just as it is for most others I've met.

No one I've known with a calling, however, had income as a top objective. When calling people decide which position to take within their field, pay differences between alternatives seldom get much attention. Calling people want compensation to be "fair" or "at market." If that criterion is met, money stays in the background. They emphasize other things. Some calling people were in fields with high potential compensation; others weren't. But in both cases, many of these people realize incomes at the top of their professions. Financial success has come from accomplishments in the work rather than through conscious intent.

I certainly don't believe that money is bad. I do argue that if you want a calling, money seldom should be a big factor in career choice. Whether you're going for a calling or not, it never should be the only factor. If a new career field or a new job doesn't seem appealing but comes with a big paycheck, be on guard. Consider how the field or position would affect your outlook, motivation, performance, and perhaps ultimately your pay.

Even if you're seeking a calling and want to put money in the backseat, are there situations where money might play a bigger role? Perhaps you're about to graduate, have significant debt, and hope to pay off the loan. Or maybe your spouse stopped working to care for a new baby. Or perhaps you just became financially responsible for aging parents. Circumstances like these will naturally increase money's weighting when you're making a career choice, but if it becomes dominant, it can derail your journey to a calling. It might lead to unhappiness.

There are fields where money is out front and where people therefore may have a greater tendency to take a career or job attitude toward work. Even there, however, money doesn't have to drive career choice. Let's take as an example some parts of the finance industry. If you work seventy or eighty hours a week or more for an investment firm, dislike the experience, and hang on for the pay today and the promise of greater pay tomorrow, you may have a job mentality no matter how much money you make. But if you're in that role at the same firm and what matters most to you is the craft of investment choice and the potential to create value for investors, you may be approaching a calling—one that can provide outsized financial rewards.

Money motivates most career people, and their high ambitions may lead them to success. But their focus on money is risky. If they take a new position because it pays more and they then hate the work, their decision may have an adverse effect on their advancement and ultimately on their compensation. They sometimes seem to intuit this and sweat their choices.

Money is important to job people, but if seeking money leads to the wrong choice, they may find themselves in an unappealing situation. They may not do well and be at risk.

## Prestige and Power

Prestige can come from association with admired institutions. It can come from significant accomplishments and the titles that go with them. It can create appealing options for the future. By itself, however, prestige is hollow. Power, either a contributor to or a result of a prestigious position, is similar. Power can enable positive accomplishments. Power also can lead people to feel pressure and can lead to dissatisfaction if everything's not working well.

There's nothing wrong with prestige or power, but the question for career strategists is how much the desire for those things should affect decisions. You're taking your eye off the ball if you accept an offer you don't like simply for the sake of prestige or power. You may be missing something better.

People with callings are proud of their accomplishments. Like everyone else, they enjoy recognition, but prestige seldom drives their choices. They welcome power if it helps them meet their goals for the work. The irony is that calling people who de-emphasize prestige and power often are highly accomplished and therefore end up in prestigious and powerful positions. They do well by doing good.

Career people may make choices to achieve recognition and prestige, which can speed advancement into positions with greater power. Job people seldom care much about prestige.

Let's look at the story of businessman Karl, a man who found a sensible balance between money and other things.

## How Karl Balanced Money's Role

You might imagine Karl's face on a recruiting poster if it weren't for the mustache. He left the Navy, got an MBA, and moved through several positions with increasing responsibilities. He then became COO of a privately held $300 million manufacturing company. When the owners signed an agreement to sell the company to a large foreign firm, Karl decided he no longer wanted to work there and resigned.

Within a month, Karl became CEO of a start-up in a related industry. He was optimistic about the business, but it was July 2008. Lehman Brothers went bankrupt two months later, and the air went out of venture funding. Karl kept the company going for two years, taking no salary in year two. But without enough trial customers, the company couldn't attract investors, and the outlook was grim. Karl decided he had to find something else, a position with a regular paycheck. Here's how he explained his decision:

> I had bled myself white, living on savings. But it was less important than I'd thought it would be. When I became COO [at the first company] it was a big step up, and we found a way to spend almost all of it. But then with the new thing, we found it didn't take all that much to be comfortable. I've lived below my means, and I'm glad I did that. Now I'm forty-four. This is the power decade. I've got to put it in gear.

Karl had a strong reputation, and people wanted to help. He found six potential opportunities, all related to personal contacts. One resulted from a former shipmate, the others from business acquaintances. From those six came four good offers.

With two children in middle school, Karl came to realize that an important objective was to contain business travel. Three of the four jobs required travel almost every day, whereas the fourth required only one or two travel days per week.

That position was at the company he'd left two years earlier. The sale hadn't gone through, and the company remained independent. He'd be reporting to a man who'd reported to him before, but both that man and the CEO were expected to retire in two or three years. Not only did this position have manageable travel, but Karl judged it to be the best opportunity. He knew the business and might someday run the company. The offer had 10 to 20 percent lower compensation than the others, but it was more than enough to support his family, and the difference in pay was secondary. Karl accepted the offer.

Karl's thinking pulled together the different considerations about money in a sensible way. Though Karl faced tough financial circumstances, he didn't let money lead him in the wrong direction. He left his start-up to make ends meet, but judged that the lowest-paid offer was the best long-term opportunity with the least travel. He found a good balance.

Everyone realizes benefits from work. The question we're dealing with here is what importance to put on those benefits in career choice. Another kind of values remains—the conditions of work.

## Conditions of the Work

I've seen two conditions of work play important roles in career choice: organization culture and sacrifice. These two values don't differentiate people on the job/career/calling scorecard in the same way as the ones we've already discussed. No one wants a bad culture, and no one seeks sacrifice. What's interesting about these values is what different people will put up with and why.

### Organization Culture

For people engaged in career planning, organization culture generates a great deal of interest. When I ask MBA students to imagine a perfect position or a horrible position and the characteristics of each, over half mention culture; for some, culture sits at the top of the list. These students believe it's critical to their future happiness, and many are worried they'll end up in a place where they don't fit. Of all my blog posts on hbr.org, I received by far the greatest number of comments when I wrote about culture. Most commenters felt that it matters greatly. Some comments were poignant, reflecting what sounded like significant personal disappointments.

The right culture can stimulate success. For calling people, that culture emphasizes service and makes their role in providing that service clear, provides avenues to build out a highly valued craft, and enables everyone to contribute to institutional health. For career people, that culture provides a good prospect of success and creates a good platform for future advancement.

Across job, career, and calling people, I've seen the majority emphasize the downside risk from a bad culture more than the upside from an exceptional culture. What defines a bad culture varies from person to person, though it often includes issues with supervision, autonomy, rigidity, and needless sacrifice.

Both calling and career people can become distressed if they believe that their employer has a bad culture and that the culture is inhibiting success as they define it. Job people who are less engaged in general don't find culture as important in their calculations unless it's making their work lives unacceptable. That often has to do with sacrifice, the topic to which we'll now turn.

## Sacrifice

Sacrifice can come in three forms: intensity, travel, and moves.

You may work long hours; your hours may be unpredictable; the work may be intense; you may have to be on call when you're not at work; you may face an up-or-out evaluation system.

Business travel can be physically demanding, with early planes followed by late planes, too much to eat or the wrong things to eat, and no routine exercise. Travel can take you away from family and friends and make it hard to have a personal life. A special challenge can be organizing your life (paying bills, for example, or picking up dry cleaning).

Moving to another city can be exciting. It also may be hard to get settled and develop new connections. You may like where you already live.

These sacrifices can complicate family situations. A move may uproot a trailing spouse, cause him or her to look for a new position, and require a search for satisfactory schools. Caring for children (or family members needing assistance) may prevent long hours or significant business travel. I heard about a special case from the English wife of the CEO of a US company. She told me, "We had to leave a cat behind when we moved to Hong Kong. After we returned to England and got reestablished there, [my husband] had a very good opportunity in the US. I was wary, but when he said we could bring both cats with us, I was ready to go."

No one seeks sacrifice, but it comes with the territory. On one hand, people enter demanding fields to accomplish important things, but performance may suffer if continued sacrifice lowers personal energy and creativity. It can lead to burnout. On the other hand, people who always refuse sacrifice will greatly limit their opportunities.

Managing sacrifice was an important consideration in a third of the decisions I've studied. Some people declined moves to other cities that would have advanced their careers. Others thought carefully about the required sacrifices before accepting offers, and others changed jobs to reduce hours or travel. Sacrifice mattered even though these people were motivated and had invested in their work lives. I think that's a good thing. Giving due consideration to sacrifice is a topic we ignore to our peril.

Like everyone else, calling people face trade-offs. Success is important, and they can't succeed without sacrifice. If they're in a position that meets their values, then the work may not feel like "work," and at least some sacrifice will fit into their lives. But they too must find a sustainable pace.

Career people tend to a similar view, but their sacrifice is intended to lead to advancement. If that happens, they feel good and may work all the harder. If they don't advance, however, the result can be unhappiness, and the importance of sacrifice can grow in their calculations.

Most job people tamp down sacrifices. They free up time for things outside work. They resent it when work impinges on personal time in unexpected ways.

So what's different about the people with callings? Their ambition springs from the work itself—service, craftsmanship, and institution building. Accomplishments in those areas often bring happiness and a good measure of satisfaction. Calling people accept sacrifices to achieve those accomplishments. They seldom make decisions whose main purpose is to increase pay or prestige. By focusing on the work, they can be highly successful, and that success sometimes leads to the pay and prestige they never emphasized. Many create resilient positions. Their records of accomplishment, the skills they've built, and the respect they enjoy from professional acquaintances can make it easier to find something new if they need to. Their values and the results of following those values lead them to what business strategists call "sustainable competitive advantage."

## Uncovering Your Values

A calling is the gold standard in career strategy. Most people want callings. I hope you do. If you'd like to find a calling or at least explore the possibilities, take these steps to be purposeful in thinking about values at work.

## 1. Reflect on the Value Categories

What values motivate me and may create my calling or what motivates your best friend won't be the same for you. It certainly won't be exactly the same. These values are about you.

Think about craftsmanship, service, institution, money, and prestige. Let these broad categories stimulate your thinking. What narrowly defined aspects of these three value categories match what you most care about? Which ones might stimulate your ambitions? Which ones might be so important that they'd overcome questions about sacrifice, or overcome those aspects of organization culture that you don't care for but that don't make it hard to reach your goals?

Take craftsmanship, for example. How might it apply to you? Visualize yourself as a craftsman who enjoys the work and achieves excellence. What might you be doing? Would you be the best trial lawyer in the firm or the best at contract negotiations? Within trial practice, might you be the best at making opening and closing statements before the jury or the best at cross-examination? What would make you proud?

Or if you're thinking about service, remember the specific kinds of service you just read about: Brian's hope to improve diets, Nathan's commitment to quality education for the underprivileged, and Charlie's goals to increase the impact of the sales and marketing team. You'll need to get to specific goals like these to find useful direction and motivation.

## 2. Learn from People You Know

The stories of people in this book can stimulate ideas and help get you started. Personal experiences, however, can beat stories in a book by a wide margin. You'll gain deeper insight from people you know.

Talk to colleagues, friends, acquaintances, or others whom you don't know well who seem to have a calling. Describe the job/career/calling model and ask where they see themselves on that spectrum. Ask what inspires them and provides a sense of accomplishment. Ask what made them recognize this. Probe how their values have influenced their choices about work.

### 3. Determine Your Values

Draw on your personal reflections and what you've learned from calling people. Describe the values you care most about. Which ones could provide new sources of energy? Which ones could expand your ambition?

Values can't all be equally important. Assign them to three categories—high, medium, and low. If you find it hard to do that or to rank within those three categories, try this technique that one man used to help do his ranking: "If I only could meet one value in my work," he asked himself, "what would that one value be?" And then, "What if there only were two?" And so on down the list.

When you've completed this step, you'll have a *prioritized list of your values related to work.*

You'll use this list to help imagine fields or roles where you might realize those values. Keep it handy. It can lead to the objectives you'll need in order for you to pick one job offer and not another one. It provides standards against which to reflect on progress over time.

These categories remind me of companies I've known. Most companies that do best over time are founded on visions of becoming excellent at key functions, providing high-value products or services, and building powerful institutions. They pay attention to the bottom line, but they don't unduly emphasize next quarter's profits. They're like people with callings. Companies that put financial returns in the driver's seat may look good for a while, but they ultimately can be at risk if their service, craft, and institution are weak, just like some careerists. And you won't hear much about uncommitted companies that sound like job people. They won't be around for long.

The body of research on callings is growing. One book on this topic is *Make Your Job a Calling,* by career advisers and professors Bryan Dik and Ryan Duffy.[4] If you want to read more about callings, that's a good place to go.

I'll add a final thought about values in work. You've seen that people with callings emphasize the work itself and de-emphasize what they take from work—not every minute of every day, but most days. If you already have that orientation, this book will help you identify the fields or roles where you stand the best chance of discovering a calling (or recognizing that you've already found it). If you've never thought about values in work but are comfortable with this approach, this book will help you get started.

But what if you don't naturally emphasize what you put into work? What if you see yourself as a careerist now, and it's hard to see how to shift gears? Or what if you're on the fence? If that's your orientation, this book can help in two ways. When you see the benefits of emphasizing the work itself, I hope you'll try to move in that direction. When you do, I hope this book will show you the path to follow. But if prioritizing values in the work simply isn't for you, you'll get plenty of ideas here about how to succeed as a careerist.

# Chapter 2

# STRENGTHS

**KNOWING AND DEPLOYING STRENGTHS** is a big part of business strategy. Executives setting corporate vision begin with their institution's strengths. Those strengths can include very different things: functional areas, such as highly productive operations management; assets, such as intellectual property; and special relationships, such as long-term supply connections. An expansive new vision may lead to programs intended to develop or acquire additional strengths. With a shorter time frame in mind, smart product strategy reflects a full appreciation of how well the product meets market needs relative to competition.

Knowing and deploying strengths also is big in career strategy. Developing the strengths required to meet aspirations is a principal goal of the long-term action plan. In a job search, you bring the strengths you already have or those you could develop quickly on the job. They're why someone will hire you.

Not only do strengths affect your competitiveness, but what comes most easily to you may not feel like work. It may be fun. Psychologists have researched the connection between strengths and callings. Most conclude that people working in areas of personal strength not only accomplish more but are happier. Working in a field or role where you regularly deploy your top strengths puts attention on in-the-work motivations and gives you the best shot at finding your calling. Professor Martin Seligman of the University of Pennsylvania coined the phrase "signature strengths," which nicely captures the kind of insight I hope you'll uncover.[1]

The opposite of the feeling of accomplishment people can experience from regularly using signature strengths is the collapse of passion that can come when someone commits to a field of work and then discovers that he or she isn't well suited to it. If you're contemplating a move to a field where you don't have the required capabilities or can't expect to develop them on the job, you have grounds for caution.

At the outset of this chapter, let me make clear what I mean when I use the term *strengths.* Strengths include innate talents and aptitudes, such as facility with numbers or the ability to get to know people easily. Those intrinsic talents are the core. They greatly influence long-term aspirations. Strengths also include developed skills and knowledge, such as what people learn by majoring in fields like accounting and nursing or what they learn on the job. Those pieces of knowledge most affect near-term performance in a particular position. Ideally, you'll develop knowledge that nicely deploys your core talents.

A talent can lead to success in diverse fields. For example, a woman's talent at mathematical computation might be the foundational strength for careers like these: physicist, software programmer, high school math instructor, stock trader, tax attorney, and professional gambler. That's a wide field of play, and I've only scratched the surface. In addition to her talent, the knowledge she would gain through training and practical applications in any one of these fields would build strength in that field. That experience also might build capability for other fields where math was important, but if she moved to one of them, she'd be relying more on her core talent than on what she'd learned from her past work.

Or imagine a man whose top intrinsic talent is imagining appealing ways to present visual information, and who has learned how to communicate persuasively in writing and has several years of experience with websites. He's now an expert at creating brand imagery through websites. If he transitioned to creating brand imagery through other media, that small step out might tie closely to his talent and to the knowledge he'd gained through his work. A bigger stretch would be to a field that derived from his foundational talent in presenting visual information but that didn't need his acquired skills in writing and websites—for example, magazine illustration or fine art. Also possible might be to move to a branch of marketing that had nothing to do with his visual talent. He'd be leveraging his marketing know-how, but leaving visual presentation talent behind. That move might work well, but before making it he'd be wise to consider how happy he'd be and how well he'd do.

Considering that understanding strengths is critical to career strategy, you might assume that people put plenty of effort into understanding their strengths. That's not what I've found. Most people can't easily answer questions about what makes them special or about what makes them highly qualified for a field of work they find intriguing. Most arrived at an industry or a profession that related to their strengths, but they missed the opportunity to let their strengths consciously drive career strategy.

Others developed an insightful view of strengths and used it to make better decisions. This chapter shows you how to do that.

## Two Strength Stories

We'll begin with two stories about strengths. Corporate officer Pallab came up with fresh insights about strengths that radically shifted his career strategy and led to a good result. Attorney Jerry had a very different experience. Misunderstanding his strengths, he set unrealistic goals and suffered the consequences.

### Pallab's Surprising Strength

At fifty-two, Pallab was the marketing SVP and one of the top ten people in a ten-thousand-person organization. He was one of the CEO's go-to people. When his company was acquired by a Fortune 500 company, he was pleased when the acquirer asked him to stay on. However, he soon came to realize that he now was one of the top three hundred people in a hundred-thousand-person organization. In marketing alone, he was one of fifteen VPs. Fifteen! Pallab had less autonomy, he was uncertain about his future, and he was unhappy. He described it like this: "The money and the lifestyle are the same. I don't feel like I'm as important as I was. Before, I was running point for the CEO on high-impact areas. Now, my job isn't large enough, and I'm not privy to a lot of executive decisions. We are so large and matrixed that everyone's dispensable. I've shrunk."

Pallab wondered whether he was running out of time to accomplish the things he'd hoped to do in his life. In the near term, moreover, he knew his job might be at risk. He wasn't well connected and had no sense of where he stood. He also worried that he might stay in more or less the same position for the next decade and watch others advance.

He needed both a new career strategy for the long-term and a job search plan. Not sure what to target or how best to present himself, he focused on his strengths. Although he found the competitive mind-set easy to grasp, he had a hard time coming up with the distinctive strengths that would make him truly competitive. He went through multiple drafts over several months. The question I kept pushing was this: "What makes you special?"

His first thought was stimulating growth, especially in emerging markets. That was one part of a potentially strong story, but it wasn't clear what made him good at that. It sounded like what others might say.

A month later, he was thinking about these characteristics: knowledge of how to market the industry's products, B2B marketing, bridging cultures between developing and developed countries, and creating teams to attack new markets. This was much better, but would it really distinguish him from people competing for the same positions? Rather than claiming he could develop breakthrough marketing plans, for example, what was it that made him especially good at that?

Throughout this period, Pallab was conducting a low-key job search. Nothing had emerged after three frustrating months, so he reengaged with the process of understanding his strengths. Searching through his personal work history, he discovered something new: empathy. He'd never before thought to describe himself as being especially empathetic. However, when he reflected on his biggest successes and what had led to them, he landed on his talent at appreciating others' interests, feelings, and needs. By exploring patterns in his past experience, he discovered empathy.

Once he thought of empathy, he quickly saw how to link it closely to success at work and thus to job requirements. Here's what Pallab wrote:

> I have empathy. I understand other people and their needs, desires, and hopes. This capability is especially evident across cultures; at both the country and regional levels, I bring the developed world to the developing world (and the reverse). From this come three business strengths:
>
> - I understand both consumer and business markets. I create product offerings that appeal to the market, set marketing strategies

and tactics to communicate with markets, build sales programs with individual customers, and determine what prices will work.

- I understand the people in my organization. I inspire people and build teams. My teams get a lot done, and my people finish assignments with me having greater personal capability than they did at the start.
- I understand people in other organizations and build cooperative relationships, both among the units in my corporation and partnering networks with others. Everyone wins and is committed.

Empathy was real. Empathy helped him succeed. He could back up the empathy claim with stories and accomplishments. He was confident that few others in his field could match him on empathy and that still fewer would think of mentioning empathy when describing themselves.

Pallab finally knew what made him special. I'd like to say that his newly discovered strength immediately led him to a new strategy and then to a successful job search. But it didn't. He didn't fully trust what he called a "soft" concept like empathy. Even though he'd intended to lead with empathy, he never really did. And no appealing opportunities were on the horizon.

Events intervened. Pallab's supervisor was fired, and that position remained vacant while top management considered the possibilities. They told Pallab he was a candidate, but never talked to him about it. Three months later, he too was terminated.

Because nothing else was working, he now centered his search on empathy. He mentioned empathy on his resume, and how that led to accomplishment. He brought up empathy in discussions with search consultants and prospective employers. He showed empathy in the way he conducted his side of conversations—demonstrating good listening skills and giving good responses to what he heard.

Within two months, Pallab received an offer he liked—from a company in a related industry about the size of his old company, with a role similar to the one he'd had there. When Pallab asked the CEO why he got the offer, the answer was empathy. No kidding! The CEO had founded the company and had very clear views on most issues. Most of his direct reports were cautious about questioning his ideas, but he knew he needed to be challenged in the right way. He believed that he and Pallab could establish a productive working relationship.

Other factors contributed to his case. Pallab's marketing know-how was the ticket to entry. He wouldn't have been considered for the position without that. His overseas experience was important to this international company. His thorough preparation before each meeting showed he was serious. But it was empathy that made him stand out. If Pallab hadn't emphasized empathy, the CEO might not have appreciated that it was what he needed and that Pallab was the one to provide it. Pallab might have spent more time unemployed and then ended up in a less appealing position.

In Pallab's case, the winning strength turned out to be a personal characteristic, but I'm not saying that's what it must be. Your strength can be a narrow piece of knowledge or a particular capability. It can be a more general capability, backed up by a very specific and credible strength—for example, general management strength underpinned by the ability to structure organizations to make people truly accountable for results. What matters is finding what makes you especially qualified for your target position or field of work.

The second strengths story is about attorney Jerry, a man whose career went off track because he paid little attention to strengths and targeted a position for which he wasn't well qualified.

### Unemployed Jerry, Misunderstanding Strengths

Jerry was general counsel at a $2 billion privately held company. His competence, his focus on what was best for the company, and his professionalism created a deep bond of trust between Jerry and the seventy-one-year-old founder. Over time, Jerry had become his confidant across legal issues, business topics, and even some personal matters. Jerry sometimes felt like the CEO's deputy.

The recession came. Sales declined, profits turned to losses, and there were concerns about the company's cash position. In the midst of this, the founder had a heart attack and died.

Jerry was appointed acting CEO, reporting to the estate's executor. Even though Jerry carried the CEO title, the executor made every material decision. As she and the other heirs got up to speed, the priority became to ensure that they got their money out. The result was a hasty sale to an investment group at a low price that left most management options under water. The acquiring fund emphasized consolidation and cost cutting rather than business building. Over time, Jerry and most of his colleagues lost their jobs. At fifty-one, Jerry was unemployed with a much smaller nest egg than he'd expected.

Jerry welcomed a few months off. He was about to become board chair of a local charity and looked forward to getting started on that. More time with his wife and children would be good too; as he said, "I looked at it as the gift of a sabbatical. Early on, I had the air of enjoying myself, the best experience in my life. It really was. The charity work, tennis lessons, and travel. I was happy. I didn't feel pressure."

Jerry was more focused on long-term reflection than active job search in the first year, but he was surprised when nothing appeared. Nothing! He hadn't asked for help. He had assumed people would take the initiative. As the second year began, Jerry began a search, something he'd hoped to avoid. "There's a similarity between a job search and dating," he told me later, "and I didn't enjoy dating."

At the start, he didn't initiate a discussion of what he wanted to do. He recalled how he answered when asked: "I told people I wanted a CEO's position in a healthy and well capitalized company, a company on a growth trajectory. I wanted one based here in town. I wanted compensation similar to what I had been making the last couple of years."

Little happened, and he was out of work for almost two years. Then a casual acquaintance from the neighborhood asked Jerry about a general counsel position at another private company. Two weeks later, Jerry had the offer. He accepted it, because it was the only one around. Here was his rationale:

> I was tired of paying each month for a poor health care plan. I was tired of liquidating mutual funds every few months. I didn't feel right about that. Not the right role model for the kids. And I felt stress when my wife didn't seem sure that we could continue to send the kids to a good summer camp or perhaps even to pay private school tuition. I was comfortable saying not to worry, that those things would work out. She accepted that in year one, but in year two she really didn't.
>
> As the first general counsel, I have to roll up my sleeves and perform legally in a way I hadn't for fifteen years. I'm now practicing law. Before, I was managing, not drafting or negotiating on the phone. They had a competitive financial package, but it might not be as good as it looked given the hours I now work. If I had had what I wanted in the bank, I don't think I'd have taken this position, because the chief legal officer position is a most stressful thing.

A year into his new job, Jerry was reasonably content with where he'd landed but emotional about the two years when he was out of work. After we talked through his experience, Jerry recognized that he'd overestimated himself and assumed the world would come to him.

Jerry's relationship with the company's founder had been unique. Then, as interim CEO, his limited authority meant that it wasn't a true CEO role. At the one company where he discussed a potential CEO position, he grasped the unhappy fact that he wasn't prepared to run a company in a new industry with a new organization. "The more I listened to their questions," Jerry recalled, "the more ill-prepared I felt. I didn't know for sure I could deliver in a business role. I had a false sense that I could hang up my legal hat and focus on the business side."

Moreover, CEO positions are few and far between. When he factored in his goals related to location and compensation, he found that few companies would fit. As he said, "It was almost comical. With that compensation goal, it couldn't really be a local company. I was sincere at the time. If a dream job had come up in Seattle, for example, I wouldn't have accepted it. We like where we are."

What if Jerry had targeted another general counsel position with involvement in business issues? That would have matched his strengths and background. It would have been a credible target. We can't know what would have happened, but he'd likely have had more options to choose from. He wasn't unhappy with his new position, but he might have found one he liked better. He might have found it sooner.

Strengths matter greatly in careers, as is evident from these two stories. The question is how to get a good handle on your strengths.

## Uncovering Signature Strengths

One way business leaders try to uncover new business opportunities is to list their company's competencies and test them against what other companies do, both in their industry and in other industries with related functions. For example, a telecom company evaluating its call handling skills could learn different things from other telecom companies, airlines, and computer help desks. The company would determine which of its strengths are distinctive and then look for ways to exploit them.

Think about personal competencies in the same way. Develop your own list of strengths and evaluate yourself against that list. What are you best at? How do you compare to peers? What's your competitive advantage? Here are productive ways to stimulate that thinking, so that your experience can be more like Pallab's than Jerry's.

### 1. Self-Assessment

Your strengths are what you bring to work. List what first comes to mind.

Reflect on your earlier jobs and your time at school. What did you enjoy most? What were you best at? Maybe you have talents that were tangential in the past, but that could become significant if recognized and nurtured. Even activities with no direct connection to current endeavors may influence your future. Music lessons when you were a child may have built habits and skills that will be useful in lines of work having nothing to do with music. The same may go for high school athletics, bridge tournaments, or organizing events for religious or civic institutions.

Recall the successes that make you proud. What caused them? What was it about you that enabled you to succeed? At this stage, you're searching for clues about talents that suggest appealing directions. That line of thinking unlocked Pallab's strength inquiry.

Your resume will stimulate ideas, but it's neither a summary of your current strengths nor a predictor of your promise for the future. It's evidence. Resumes usually present achievements that sound like learned skills and only suggest intrinsic talents. A prospective employer wants the strength and views the experience as proof of that skill.

Here's an example of some of the strengths a manager in computer solutions sales and marketing might have: a natural talent for listening to and understanding customers, the knowledge of software and hardware that enables her to meet customers' information needs with computer solutions, a natural talent for coaching junior salespeople and building teams, and developed skills in proposal writing. Some strengths on this list are exactly suited to the position itself; others are broader, extending more easily to related positions.

Although generic strengths are simple to state, they're seldom much help. Seek distinctive strengths that closely tie to what's required for success in a particular line of work. For example, your strength is not just in bioengineering, a field crowded with thousands of others, but in the specific parts of bioengineering where you're unusual. You'll be on the strongest footing if you can recognize the intrinsic talent that led you to bioengineering in the first place and how that talent has distinguished you from others in the field. You'll have arrived at your own version of what empathy was for Pallab. Narrow and deep characteristics that make you truly stand out will naturally aim you toward some fields and roles and not others. They're what a prospective employer is most likely to notice and remember.

### 2. Performance Reviews

Look back at past performance evaluations—both the formal documents and what you heard informally—for ideas about skills.

Although you can gain valuable insights from feedback, view it as input rather than as the exact answer to your inquiry. The written words in that feedback may need interpretation in the context of how the HR processes work. You may or may not fully agree with them. Your past positions may or may not be highly relevant to the career you're planning.

### 3. Strength Surveys

Take one or more of the publicly available strength surveys.[2] Surveys can make you confident in a characteristic you already recognized. Or you may notice new talents or features of your personality. Most people I've known who used surveys like these found the exercise worthwhile, but they needed more than a little follow-up reflection to understand what the results really meant and how to apply those results.

## 4. Input from Others

Ask current or former colleagues, search consultants, or career counselors for honest feedback without pulling punches. They may mention strengths you don't recognize, raise questions about the strengths you do mention, or ask questions that help you visualize new strengths.

Get the ball rolling by asking questions like these: "What am I best at?" "What strengths might I build on?" "What are my weaknesses?" "What jobs should I avoid?" "What jobs should I target?" Bring your initial list of strengths and your resume to help them be effective counselors. View this as something like a market test, and learn all you can from it. Make it easy and risk-free. Don't debate or argue about what they tell you.

If you'd like to deploy a formal survey-style methodology to gather this input, consider the Reflected Best Self (RBS) exercise developed at the University of Michigan.[3] Its underlying premises are that people can learn about strengths from others who know them and that focusing on strengths (not weaknesses) can provide the most productive platform for personal development. As designed, the RBS end product is intended to help people get ideas to restructure their current positions rather than to help them find completely new directions, but position redefinition certainly can be part of career strategy, and the strengths insights from this exercise can apply to big-picture strategizing as well.

## 5. "Hire" Yourself

Consider a position that interests you in the long term and think about whether you would hire yourself. Ask yourself, "Why would I be hired for this job?" Ask, "Why would I fail to get this offer?" By putting your strengths assessment in the context of a situation like this, you may become aware of strengths and shortcomings that you'd otherwise miss.

### 6. List Signature Strengths

Let each of these exercises be a test of the others. If the same strengths appear from multiple sources, you're probably finding something that's well established. If a strength appears only once, it may not be that important, or it may be that you've never been in a position where it shows.

Be sure to capture important talents, even if you've never used them. List any area where you believe you're unusually capable, whether or not it's obvious how it would affect career strategy. There'll be time to consider that later.

Take the strengths you've identified and list them in order of their importance. This *ranked list of strengths* completes Chapter 2. You'll use it in different ways as you progress through the book. Your strengths may suggest appealing new opportunities, personal growth priorities, and how to direct a job search.

I spoke to several search firm consultants as part of my research. One of them emphasized the importance of knowing strengths and shortcomings. Here's the way he put it: "A small percentage of the population has an authentic understanding of themselves. But of those placed into meaningful jobs, I'd say that more than half do. It's almost a condition to be placed as an external candidate for a big job. The ones we present to our client are usually the people who understand themselves fairly well."

At the Temple of Apollo at Delphi is inscribed the advice "Know thyself." I assume that was good advice for the ancient Greeks. It's certainly good advice for twenty-first-century career strategists.

Chapter 3

# FROM VALUES AND STRENGTHS TO FIELDS AND ROLES

**THE INTERSECTION OF STRENGTHS** and values is the place where callings can emerge, but it's often hard to imagine what the right field or role might be. People with limited work experience may have little idea what would be good candidates. People with extensive experience may have trouble thinking outside the box. Most people need brainstorming techniques to stimulate imaginative thinking about fields and roles.

## Brainstorming Fields and Roles

Use these exercises to stimulate thinking about yourself and to use that thinking to help imagine potential fields or roles. They may yield fresh ideas and perhaps a surprise or two.

### 1. Current Strengths

The journey you're already on is a good place to start. If you maintain current momentum, how might your signature strengths (identified in Chapter 2) grow during the next two years or five years or ten? Then ask yourself, "With these enhanced strengths, what fields or roles would be my natural progression?"

Broaden the inquiry. Look for different fields that could deploy your current strengths and the strengths you could develop. These fields are not as natural a progression, but they're certainly plausible. Add some stretch possibilities to the mix. Be sure to include both intrinsic talents and knowledge.

These positions constitute the first list of potential fields.

## 2. Extreme Strengths

Dramatically upshift. Take what you believe is your top strength, assume you're absolutely first class at it (whether you really think you're good or great), and imagine what field or maybe what two or three fields would then be naturals. What might be possible if you're absolutely at the top? For this moment at least, assume you have few or no peers. Then go through the same process with a second important strength. Perhaps do this a third time. The possible fields or roles you discover here may be different and exciting.[1]

## 3. Extreme Values

Conduct a similar exercise with values. Start with your most important value at work (identified in Chapter 1), assume that it dominates all others, and then imagine what field or what two or three fields would best position you to meet it. Assume that meeting this value is everything to you. Assume you could make it happen. What might be possible? Do this for a second value and perhaps for a third.

## 4. Dream Jobs and Nightmares

Write down what you'd consider a wonderful position, a dream job. Describe a second perfect position. The sky's the limit. Then imagine the opposite—a nightmare. This horrible hypothetical job shouldn't be one that no one like you would accept; to learn from the exercise, you or someone like you might settle for it if there were no other possibilities.

For both dream jobs and nightmares, visualize a specific field (such as electronics product management, opening a restaurant, or being a college athletic director or an undertaker). Create a vivid picture of life in that field—where it's located, what you do each day or each week, how the organization works, the work environment, what impact you have, what you're learning, and so on. Be expansive.

The perfect positions may be good ideas by themselves. However, the more important purpose of this exercise is to provide points of departure for further brainstorming. Notice the features of the perfect positions you find most appealing. In the horrible jobs, notice the features that you most want to avoid and consider whether you should be seeking their opposites. Use all those characteristics to suggest other possible fields and roles.

## 5. Personal History

People often discard activities they found interesting earlier in life. That's natural, sometimes a sign of maturity. But people can leave things behind that should be part of their future.

Reflect on your time in high school. Recall what you liked best in class, what extracurricular activities you enjoyed, what else you did after class, or how you spent the summers. Did you enjoy tennis, student government, or your role in the school play? For any of that, what might it say about deep interests that have been below the radar since then? Do the same for college, especially freshman year before you settled into a routine. Recall what you liked best during your first year in your first job. How did you spend time after class or after work? What are you doing now in your spare time? What might that say about your interests and priorities?

Revisit pivotal career decisions and how they turned out. Why did you make those decisions? How important are those criteria now? These decisions are personal case studies.

Make a list of all these "likes," and consider whether any of them could be part of your future. What fields or roles do they suggest?

### 6. Article

Draft an article for publication ten or twenty years in the future to describe your career, perhaps for the *Wall Street Journal*, your local newspaper, your school's alumni magazine, or an industry publication. What would you like to be said about you? What would you want to be known for? With that in hand, shift to how that might translate into fields or roles.

### 7. Others Like You

The exercises to this point have been inward looking. They've sought personal insights to help you identify fields. But some potential fits might never come to mind. Maybe you simply won't think of those fields, or maybe they're too remote from what you've been doing. How to look for them?

Come at them from the opposite direction. Look at what other people like you are doing—for example, social friends, colleagues from prior jobs, or alumni from school. Look at LinkedIn listings for people with similar backgrounds. Or read into what highly successful people you admire were doing when they were your age or at your stage of their careers. One man told me he got ideas by reading the obituary section of the *New York Times*. The people from all these sources are (or were) something like you. Their career paths may stimulate ideas about yours.

Then ask yourself how well these ideas would fit with your strengths and values. You'll discard many, but a few may be keepers.

You'll get the most out of these brainstorming exercises if you put aside questions about what's easy or hard. Include possibilities that flow directly from what you've been doing, but also consider which ones are most intriguing. They might be possible—if not now, then at some point in the future.

## Three Students Looking for New Fields

The last step in the field/role brainstorming process is to decide which ones are promising enough to investigate in depth. Before we get to that, however, take a look at some examples of these exercises in action. Three MBA students at roughly the same points in their lives used these methods and identified promising new fields, but they made very different decisions about what to do. I'll first describe how Juliette uncovered a surprising new direction and developed a plan to explore it in depth.

### Juliette's Surprise from the Back of Her Mind

Juliette, twenty-six, entered business school after four years in a technical discipline. The MBA, she assumed, would position her to shift to technology management. And that's exactly the job offer she got in her second year: technology management with a well-regarded company and a good compensation bump. What's not to like about that? She had a month to accept the offer.

When she paused to reflect, however, Juliette wasn't 100 percent sure. She began to wonder. Should she really return to that field or try something else? And if so, what might that be?

Juliette went through two of these brainstorming exercises in depth—dream jobs/nightmares and personal history. When she did that, an interest emerged. She noticed how excited she'd always been when searching for unrecognized pieces in antique stores and galleries. She liked the art, and she liked the hunt. She had no formal background in art or antiques, nor in retailing or consumer marketing. She simply liked it and thought she was good at it. She'd never before thought of a career in that area. From the pride in her voice when she told me about this, however, I could tell it had been more than an exercise.

There was no formal recruiting at school in that field. Few positions blended art and business, but she spotted one possibility in an ad—a curatorial position with a large auction house whose job spec included an MBA. She applied for the position and was invited to interview in New York.

She began to prepare, but again paused to reflect. One issue was timing. The auction house interviews were after the date when she had to accept or decline the technology management position. And the auction house was a bird in the bush; she might not get that offer. A second issue was financial. The compensation was less than half of her other job offer, she'd accumulated $100,000 in student loans, and New York was an expensive place to live. Finally, she really wasn't sure she wanted the art/antique career. It was an intriguing idea, but a very new one. She wasn't seeking to flee from the technology world, and her new management responsibilities would challenge her in a good way. So Juliette dropped her name from the auction house interview schedule, accepted the technology offer, and left school with optimism about her future in that line of work.

But that's not the end of her story. She didn't abandon the art/antique idea. If the auction house didn't work now, what else might be possible?

Juliette developed a plan to set herself up as a small-scale art and antiques dealer—looking for objects to buy and sell. She intended to work on this during vacations and weekends, see how she liked it, and determine whether she could find a winning business proposition there. Worst case? Over several years, she'd have bought some things she liked and could keep or resell. In effect, she'd be conducting a serious career experiment.

Without having stimulated her thinking by looking for past interests, Juliette wouldn't have thought of any of this. Most likely, she'll pursue technology management for the long term. Remember, she enjoys it. It's no compromise and might indeed become her calling. But she may discover a way to enter the art and antique world. As long as she follows up on this experiment, she'll be exploring it on the side while building her base career. That's a good result at this stage of her life.

When I assembled these brainstorming exercises and began to try them out, I hoped that they'd lead people directly to callings. That can happen with fields people already know; they're recommitting rather than relaunching themselves. When it comes to completely new lines of work, however, that result is rare. These exercises almost always lead to fresh ideas as they did for Juliette, but few people make radical shifts without trying things out first.

People sometimes not only come up with that big new idea but also commit to it and begin making that change. That's what twenty-eight-year-old MBA student Mei did.

## Mei's Challenging New Direction

Mei majored in business with a focus on consumer marketing. She liked studying how people think and how to appeal to them. You might assume that her first position out of college would be with a company known for consumer marketing, but no. She wanted to return to her hometown, and few consumer marketing businesses were there. After five months, she found a marketing position with an industrial company that sold commodity products to consumers. Not a bad place to start, but not a perfect fit either.

After several years, Mei missed the exposure to sophisticated consumer wants and needs. Hoping to stimulate a career switch, she enrolled in a two-year MBA program, attending on nights and weekends while continuing to work. That was the best near-term financial solution, and she thought she'd benefit from two more years of work experience.

After a year and a half, however, Mei still lacked a plan. That's when she took my course. She went through the strengths exercises, brainstormed fields of work, looked to her past for ideas, and reread the "obituary" exercise she'd done as an undergraduate eight years before. There were three results from these inquiries.

First, it became clear to her that she wanted a change. She'd known that before, but now she became determined to make that change happen.

Second, she solidified what she liked most. That included involvement with the way people think and make decisions, public speaking, and project management. These weren't surprises, but now they stood out.

Third, she prepared a list of possible fields she liked—nonprofits, management consulting, TV, entertainment, consumer marketing, and diplomatic service. She hoped to "create something that inspires people, moves people, and would stretch myself creatively." She was interested in positions with international travel. These ideas weren't new either, but never before had she seriously contemplated them as real possibilities.

In Mei's case, her long list of possibilities made it hard to develop a plan for any of them. I encouraged her to determine what underlying goals unified the list and to use those to narrow down the list. She later told me this: "This was the hard part of class. None looked attainable. Frankly, it was overwhelming to prune the list because I was interested in everything. I didn't want to box myself in. I was so afraid of making the wrong decision that I almost didn't want to make a decision at all."

The next exercise helped. Each member of the class counseled another student and then led a short class discussion of his or her conclusions and recommendations. The classmate assigned to Mei came up with what she called a "gut check": she asked Mei to react to a variety of ways to interpret each potential target and to judge which ones she wanted most and which others weren't a good match. This connected with Mei in a profound way:

> Until then, I'd never talked to anyone about my aspirations. She was in my face in a pleasant manner. She forced me to think about it, reflect on what's realistic, and do something about it. The gut check helped clarify that I enjoyed entertainment/media more than international work (not too surprising) or consumer products (mildly surprising). I couldn't imagine being happy at a nonprofit with a standard nonprofit salary—maybe later in life. Although I wasn't surprised I liked entertainment and media, it forced the question again: Why am I still at my current job?

Mei pruned her list back to two possibilities—entertainment/media and related consumer industries on one hand and management consulting on the other. Over the next month, she spoke to people who were consultants and concluded that consulting failed to meet her desire to see results from her work. (I could debate this, but that's where she came out.) So she de-emphasized consulting. Mei now had a single target.

The entertainment target probably meant she'd have to move to California or New York. After several years in her hometown, she liked that idea. But it also meant that she'd have to travel to meet relevant people, making the search harder still.

Graduation came, so Mei was no longer attending school while working full-time. With a clear long-term direction, she now had time to launch the job search that would change her career. She expected to begin that search, as did I. But she couldn't get started. "It seemed daunting," she said, "and what I really wanted to do seemed far-fetched. I'm baffled how to motivate myself and focus on the search."

Then a recruiter called who'd noticed Mei's new LinkedIn profile that included her MBA degree. The recruiter was helping a company in town fill a position similar to Mei's, except that it was a supervisory role. Here was her assessment at that time:

> The pros are a promotion in title, an increase in salary, immediate change from my current job, and the people. The cons would be potentially wasting time and missing out on the potential to grow in an industry I might enjoy more. My gut tells me to reject the offer, while my practical side says to take it since I may be able to find work more easily with management experience under my belt.

This was a pivotal point in her career. If Mei didn't shift fields now, when would she? Here's how she described why she turned them down:

> My new work wouldn't be all that different than my current work, so the only benefits would be title and salary. Two years was also too big of a commitment when I want to know what else is out there. Since I went back to school to change my career, hopefully I can make that happen. So the job search has started in earnest.

This was courageous. Mei turned down a promotion, first-time supervisory role, and a raise. When she did that, she also was deciding to double down on job search. Having declined to move up in her current field, she had no choice. And six months after that, she got two offers the same week. Both were consumer marketing roles. Both were in California. And both came with compensation boosts similar to the offer she'd declined. Mei's fresh start resulted from a new strategy, a commitment to it, and the hard work required to turn strategy into opportunity.

You've read about Juliette's plan to explore a new idea and about Mei's decision to go all in. Here's another student with yet another kind of conclusion—government employee Tommy, thirty-two.

## Why Tommy Couldn't Do It

Tommy also was in a nights-and-weekends MBA program while he continued to work full-time and earn close to the median income. He also was in an employer-sponsored program that loaned him the money to pay his tuition. After he graduated, 20 percent of the loan would be forgiven each year, and he'd likely get promoted to a managerial role. It wasn't easy to get into this tuition program, and Tommy was proud that people wanted to invest in him.

Tommy entered school expecting to follow exactly that plan, but as time passed he became intrigued with the fields his classmates were considering. The brainstorming exercises led him to realize that although his current work was a good fit, he'd prefer a position that required more intellectual exploration. I wasn't surprised. Tommy was an unusually gifted thinker. He considered what that might mean and determined he wanted to get a PhD and become a professor. If he were going to do this, he wanted to get into a top program, but it was too late in the year to complete a high-quality PhD application. So he decided to return to his employer for a year and take the time he felt he needed to prepare that application. He formulated a contingency plan that was among the most thorough I've seen to capture the different ways all this might go. Everything was well thought through. He had a solid plan of steps to construct that application when the class concluded.

A few months later, however, Tommy changed his mind and recommitted to his employer. He felt it would be hard to transition to management while preparing first-class PhD applications, so he decided he'd have to stay in something like his old role. That was one problem. He wasn't sure, but he thought he might like to try his hand at management. That's when he looked closely at the financial implications. Even if he landed a PhD fellowship, he expected to be almost $200,000 in debt when he finished school several years later. If he then got a tenure-track professor's position, he might begin with income not greatly higher than what he earned in his current work, and he'd be paying off his MBA loan with interest. And although he'd enter the program with enthusiasm, he also knew that some PhD students drop out and never get the degree. He ran the numbers and concluded, "I'd be in debt until I was fifty." He just couldn't accept that scenario of his future.

I was disappointed when I heard this, but how could I disagree? The prospect of being in debt until fifty would be hard for anyone to face. And Tommy wasn't fleeing a bad situation. His employer liked him and was funding his MBA. Tommy liked his current work. I assume that over time, he'll be quite a success there.

Juliette, Mei, and Tommy all identified promising new aspirations, but they came to very different conclusions about whether to take the steps required to pursue those aspirations. Career strategies, as you'll see throughout this book, are individual things. I'll have more to say about commitment decisions like these later in the book.

These three MBA students came to these exercises at a productive time—when graduation was approaching. What kinds of situations will stimulate deep thinking about your future?

## Stimulating Situations

These exercises will be most powerful if you use them when you're ready for inspiration. When might that be?

Inflection points can be stimulating. Maybe you've been offered a transfer, were denied an expected promotion, or are out of work. Maybe you're about to graduate, or there's a big change in your personal life. Use the need for a decision to prompt your inquiry into purpose.

Unfamiliar places can stimulate creativity. Perhaps you're on vacation, taking an unusual business trip, or visiting the town where you grew up. You may be open to new ideas and possibilities. Good ideas may be working in the back of your mind. Be alert for signals and clues, and you may get surprises.

My students provide good examples of both of these situations. Most hope their two years in school will create new opportunities, and thinking through opportunities becomes especially important when graduation is on the horizon. Students who work full- time during the day and attend class on nights and weekends don't need a new position in June, but they're in a different world when on campus. Being there and being around the other students liberates thinking. Even the most satisfied reflect on how well their current work matches their aspirations.

One person who found insight at a special place and at a special time in his life was Reverend Alan.

## Where Reverend Alan's Calling Came

After college graduation, Alan got the opportunity to study abroad. He was excited about that, but as the year wore on, he felt unattached and uncommitted. He worried about what he'd do with his life. In a personal crisis, he sought inspiration while camping in a remote desert. It wasn't that dangerous a place, but it was a long way from civilization if he met up with the wrong people or had an accident.

Alan thought back to his childhood and to his time in school. He recalled discussing public issues with his grandparents around the dinner table and his mother's involvement in their church's social welfare programs. He'd been a volunteer EMT. He'd held what he called "office hours" on relationship counseling at high school lunch. At his university, he'd migrated to a psychology major once he realized that organic chemistry was too high a barrier to his becoming a physician.

In the desert, Alan came to the realization that he should "return home and serve my people." He wasn't sure what those words meant, and he didn't know where they came from, but he knew that this epiphany was big. He described it this way:

> I never heard those words—"return home and serve my people"—before that moment. I was looking for a lot of direction. I was on a self-imposed retreat, just myself and a friend. I was putting myself

> at risk. It wasn't that safe. I really had no idea what I wanted to do with my life. I call it an awakening! Like becoming aware of myself, correcting a potentially disastrous move. The organism I am was trying to pull me back to center. The event is really a coming home to myself, my inner guide, my purpose. I remember hearing those words, but I didn't assume they were external, at least not in the form of a booming voice.

The only immediate decision Alan made then was to return to the United States, but the purpose of serving people in his home country has become the guidepost of his life.

Coming back was hard. Alan moved into his family's home and for a year took odd jobs, including four months working on a farm during harvest. Drawing on his psychology degree, he found a counseling position in homeless shelters. A few years later, he recommitted to his religious roots, attended seminary, and was ordained. He became assistant minister at a church in a city he and his wife loved, but moved to a church in a distant city because he felt he could accomplish more there. Alan emphasized his purpose in these decisions. As he said: "Serving others is fulfilling. If we work for our own good, it's just a job. If we work for something larger, it's a calling. I've looked for adventure. But my responsibility is not just to have a great adventure but to use what I've learned to change the world or some slice of it."

Few will seek insight in a remote desert, but we can learn from Alan's experience. He was open to inspiration, and the remoteness of his camping experience triggered the insight that led to his calling.

## Brainstorming Step 8

Now you're ready for the last step in the brainstorming process. Use the ideas from all the techniques in this chapter to determine which fields and roles to explore and perhaps (as you learn more about them) decide to pursue. Check your thinking by asking yourself these questions.

If I were in this field or role,

- Would I be taking full advantage of my talents and skills?
- Would I naturally emphasize the content of the work and the results of the work?
- Would I put the rewards from work in the backseat?
- Would I be willing to sacrifice to succeed?

Every field for which you can answer yes to most or to all of these questions is a candidate. Complete this step by listing *your potential target fields or roles for the long term. Prioritize the list.* This ranked list is the end product of Chapter 3.

Throughout this book, my goal is to establish step-by-step processes to help you work out your winning career strategy. That's certainly true here. Moving from Chapter 1 (values) and Chapter 2 (strengths) to Chapter 3 (translating values and strengths into potential fields or roles) is a sensible thought process. It should put good ideas on the table. Those fields or roles become the topics to investigate thoroughly and try out if appropriate, as you'll see next in Chapter 4.

Chapter 4

# INVESTIGATION

**BUSINESS STRATEGISTS GET THE FACTS** before making big decisions. For a big capital project, there'll be alternative engineering designs and associated cost and performance estimates. There'll be an appraisal of the market and other factors that would affect the investment's performance. With a shorter time frame in mind, excellent marketers put in the time and effort required to know customer needs and how well both their product and competitive products meet those needs. They may commission technical tests and conduct market research to get to the bottom of product performance. No one wants to make a mistake he or she could have avoided with better information.

As a management consultant, I did a lot of that kind of research and fact finding. Our hope was to clarify the situation, the outlook for the future, and the pros and cons of the alternatives. Client executives might still disagree among themselves about what to do, but they no longer disagreed about the baseline situation. Their policy debate was well informed.

Individuals also get the facts before making big purchases. You wouldn't buy a house, for example, without doing the research first. You'd investigate the local market, the value of comparable houses, the commute to work, local schools for children, and other pros and cons related to how the house would affect your life. That's common sense.

Career choices are ultimately more important, yet I've seen many people fail to learn what they need to know to make the best choice. They may enter a graduate degree program with only a faint understanding of what that field would be like. They might accept a job offer knowing little about the institution. Don't let that be you. Be at least as rigorous in your personal strategy as you'd be when assessing your employer's strategy choices. The right thought process based on the right information is what it takes to make winning career choices.

The attention was on you in the first two chapters—on what you'd most want to do in your work life and the strengths you bring to work. Chapter 3 began to link these internal perspectives to potential fields and roles. Chapter 4 now looks outward. It shows you how to investigate the fields and roles you find intriguing.

I'll kick off the topic of learning with a story of Sean's first-class research into a job offer and how that research led him to a surprising conclusion.

## Where Sean's Research Led

Sean had been a management consultant for nine years. He liked the work, was a thoughtful guide to junior people in the firm, and enjoyed warm client relationships. He expected to be there for the long term.

Yet Sean took calls from search firms. He'd gone to a few initial meetings, but never any further. Those visits kept him in touch with what he called "the market" and his position in it. He also developed acquaintances with search consultants. One of those contacts might lead to an executive position at a large company, a vague aspiration of Sean's.

Sean found one of these calls intriguing—to be the chief administrative officer (CAO) of a Fortune 200 company. It was a new position intended to last two or three years. During that time, he'd restructure most of the corporate functions to increase productivity and learn the rest of the company. If all went well, he was told, he'd then have the opportunity to run one of the company's businesses. This sounded like the perfect setup, and he had good familiarity with the functions he'd be leading. Sean talked to his wife, and they decided to explore it in depth.

After a thorough tour of the company's annual reports and other published articles about it, Sean was ready for his first visit to headquarters. He sailed through the interviews with flying colors. A couple of days later, the CEO called and asked Sean to make a return visit to meet each of the functional heads who'd be reporting to him. Sean began to define how to add value in the CAO role and prepared a draft action plan. After a third visit, Sean got the offer. He'd been competing with capable people, and he was proud he'd "won the contest."

Sean was interested. He'd learned about the company's situation and outlook. The company had been sputtering, and Wall Street had hammered the company's shares. That might have been cause for concern, but Sean became confident that the company would rebound. If that happened, he'd be a senior member of a winning institution, the company's share price would go up a lot, and his stock options would be worth a great deal.

But Sean hadn't learned enough about the job itself to decide. On his next visit, he would explore whatever topics he liked and perhaps decide to accept.

Sean's priority was culture and role. He asked questions like these: "What are you excited about?" "What are you proud of?" "Who are your close friends in the company?" "How does the group function together?" In those conversations, he learned who the company's heroes were, what made them successful, and what his biggest challenges and opportunities would be. He and the people he met were jointly determining how to make the new role successful. He was raising topics they'd never considered. It felt as though he already worked there.

People interviewing for jobs sometimes worry that probing questions might make others uncomfortable and put an offer at risk. That's not what I've seen in general. In this case, doing that solidified the CEO's conviction that Sean was the right choice. His earnestness and courtesy made tough questions come across as showing insight and interest in their success rather than as being critical or threatening. He was irresistible.

Sean also used the time to confirm what he'd heard at the outset, that this position could put him on a path to lead a business. He was close to a yes. As he put it:

> The deal played to who I am. I liked the people a lot. It was a position I'd be proud to have. I don't mean the power; I'm not into that. But if I was at a party and someone asked what I did, well, it'd be a job I'd be proud to mention. There was a lot of financial upside. I was eight toes out the door.

A couple of days later, however, Sean turned down the offer.

One reason to decline was the move. Sean's wife had been excited at first. But as she thought about it, she realized that she enjoyed her community, was involved in the kids' school, had a rewarding social circle, and had begun a term on a volunteer board. Without question, she'd move if he wanted to, but she preferred to stay put.

Second, Sean felt that the new role was a misfit in the company's deeply ingrained culture. He questioned how he'd be viewed as the first CAO, given everyone's sharp focus on bottom-line results. It was a highly performance-driven environment, with autonomous profit centers. Corporate staffs were seen as overhead. A red flag: because the role wasn't like any other at the organization, the higher-ups hadn't thought through what metrics to use to evaluate his performance. He said that was the most important thing he'd learned: "I asked how they'd keep score, how they'd know I was making a difference. We never got to satisfactory answers. They weren't hiding anything. This CAO position was new. They didn't know."

Sean was concerned that he wouldn't really be accepted and therefore that the CAO role would not, in fact, be a springboard to the line job he wanted.

Last, he liked consulting. It may not have been a full-scale calling, but he certainly wasn't dissatisfied. If he'd been unhappy, he might have accepted the offer. But why leave a position he liked for something carrying the risk that even if he did well, it might not lead to his long-term goal?

Sean looked in depth at the topics we'll examine later in this chapter. He got excited by what he learned about the company's outlook and by the positive experience he had with the company's leaders. But what he learned about culture and role made him cautious. And both he and his wife took this time to reflect on how they really felt about moving. That's a lot of valuable learning in a short time.

Armed with the same facts, others might have made a different decision. But Sean's decision was the right one for him. Career decisions are individual things, and different people bring different objectives to those decisions.

We'll now explore ways to research fields and roles and get to the kind of insights Sean found. I'll provide suggestions for how to learn from public sources of information and from people who can give you the inside picture. I'll spotlight how to explore four topics that almost always come up: culture, role, sacrifice, and industry outlook. I'll conclude the chapter by showing a different path to learning: career experimentation. Experiments are especially important before making radical career moves.

## Designing Your Learning Program

Pursue both public and private sources of information.

### Public Information

Mastering public information is the admission ticket. Read everything you can find about the field of work you're considering. If you're preparing for job interviews, research both the field and the institution. Interviewers expect people already to be familiar with this information. Professional networking contacts do too, especially people who aren't close acquaintances.

Institutions in the field you're evaluating are likely to have websites. That's an easy place to start. You gain an overview of each company, and with some companies you can get a lot of detail. Some have a section on careers, and if the site is thorough and well designed, it can be helpful in the first steps in your exploration.

For a public corporation in the United States, look for its annual report and the annual Form 10-K (usually found on the website in the investor section). The 10-K provides a full set of financial information along with a thorough discussion of the business—from detail about facilities, markets, and competition to the business's opportunities and risks. Keep in mind that these reports, formal vision statements, and other company-generated documents are partly marketing and public communication tools. Look at several companies' 10-Ks to investigate a field.

There also may be good articles or books on the institutions, fields, or professions you're investigating. There may be online reviews of what it's like to work at an institution you're considering.

This easy-to-find public information is the baseline. It's essential to be familiar with it, but it's seldom enough to yield deep insight.

### Your Private Research

After reading up, do a reality check. Learn more than what's available to the public.

Meet people in the field. Meet people who know the field because they have relationships within it, for example, customers, suppliers, or partners. Not only can these people paint a vivid picture of what it's like in general, but they also can answer questions and tailor their information to your interests.

If the field you're considering relates to what you're already currently doing, you may already know people to contact. You may be able to identify potential contacts through your school's alumni records and through social media. Some cold calls won't get a response; others will.

Prime the pump. Most people will find it easier to react to your ideas than to come up with ideas completely on their own. Make it easy for them to help by describing your strengths, what motivates you, and your ideas about fields. Let them tell you what distinguishes the people who accomplish a lot and advance in these companies.

Do your own product testing. Do this firsthand with consumer packaged goods. Visit stores and compare prices, quantities, ingredients, and so on. If they're not too expensive, buy the company's and the closest competitors' products and see what you and your friends think about them. If you're looking at consumer services, visit the relevant stores or take a first step in your role as a consumer to learn about alternative service providers. With high-ticket consumer products, ask people who own them what they think and why they bought the one they did. For both consumer and industrial products, ask people in the industry or people whose work relates to the industry how to rate competitors and which ones they like best.

## Indirect Questions

Although the topics you hope to research suggest direct questions, those direct questions seldom work very well. Take the topic of organization culture. If you ask a man, "What's the culture like here?" or "Are people treated well?" he may not be sure what to say. Or he may be reluctant to tell an outsider (you) what he really thinks. Even if he answers directly, there may be a great deal of internal context, making it hard for you to understand what he means.

Taking an indirect approach is often a better tack. Indirect questions usually are easier to discuss. They provide facts from which you'll form your own opinion. In the case of culture, ask questions to gather evidence about how the organization works—for example, "Tell me about how different people contributed to a big decision" or "Could you describe the coaching you've received in the past year?" The other way to be indirect is simply to observe what's going on.

Both lines of inquiry, direct and indirect, make sense for some topics. To explore how to win as an employee in an industry or a company, it certainly makes sense to ask that direct question directly. Interviewers and others usually will like what the question says about you, and you'll learn something in the process. But go deeper than that with indirect questions. Ask about people who have succeeded and others who weren't successful. In this example, you'll learn more if you can get answers to questions like these: "What's a plausible career path at the company over ten years for a high performer who starts in the position I'm seeking?" or "Do people here learn more from on-the-job coaching or from formal training programs?" or "What's the most courageous act you've seen here?"

## Targeted Learning

Companies within a broad industry category can be very different from each other. In the electronics space, for example, there's hardware, software, and full systems solutions. Within software, differences exist among classes of software and among applications. Be clear what part of the industry you're investigating.

Functional departments or divisions within a large company may face different situations and have different environments.

Don't ignore the overall corporate setting, but be sure to emphasize the relevant division or functional unit.

Consider time frame. Established fields can change. In start-ups, everything may be different a year later. Over time, practices in one region or business may migrate toward the practices in others. If you sense that important changes are afoot, learn about both today's situation and future possibilities.

Your research will cover many topics. Here are suggestions about how to explore four of the most important.

## Four Big Topics

Sean started with an advantage: reviewing public information on a company was a natural extension of what he'd do before meeting a prospective consulting client, and asking questions about company culture and role was something like what he did in the meetings he'd have with clients during an assignment. He had an advantage, but that doesn't mean you must be a consultant to conduct a productive inquiry. You too can learn the way he did.

I'll put a spotlight on four big topics that are part of most career strategizing: culture, role, sacrifice, and industry outlook. These four topics almost always are important parts of the picture. You'll see proven lines of inquiry for each one.

I've designed these questions to be comprehensive, which means that my list of topics is unlikely to miss something that would be important to anyone, but also that there are far too many questions for any particular situation. So I suggest that you prepare for conversations and interviews by looking at these questions and thinking about which ones are important to you or are likely to come up. You can ask the questions as I've written them here. Much better will be to tailor them to your particular situation.

## Organization Culture

The first of the four big topics is organization culture. It's one of the values at work, as you saw in Chapter 1. The right culture can stimulate your success and growth. The wrong culture can create stress. It can put your success and growth at risk.

I mentioned earlier that both MBA students and readers of my blog posts on hbr.org have been interested in culture. Despite having completed classes in organizational effectiveness, some MBA students are puzzled about how to investigate culture in career strategizing. Some blog commenters were unsure how to approach the topic. Others were skeptical, doubting they could learn much until they were on board. I disagree. I believe you can learn about culture, even in the early stages.

I'm not saying that culture is simple. The opposite is true: culture is complicated. Few organizations are universally better or worse than others. You might want an institution where performance is king; others might feel that isn't fair. You might seek the clarity that formal structure and process provide; others want a wide-open environment. The culture you want is part of your aspirations.

The one exception to this is ethics, especially in regard to big questions such as temptations to cook the books, misrepresent things, or treat people unprofessionally. There aren't complicated pros and cons about ethics. Don't go where you're concerned about ethics.

Before you commit to a field of work, learn how institutions operate in that field. Before you commit to an institution, understand the culture there. Explore the topics here, and you'll have a good shot at knowing what's going on.

### Purpose

Seek a field of work and an institution with an uplifting purpose that you could find inspiring. This can include public service organizations. It can include businesses that see their products as means of improving society and putting their customers first. Be on guard against visions that emphasize financial returns. Profits are a by-product of a well-managed business. As a purpose, they aren't differentiating and can excuse opportunism.

Read published statements of the institution's vision, books and articles about the company, and relevant websites. Read them with a critical eye. If the purpose you're seeking is associated with a department within a large institution, then look into that department in a similar way.

But don't stop there. What's more important is what that purpose really means in practice, how purpose affects actions. Consider asking:

- What happens if there are gaps between the institution's actual performance and its purpose?
- When has purpose changed a decision?
- What happens if purpose conflicts with financials?
- Who gets promoted? Who are the heroes?

That last question can be powerful. The highly regarded people did certain things, and those things are likely to be a valid reflection of institutional values.

Form an opinion about whether people are proud of their product or service or proud of their institution. Do people use the word "we" when mentioning it? If people say different things about purpose or if what they say is inconsistent with the elevated description in public statements, take it as a warning.

## Teamwork

At its best, teamwork can create excitement and high productivity. It can be fun. But time and effort are required to create and maintain a team environment. The wrong environments can focus attention inward rather than on the market, breeding a weak or misguided performance ethic. Consider asking:

- How much do you work directly with colleagues, compared to individual activities?
- What team accomplishments make you proud?
- How do people compete for promotion and credit? How are members of successful teams rewarded?
- What time and effort is spent building teams?

At their best, teams are a positive part of culture, but some are problematic.

### Colleagues

Friends are good, but people don't have to be friends to be good colleagues. If they're capable, objective, and committed to the institution's success, they'll help you succeed. If not, they may not help and could get in the way (no matter how friendly they may be). Colleagues also can contribute to the institution's reputation and become members of your professional network. Most everyone wants good colleagues, but people differ in the priority they put on colleagues. Ask:

- Who are the stars? What makes them stars?
- Who in your institution do you spend time with outside work? What do you do together?
- Who in your institution do you expect to be part of your professional network over time?
- Who are your mentors? How do leaders engage with you or coach?

Judge how much deference people give to senior people and whether that feels right. Consider how the talent compares to your classmates in college or to colleagues from work.

## Attention to People

You want to be treated as a valued asset the institution wishes to retain and grow. This relates to HR practices, but more important are the way people feel about each other and the attitudes of leaders. Leaders often say people are their greatest asset, but some don't always mean it. Explore that with these questions:

- Under what circumstances are people required to get on board?
- Are people told exactly what to do or given general direction? Are instructions clear or so vague that it's hard to know how to succeed?
- Do new people have time to get oriented, or is it "sink or swim" on day 1?
- Does feedback provide true insight about how to improve?
- Do people feel that raises, promotions, and terminations are fair?
- How many people leave the company each year? Of those, how many exits are voluntary?

Attention to people is usually good, but it sometimes can conflict with other organizational virtues, such as fairness, equity, and creative tension. Most people prefer a balance among these different considerations.

## Communications

People in some organizations say what they think. They're direct and blunt. In situations like this, life sometimes is rough, but you'll usually know where everyone stands. Politeness or politics reigns in others. People are careful in what they say and how they say it. They avoid controversy. Little tension is in the air, but that lack of true communication can mask important subjects. Strong feelings can simmer below the surface.

How people communicate with others—and how they expect you to communicate with them—will affect day-to-day life. Consider asking:

- Do people say what they think? Are they direct, even if others are hurt or offended?
- Do you know where your colleagues are coming from? Are people careful about what they say and how they say it? Do they avoid controversial issues?
- Is everyone encouraged to participate in discussions and have dissenting opinions? Does the boss listen?
- Except for sensitive information, does everyone know what's going on? Are lots of things confidential?

Consider how well people's communications styles fit with your preferences.

## Performance

An organization centered on accomplishments has advantages. People are promoted and rewarded (or not) depending on what they achieve rather than on who they know. Things are reasonably clear, and you know where you stand. An unyielding focus on accomplishments, however, may not be fair if accomplishments are hard to measure or if many factors that affect performance are outside the individual's control. And a performance focus may encourage short-term thinking.

Other organizations interpret the causes of better or worse performance and evaluate people in that light. The people who create those performance systems are hoping to be reasonable and fair. But the systems can be confusing, with less clarity. They can lead to less drive for success.

Learn about performance management and how supervisors judge performance. Ask:

- What determines performance evaluations? How does compensation relate to financials? To purpose?
- How is negative feedback communicated? Is it private, respectful, and focused on improvement? Is it public, negative, and embarrassing?
- Do performance measures reflect differences in difficulty? Are measures adjusted when employees have limited influence on results?

Some like it when there's no doubt about what's on the line. Others prefer a more nuanced view.

## Processes and Productivity

Some organizations operate in a structured way, emphasizing principles and procedures. They make decisions only after touching all the bases. They may have policies about work hours and dress codes. Others emphasize autonomy, flexibility, and freedom. Although most people want freedom, it sometimes leads to complexity, low teamwork, and business risk. Too much freedom can put an institution on the road to failure. Raise questions like these:

- Are the right people involved in decisions at the right time? What bases must be touched? How long does that take? What happens if people skip steps?
- Do leaders have open doors? Do people drop in with questions, or are appointments required?
- What policies guide day-to-day activities (for example: dress code, work hours, office environment)?
- How many layers are in the organization? How many people report to key leaders? How many report to the leader of the department where you might be working?

Look around the office while you're there. Is it orderly or disorderly? Do administrative people seem happy? Is the hiring process professional and respectful?

That's how to explore culture. Remember that this is a comprehensive list. You'll need to narrow it down to match your particular situation. We'll now turn to a second big topic that's a close cousin of culture: role.

## Role

Your role is what you do. It's who you are there. In the right role, you have a good shot at accomplishment and growth. The wrong role can breed disappointment. Here are the elements of a productive inquiry into role.

### Know the Role

Master the written job description ahead of time. But know that written job descriptions only get you started. Some are hard to understand, others are out-of-date, and some don't closely match the way things really work.

Ask directly about your prospective role, and come to meetings with questions to clarify what you already know. Test it with detail. For example: What happens day-to-day (and month-to-month)? What are the closest relationships? What are the responsibilities?

One way to learn about role is to learn what the role wouldn't be. Ask about related functions and learn which ones aren't part of the role.

### Understand What You Could Accomplish

Your career progression will rest on accomplishments. The role suggests what those accomplishments might be. Think about whether they'd make you proud, whether they'd meet your aspirations for personal impact.

Setting yourself up for impact requires the right authority, responsibility, and access to the people you'll need to succeed. Pay particular attention to your future boss and whether you sense that he or she will support you in reaching for high impact.

Test this with detail. Imagine the day-to-day tasks and how you'd succeed. Imagine who you'd be working with, whether they'd be able to help, whether they'd be inclined to help and, if not, what you could do then. Get a feeling for what decisions you could make or what initiatives you could take on your own.

### Understand What You'd Learn

Describe what would be your "curriculum" in the role, what you'd learn at work. Identify who'd be your coaches. Learn whether they'd see coaching as important and think about how good they'd be at guiding you.

Role ties to organization culture; if there's a restructuring and roles change, you'll be better off if you're comfortable with everything else there (that is, the culture).

The way I've described the inquiry into role has focused on learning about an offer. Absolutely be sure to know the role you'd have if you accept an offer. In a less specific way, the same three topics also apply to researching a field you're thinking of targeting in your long-term plan.

Related to culture and role is sacrifice, the next of the four big subjects.

## Sacrifice

Whether you're considering a new field or evaluating a job offer, know what the sacrifices would be and how you'd manage them—before taking the leap.

I'll begin with brief stories about CEO Steve and corporate officer Susan. He accepts and manages sacrifice. She outsources it.

## Honoring Steve's Boundaries

Almost all CEOs work long hours. Many have substantial business travel. What's unusual about Steve is how much travel he has and how aggressively he manages the consequences.

When offered the CEO position in another city 250 miles away, Steve said he'd do it only if he didn't have to relocate. With children in school and local connections, he and his wife were rooted. When the board agreed, he knew he'd be away from home almost every work day. He accepted that job and its travel, because he felt he could set three boundaries to handle the impact.

He scheduled meetings to allow him to leave home Monday morning (instead of Sunday evening) and return Friday midday before rush hour.

He set up easy living arrangements in the new city. He'd considered renting an apartment, but decided he wanted no responsibility for housing there. He told me how that saved him time and kept him focused on work:

> I stay in the same hotel every week, in the same room. It's close to the office. I keep clothes and toiletries there. My deal with them is that I don't have to pack up my stuff—they do—if the room will be in use when I'm not there. This way, I don't have to mentally leave for work the day before by packing, and I never have to carry a bag.

And he regularly stays in touch with each member of his family: "I speak to my wife two or three times a day. At least every other day, I speak to each of my daughters. I text-message each girl every day or so. I've killed myself to make all birthdays and all school events. I'm away every week, but I work hard not to be away when away."

As CEO, Steve has unusual flexibility to contain sacrifice. Now let's consider a different approach to sacrifice—how Susan balanced career and child care.

### How Susan Merged Motherhood and Work

Susan had just gotten the opportunity to run a business that was being acquired, and her first role would be to merge it with the new parent company. She'd long hoped to lead a business, and this was an exciting opportunity for her. Her husband was starting a company, and no one could know how that would go, so the income that came with her position was important too.

The timing, however, was something else. The offer came three months before their first baby was due. When Susan committed to the job, she also committed to providing first-class child care to ensure that her time with her children was high quality. Five years later with two children, she described her approach:

> I can't say how many people come to me and ask how I manage it. We've gone to a second nanny, so that when I get home each day, I don't have to do housework. I'm not the business side of parenting like so many other moms, but something more like a traditional dad used to be. I spend quality time with the kids every evening and on the weekend. I read to them. When I got home each day, if my job was to clean up, feed them, and then clean up again, I don't think I'd do as good a job as a mom. I'm sure I wouldn't be happy.
>
> This works because we have great nannies. We've gone through several to get where we are. At one point, we interviewed thirty before hiring one. We make sure to create a positive environment and pay enough so that they feel valued. We don't go on expensive vacations and we don't go out a lot, but we do spend to support our two careers.

Susan and her husband hadn't fully thought all this through when she accepted the job offer, but they were resolved to do what was required. Their practice has worked, both professionally and at home. Not everyone can afford to do what Susan did, but everyone can step back and think through the challenges and how to deal with them.

People often have more opportunities to limit sacrifices than they first assume. If a position you like comes with a challenging sacrifice, imagine what Steve or Susan might do and whether something similar could contain your downside. Follow these steps to think through sacrifice.

### 1. Know What's Really Required

Learn about hours and intensity and what makes them necessary. You may assume that certain activities are compulsory when they actually aren't. For example, junior consultants at McKinsey & Company sometimes believed late hours were a must. If they'd asked me, they'd have learned it depended on the situation. It wasn't always necessary.

Learn what travel is needed. People sometimes assume that the only way to do their job is to be away all the time. They don't realize that they might be able to organize their schedule, files, and responsibilities to allow them to work in the office or at home a day a week or more.

Learn whether a move really is necessary. Rather than moving, you may be able to accept a new position with a flexible work arrangement and the associated travel.

### 2. Identify Boundaries

For the sacrifices that you must contain, imagine guidelines to govern your behavior most of the time. Get specific. For example:

- Attend important events at your child's school
- Be home in time for dinner (but after that, do what's required to stay on top of work)

- Be with your spouse for birthday dinner
- Work late on business trips to free up weekends
- Set vacations in advance and plan your schedule accordingly

Ask others about their personal boundaries. Consider whether you could succeed with the boundaries you've imagined.

### 3. Decide Whether the Sacrifice Is Acceptable

You'll have to do hard things to accomplish a lot, but some sacrifices may be unacceptable. Do the benefits outweigh the costs? By getting clear on what the sacrifices really are and whether you can define sensible boundaries, you'll be in a position to make that call.

There are two good times to consider the topic of sacrifice. The first is when you're getting started on long-term strategy or on a job search. Sacrifices differ across fields and roles. What you learn about sacrifice may influence both which fields and roles you target in the long term and which opportunities you seek now.

The second time is after you have a job offer in hand and the employer is hoping you'll accept. Employers expect you to evaluate all aspects of their offer, including intensity, hours, travel, and certainly relocations. They may be flexible on some of this, though that will depend on the role and on the institution's culture. To prepare for that discussion, try to sit on their side of the table and think about how to make things just as effective for them with your desired boundary in place. An open discussion of these issues will be in your best interest (and often their interest, too). It's seldom wise to initiate a discussion of sacrifice during job interviews, but be prepared if they ask.

The last of the four big topics is the outlook for the industry or company you're evaluating.

## Industry or Company Outlook

You'll benefit from being part of a buoyant field or an ascending institution. You'll be at risk if your field or institution is in decline.

As I write this book, a contemporary example is law school. For years, people could enter law school expecting to find a legal job when they graduated. With new attorney hiring down, however, some new lawyers aren't finding those legal jobs. It certainly makes sense for the right people to enter law school today, but others who aren't sure they want to be attorneys might think twice before making that commitment. The opposite example is a growth industry like organic and natural food. People who entered that world a decade ago have enjoyed the ride as consumers' preferences have changed and companies are growing to meet those needs. They're benefiting personally from that experience.

These situations will change. There'll always be a need for lawyers, and the growth in organic food can't continue at the pace it's enjoyed. But those are the kinds of trends I encourage you to learn about before making your commitment.

As a strategy consultant, I often worked with a team of people for months to develop a highly confident view of the future of an industry or a company. Few can commit an effort like that to career strategizing. Whatever level of depth is appropriate in your inquiry, doing your own industry or company assessment also will equip you for networking meetings and job interviews. The challenge for me in writing this section has been to think about how you can get your feet wet without conducting the full industry study one of my consulting teams would have conducted. Follow the suggestions here.

### Efficient Sources

Two online publications by the US Bureau of Labor Statistics can help you get oriented on a field of work—the *Occupational Outlook Handbook* and *O*Net OnLine.*[1] Dry but useful, they provide getting-started information—for example, the nature of work, wage levels, and employment—on hundreds of occupations. Pay attention to forecast changes in employment; they may suggest whether you'd be swimming with the tide or going upstream.

Other efficient sources, mentioned earlier in this chapter, include public financial reports in companies' 10-K documents and books and articles about companies and industries. And, as I mentioned, get familiar with the institution's products by buying and using low-budget consumer products or talking to people who use either consumer or industrial products.

## Topics to Explore

Look into how the industry operates, making the elements of industry structure your checklist of topics to explore (often called the "Porter Model" due to the powerful way my classmate Michael Porter demonstrated how to evaluate industries):[2]

- Markets
- Competitors in the industry
- Distributors and/or retailers to the market
- Supplier industries
- Barriers to entry or to exit

And there are forces outside the industry that can affect it:

- Substitute products
- Regulation
- New technologies
- Style, taste, and other cultural developments
- The overall economy

You can't go wrong with this list. Explore these topics, and you'll develop a feel for how the industry works today. Look for trends and for potential off-trend changes. Develop your own perspective about what those changes mean and how they affect the attractiveness of entering that field of work.

To investigate an individual company, blend thinking about the industry with specific facts on the company itself. The following is a good checklist of topics to explore about individual companies:

- Financial performance—past, present, and possible future
- Competitive position with different customer groups
- Cost position relative to competitors
- Organization strengths and shortfalls
- Opportunities for improvement
- The big challenges
- Overall, the company's standing in the industry

Industry outlook is an input into your decision, not the final word. If you're excited about a field, it may be right for you even if there are headwinds (though be careful if you expect a hurricane). And if you enter a high-growth field with great opportunity but aren't excited about it, you may not be successful, you may not like it, and ultimately you may leave.

## Learning Expectations for Executives

People seeking executive positions present a special case. Hiring officers will be more open with them about problems and opportunities. They also will have higher expectations about learning. They'll expect candidates to have a plan to get started before they get the offer.

Senior executive Ian provides an excellent example. He led a financial company through a turnaround and then its sale. After several months of time off, he was ready for the next opportunity.

He used a structured screening methodology to explore the possibilities and then did a deep dive on the company where he got an offer.

### Ian's "Due Diligence"

Ian approached opportunity search in the same way that private equity firms seek good investments. He conducted what he called "R&D projects." They worked this way:

> I put together a grid, an inventory of projects, and ranked them on whether they were important to me and their prospects. I was trying to run experiments. I'll devote X amount of time to it. If it doesn't work, I kill it. I was more concerned about false positives than false negatives. With a false positive, I'd spend time on something not going anywhere. I'm a systematic person. It helped me structure the days. I'd feel good about myself or give myself a kick in the butt.

Ian thought about his future and developed four criteria to evaluate the possibilities: "To lead an organization again, for the institution to be challenged and facing a major change, industries I knew well, and in the city where I already lived." He knew that major change could be tough, but felt he was well equipped for that and knew he'd be most likely to find that kind of opportunity. As he later told me, "I'd have been delighted to go into a high-performing company, but typically I don't get that phone call. I get the call when things are messy."

Ian identified promising situations, learned about them, evaluated what he'd learned against his criteria, and decided which ones to pursue in depth. As he put it, "If an experiment or opportunity did not get enough points on the scale or have momentum, then I spent less time on it, protecting my time. Eventually a few leaders emerged, and ultimately a winner hit." The winner had begun with a call in February from a fund that had owned an interest in the company where Ian had just been CEO. That fund owned part of another financial services company that was in distress and needed a new leader.

This fund and its coinvesting partner had just commissioned a search for that leader. Ian followed that firm's process, and by early May he got the word that he was the leading candidate. He then began to negotiate the details, hopefully turning their intention to hire him into a concrete offer, working with them to define the role correctly, and gathering the information needed for Ian to decide whether to accept. He described it like this:

> They were surprised when I sent them a list with over a hundred questions that I built off an M&A due diligence list. If I'm going to move and invest some money in the venture, then I have to treat this with no less than the same seriousness as I would when considering putting up capital.
>
> I told the investment firm partner (whom I didn't know well) that I didn't expect answers to all the questions, but the fact that they can or can't answer questions tells me something. If he answers questions quickly, that tells something—run for the hills or maybe it's good. If they were not able to answer the questions, then I could evaluate that information as either a red flag or weakness that I would need to address.
>
> The partner was put off by this list or at least said he was. It was a way of negotiating on his side. It's part of the game. He answered 30 or 40 percent of it. Regardless, I knew he'd conclude at least that I was taking this very seriously, and I'd ideally begin building trust that I was thorough.

Ian's extensive due diligence shifted the discussion a bit in his favor, because it allowed him to be not only a seller but also a buyer. As he said, "I don't need this job."

Ian learned why the company was financially challenged. It was growing, but prices and margins were among the industry's lowest.

He saw "colossal economic leverage" from price increases. He also saw IT's critical role in pricing and how complicated it would be to change IT. From the next round of conversations, Ian saw how the misguided pricing resulted from process and organizational shortcomings. So he put a lot of effort into understanding that.

The source of the problem and a plan to fix it were the main findings of Ian's due diligence. He concluded that "the culture was antagonistic. Lots of disconnects. I could see the high level of distrust in how people answered questions about themselves and others. There was frustration with the inability to get stuff done." He outlined a plan including replacing one of the top officers and shifting other roles. "Most important," he said, "was to get senior management to function as a team. That would have a multiplier effect." He planned to make this happen by focusing everyone, in a transparent and methodical way, on two or three high-priority problems and achieving early successes. "When we pulled it off," he said, "it would allow us to do ten other things."

As he looked back two years later, Ian was pleased with his due diligence: "It was a twofer: evaluation and diagnostic. My decision and my first ninety days." The way he conducted his side of discussions made the company's owners confident that he was the right choice. What he learned made him confident that he could lead the turnaround, and that allowed him to accept the offer. He followed most elements of his original plan with good results. The organization now functions well, the pricing function and IT are very different, and profits are up. They're shifting from a turnaround mentality to a focus on long-term business development. Ian's aggressive learning is paying off big-time.

Ian met all his original screening criteria but one—the company's location. When he got started, he knew that few companies in his target field were located in his city. It was a sacrifice to commute across the country for more than a year and then—once it was clear that the company had a bright future—to move. He accepted this. The secret to using criteria like these, he said, is to "be as clear as you can, but never doctrinaire."

What you've seen so far is how to conduct research, how to do a study. That's where most people spend the most time. By itself, however, that research seldom works well when you're considering dramatic changes. That's where experimentation is essential.

## Productive Experimentation

If you're thinking of moving from a corporate office to launch a new venture in that field, that's a big change. If you're about to leave the corporate world to open a retail store, that's huge. You're starting over, leaving much of your past behind. If you're considering a very new direction, you'll make a better-informed decision if you can try it out before committing. As INSEAD professor Herminia Ibarra has written, big changes can require changes in personal identities, and people usually need to experiment with those changes first.[3]

I'll start with Nina's story. It shows the power of a full-scale experiment, even though at the time she didn't realize that that was what she was doing.

### Nina's "Experiment" to Become a Picasso

Nina grew up in a conventional environment. Her family's expectations were that she'd go to college, come home, get married, and have a large family. She had no interest in that. As she said: "The last thing I wanted to do was to come home. I was raised to go shopping and have a family. My main motivation was to be free to make my own decisions, not to have the pressure from my mother to do things her way. In my mind, that meant I had to get a job."

Nina found a position in advertising, a loose connection to the studio art classes she'd loved in college. She liked that and transitioned to corporate life on the marketing side. She accomplished things, moved up, and was well paid. She was proud of these successes.

Though her focus was very much on that career, art kept reappearing. Nina took occasional weekend painting courses and painted in her free time. She felt a vague longing for the field. Walking down the street, she saw the world through an artist's eyes—for example, looking at how the light hit a car window and wondering whether she could capture that in a painting, or imagining how to draw the large, weighty tree she was passing without making it look lifeless. She visited art museums on business trips when she had free time.

Nina took vacation to attend a weeklong painting seminar. Recalling her feelings the last day, she said: "I was on fire. It was like being in love. I felt like I was awake for the first time in years. I'd just turned fifty. I realized if I don't do this now, I won't ever do it."

On the plane back home, she decided to change careers. Just like that. Nina needed no big assessment. She knew. This was happening at a time when Nina had begun to question her work. She recalled:

> I was so focused on being successful that I didn't pay attention to the fact that I didn't really care about what I was doing. I didn't even want the last promotion. It was all about politics and personalities. Maybe it was that as I got older, who I was became clearer, and a bad fit became more difficult to endure.

Nina's career had become a job. Once she knew she couldn't give it her all, she didn't want to give it anything.

She checked the financial side before abandoning the high-income life for the studio. She and her husband reviewed their assets and income and what life would be like if she had no income at all. They looked at his income, their savings, and the value of their home. They estimated the cost of paying for their children to finish college. They concluded they could make it work if they sold the house and moved to a less expensive area of town. The children were largely gone, and they didn't need the room or the school district. They'd have to downscale vacations and reduce spending, but her husband supported the change. If that's what she wanted, that's what he wanted. She'd work another year to exit gracefully, but that wasn't a problem. She'd need some time to set up her art career anyway.

Seen in hindsight, Nina's art hobby had been a career experiment for twenty-five years. Weekend painting, classes, and art seminars developed skills. They also enabled her to imagine what life as an artist would be like, spending days alone in her studio. It was a low-cost way to try out what then became her calling. She gained confidence that she could become a real artist, though she didn't know at the time if she'd ever sell any art. She now has a master of fine arts degree, she's selling pieces at a premier gallery, and she takes great satisfaction from creating things. She's turned on. She's doing what she believes she always was intended to do.

One benefit to hearing Nina's story was that I got to meet her in her studio with the large pieces she was working on, some as large as ten feet high. There was something irresistible about them. I had to concentrate not to drift from what she was saying to the paintings. She got a kick out of that.

Experimentation is good for everyone. An experimental mindset is critical for big field shifts like Nina's.

Here's how to have a productive experiment.

### 1. Set Up the Experiment

A summer intern position is an experiment, as are some educational programs (such as the clinical rotations in medical school). You might take classes in an area of interest or get serious about a hobby. If you're already working, perhaps you can volunteer within your organization for an additional role that could turn into an experiment. You might be able to try out the position with a new employer before committing, an exact test of what you'd be doing. Or you might find a volunteer role with a small nonprofit that relates to the field or role you're considering.

Experiments may not demand the high level of commitment you'd have with a full-time position, but don't experiment casually. The best way to learn is to treat the experiment seriously. It might lead directly to a job offer. Success also will add to your network and record of accomplishment. Your experiment can grow skills even if you end up taking a different career path.

## 2. Prepare Your "Curriculum"

Just like a research scientist, know what you hope to learn when you start. The more explicit the learning objectives, the more you'll learn.

What might be in your curriculum? The first two chapters of this book suggest topics: your aspirations and strengths and how well this field or this position aligns with them. For example:

- What do people do day-to-day?
- What might you accomplish? How would you feel about it?
- How much would you enjoy the content of the work? Does the prospect of achieving true mastery in that line of work excite you?
- Does the work deploy your top skills?
- Can you imagine getting excited about and committed to the institution?
- What would you say about organization culture, role, sacrifice, and outlook?

- Can you imagine advancing into a leadership position? What might be a path to that?

### 3. Push to Conclusions

Periodically take out your curriculum. Judge what you're learning in the experiment and whether you need to discover anything more.

I emphasize conclusions, because experimentation can be seductive—a way to be active while putting off tough decisions. If you defer a job offer while undertaking an experiment and the employer offers the position to someone else, your deferral will have become a decision. Avoid analysis paralysis. Don't get too comfortable. Set a time frame so things don't drag out. When the time comes, write down what you've learned. Then decide.

With attractive fields in mind and a good understanding of them, you're ready to decide which one to target, the topic we now turn to in Chapter 5.

Chapter 5

# PERSONAL VALUE PROPOSITION

**THROUGHOUT THE TIME** I was preparing my career strategy class and then as I began to write this book, I sought opportunities to apply business strategy concepts to careers. Most of the concepts were good fits. None were closer matches than the way the value proposition concept in commerce can be applied to empower careers.

## Value Propositions in Business

In business, a value proposition is a statement of the target market segment, the benefits the product provides, how the product meets the target segment's needs, and price.

In the near term, the value proposition explains why a customer in the target market should buy the product. If the value proposition provides a good package of benefits and price for a market segment, it should create competitive advantage there. If the segment is large enough, that value proposition can lead to a sizeable business. Everything flows from the value proposition—from product development to distribution, from pricing to advertising.

The value proposition also leads in the long term. Product development targets are intended to create winning value propositions in the future. People determine what value proposition would be required to win before opening up a new geographic region.

To illustrate this idea, here are three different value propositions for a cruise ship, together with how the ship would be different in each case.

- We provide the best cruise experience to families with young children and charge a 10 percent price premium over average rates. The perfectly designed ship for this market segment includes large cabins to accommodate parents with children, space for entertaining day-care activities and shallow swimming pools for younger children, and climbing walls and other exciting but safe activities for teens.
- We provide the best cruise experience for people who love Broadway-style entertainment, great music, and comedy, for a 10 percent price premium. The perfect ship includes two large theaters and smaller venues to accommodate professional singers and comedians.
- We provide the most economic cruise experience, good basic quality at a 20 percent price discount. The perfect ship includes small cabins and less space for other things to make room for the greater number of cabins required to reach scale economies.

Let's imagine a cruise line's management team thinking about strategy. If they discovered one of these market segments (or another distinctive segment), if its particular needs weren't being met well by other cruise lines, and if the targeted people were willing to pay for the experience, then the cruise line could create competitive advantage by building that ship and marketing it to people in that segment. Everything would flow from a decision to adopt that value proposition—ship design, pricing, advertising, onboard programs, and so on. The company might build several similar ships if the market segment was large enough. Money would fall out of the sky.

Value propositions aren't public relations puff. They only work if they're true—if the business can operate in a way that efficiently delivers the promised benefits. That requires the business to have the right competencies—the skills and assets needed to deliver that value proposition. If those competencies are lacking, then the strategy will fail.

A related concept is an organization's employee value proposition. Several of my former McKinsey colleagues researched the War for Talent—the intense recruiting and retention competition for highly qualified people.[1] The study team conceived of applying the value proposition to help companies recruit and retain employees—viewing hiring as a strategic imperative and qualified people as a market. They defined the employee value proposition as a statement of the benefits an employer offers current and prospective employees, together with what's expected from them.

For example, imagine a multibusiness high-tech company seeking qualified engineers to join one of their product management teams. What might the employee value proposition look like? Here's one good possibility: The company would focus on engineers who hoped to move into management—its target segment of employees. It would create job responsibilities, coaching, and other learning opportunities that would make successful transitions possible, even likely. The office would be in a city that many would find attractive. The job would come with competitive compensation and benefits. In return, the company would expect these product management team members to give their work a high priority, to work against tight deadlines, and to do a great deal of business travel. It would offer the prospect for rapid advancement, but with some risk; people would become managers within a few years or leave the company. That scenario would appeal to some, not all. Like a product value proposition, it's targeted, it offers specific benefits, and the costs (in this case, the sacrifices) are clear.

## Value Propositions in Careers

Value propositions can be powerful in business. The payoff for us from this discussion is to see how the value proposition concept applies to careers. I'll first describe the career application and then illustrate it with the best example I've found.

### The Personal Value Proposition

The *personal value proposition* (PVP) is the mirror image of the employee value proposition. It's the heart of career strategy.

Your PVP is central to long-term career strategy. It's what you hope to become. It's your destination. You take initiatives to build that PVP—from career path planning to education, from network building to creating reputation.

Your PVP also is central to near-term strategy, though that PVP reflects current skills rather than where you hope to be in the future. It's a statement of why your employer should promote you now, not someone else. It's why another employer should hire you now, not someone else. It drives everything in a job search.

The PVP also checks unrealistic ambitions. If you can't imagine a winning PVP for a field you think you'd like in the future or for a job you think you want now, that may be because you don't fit. Thinking about your PVP will help rule out pursuing a field or a position where your efforts would be a waste of time. It will reduce the risk that you'll end up with a bad fit that could slow your career.

So what does a strong PVP look like? Imagine three people in their mid-thirties who all have MBAs from the same school and all work in different parts of the same multinational telecom company. Here are their PVPs:

- I know operations and can get the highest possible productivity from your network operations group. Evidence: my electrical engineering degree, my past experience in telecom operations, my MBA with an operations focus, and my current work in a wireless network.
- I'm a leader who naturally recognizes customer needs and can motivate telecom sales teams to high accomplishments. Evidence: my electrical engineering degree, my college experience as basketball team captain, my time as an infantry officer, my MBA emphasizing sales and marketing, and my current telecom marketing work.
- I'm a world-class problem solver who can find new business opportunities and bring them across the finish line. Evidence: my degree with a double major in electrical engineering and mathematical economics, my experience as an investment analyst in telecom businesses, my MBA with four Distinctions, and my current work in telecom M&A.

Each of these PVPs could enable promising long-term strategies. They could enable productive job searches in the industry or an ascending career path at the current company. Each targets a particular type of job, states what's distinctive about the individual, and provides evidence.

Imagine someone else the same age at the same company with an MBA from the same school who presented himself as a general mix of these characteristics and was seeking all three kinds of positions and perhaps some others too. He'd keep his options open, but pay a price for doing that. He'd disperse his time and effort across multiple possibilities. He wouldn't communicate as clearly. Unless he was a truly superior candidate, he'd lose to the others with their more targeted PVPs. One aspect of strategy is to choose some things and not others. This fourth person might feel the consequences of not making that choice.

This chapter focuses on PVPs for the *long-term*. In Chapter 8, we'll return to the role of PVPs in near-term strategy and job search.

You read about Steve —the corporate CEO who aggressively manages business travel—in the introduction and in Chapter 4. Steve has something more important to share with us: his PVP and how it regularly leads to significant new opportunities.

## Steve's Incredible PVP

How many people are asked to consider a new COO or CEO position three or four times a year? That happens to Steve, fifty-four. As I was writing up my notes from our conversation, I almost couldn't believe what I'd heard.

I'll set the stage by describing Steve. He's an operations leader. Many in roles like that are practical people who draw on motivational skills and personal experience to solve problems. That's not Steve. He makes things run smoothly as a big idea man. Steve spots the complexity in operational processes before most others do, and his ideas about how to deal with the complexity can come out fast. Steve makes good things happen. His business has moved from serious operations shortfalls to having a competitive advantage from operations.

Attractive positions come to Steve, far more than show up on the doorsteps of other executives with similar records. Steve gets these calls because of the way he's conceptualized his PVP and the strong professional network that's resulted. The surprise about Steve's network is its size—a grand total of three people. Can this really be possible? Can a network of three people really deliver three or four real COO or CEO opportunities a year?

Here's how Steve describes his PVP:

> It's hard to know what you're really good at. You need more than the ordinary, convenient categories. I seek the kinds of things where I fit naturally, what I enjoy. That's not consumer products, not hard science, not financial institutions, and not an enterprise that's pursuing something other than long-term financial objectives. It's operations-intensive companies who can benefit from significant performance improvement. I take floundering institutions and go build things. It's not quite turnaround, not slash and burn; but it's a far way from peaceful stewardship of assets. I'm a go-build guy.

Steve targets companies with sales ranging from $150 million to $1 billion. He doesn't want start-ups where everything would need to be established, nor a company so large that he couldn't know people down the line.

He prefers private companies. Having no experience with the special duties of a public corporation's CEO, he feels that it doesn't make sense to have to learn all that on the job at this point in his life.

Steve also emphasizes his view of the right atmosphere. "I'm not at all into sleazy places, nor into industries like tobacco, alcohol, or casinos. Ethically challenged places are no fun." Although we could debate whether those industries present ethical issues, that's not the point. They aren't right for him.

I created Table 5-1 from my notes of our conversation. It pulls together the different elements of Steve's PVP.

Steve's PVP leaves out the great majority of positions, but that doesn't bother him. He gets three or four calls a year asking him to consider a corporate CEO or COO position that's related to his PVP.

**TABLE 5.1** Steve's PVP

| TARGET | COMPANY NEEDS/ STEVE'S STRENGTHS | STEVE'S EXPECTATIONS |
| --- | --- | --- |
| • Operations–intensive industrial companies<br>• Potential benefit from significant operational improvement<br>• Privately owned<br>• Not companies requiring innovation in marketing or finance<br>• Not companies which he feels have the "wrong atmosphere"<br>• Not turnarounds<br>• Not startups | • Insight to improve performance of complex operations<br>• Leading teams to improve operations<br>• Perspectives from experiences across companies<br>• Baseline corporate functional leadership: finance, legal, etc.<br>• Reporting/communications with private owners | • Freedom to act in company's interest<br>• Profit and value driven goals<br>• Compensation at market, with big upside if meet/exceed goals |

Before we talked, Steve had never heard of the PVP concept or the characteristics of a sound PVP. But his story shows them in action. He developed his strategy to help him respond when people asked him about jobs. As he put it, "It was a polite and well-reasoned way to turn down things they were pitching that didn't fit, without my turndowns being obnoxious."

Steve accepts that he won't be considered for most CEO jobs, because most jobs don't fit his PVP. He's betting that his narrow PVP will give him an entry to positions where he's strong and that he'd enjoy.

The three people in Steve's network don't call about everything. They call about positions that connect to his PVP. It's easy to understand. It's unlike what other similarly qualified executives might say about themselves. These people believe he's a strong candidate for positions like that. Without a PVP or with a mushy PVP, Steve might not get these calls. He doesn't really think of what he's doing as seeking something new. He's certainly not in play and almost always tells the caller he's not interested. But he always picks up the phone.

We'll now turn from Steve's remarkable PVP to how to develop yours.

## Developing Your Aspirational PVP

A PVP includes four elements: target, requirements, strengths, and expectations. Think them through in this sequence, while looping back from time to time to incorporate the impact of later steps on earlier ones.

### 1. Target

The PVP begins with a target: a field or role you like and one that needs what you have to offer. Be specific—for example, not IT in general, but IT solutions development or perhaps IT solutions in supply chain management. You can think about progression within your current employer or look to the entire industry.

Pull together the streams of learning from the first four chapters of Part I.

Draw on your research to double-check your interest in the substance of the fields you're considering. Ask whether you'd meet your most important values in those fields—whether you'd care most about service, craftsmanship, and institution building.

Check these fields against your current strengths and judge whether you could do what's required in the intervening years to win in the future.

Part of getting smart about a possible target is to identify important changes on the horizon. Investigate developments in the fields you're considering—the upside they might enable and current possibilities they might close off. If everything else is equal, you'll be better off in an ascending industry, as you read in Chapter 4.

A single target simplifies everything. You can plan your future with that target in mind and pursue that future aggressively.

If you can't settle on a single target aspiration, then you'll need different plans—and therefore different PVPs—for each target. You'll take early, lower-effort steps in two or more target areas and learn from those experiences. Keeping options open can be appealing, but that flexibility comes with a downside. If you pursue multiple targets and if they require different activities, they'll expand the demands on your time and energy. Quality may suffer.. If this is where you are, you're continuing to explore. That may be the right choice right now, but at some point you'll benefit from narrowing things down.

## 2. What's Required for Success

In planning for the long term, imagine what you'll need to be able to accomplish in the future to succeed at the target. I use the word "imagine," and that's a big part of doing well at this step of the process. You can't know exactly what those future job requirements will be. Talk to informed people about the field or the role and learn about the requirements for success. You'll do best if you get several perspectives and then sit back and think deeply about what they mean. Think about what you'd be seeking if you were standing in the shoes of those potential future employers.

## 3. How Strengths Can Make You Successful

Now comes the hard part: applying those future requirements for success to yourself. You have a good sense of where you are at this time. Take a leap into the future and describe what about you would make you successful then at your target position. With this long-term perspective in mind, you may find that what's needed has more to do with natural talents than with the specific knowledge you have today or that you easily could acquire.

No one's perfect. You're strong in some areas and not as strong in others. Consider whether you could expand existing strengths and deal with the gaps.

### 4. What You Expect in Return

Your expectations about features of the position, such as work environment, money, and sacrifices, complete your PVP. They're similar to the role of price in a value proposition in business. By identifying clear expectations, you can target fields or positions with a good prospect of meeting those expectations (and avoid those that don't).

I've presented these four steps in a logical sequence—from a target to the target's requirements to how you meet those requirements to your expectations. It's a productive path. In practice, however, these aspects of PVP will intermingle. For example, your plausible future strengths may lead to targets, not the reverse. Or your expectations may knock out some otherwise attractive targets. Keep this sequence in mind, but move fluidly among the steps.

Recall corporate attorney Jerry from Chapter 2, who thought he was ready to be a CEO. He wasn't familiar with the PVP concept at that time, but he finally understood it intuitively. When I asked why he got the general counsel offer he accepted, he described a very credible PVP for that position:

> They'd never had a general counsel before. They hired me because they were getting someone with twenty years of complex experience in-house, someone who could help on nearly all substantive areas. They were looking to reduce outside counsel spending. They wanted someone with managerial and executive capability, but who was comfortable being a soldier when there was no one else to pass the gun to. And I clicked with the CEO.

Jerry got the offer instead of the law firm people the company was interviewing because of his breadth of knowledge of the law, his familiarity with the business side, the confidence that he'd be a workhorse rather than a staff grower, and the personality match with the CEO.

Educator Nathan from Chapter 1 provides another example of PVP-style thinking. Here's how he responded when I asked why they offered him the position he took, rather than other educators with far more experience:

> They were looking for someone who could come in and restructure special ed services at schools with bad track records. That's basically the job I've been doing for three years with good results. I was able to give them a step-by-step rundown of what I've done at our school and toss out a few very basic steps any school could take. I think the fact that I've successfully done the job, managed a diverse group of teachers, and was able to come into the interview with ideas made me attractive.

Begin your inquiry with values and strengths, let those values and strengths lead to your target fields, and check your strengths against target employer requirements. If you combine all that in the right way, you'll know your aspirational PVP.

Before you're done, test your PVP with these questions:

- Does the PVP tightly connect your skills and knowledge to the target?
- Does the PVP target what you'd like to do?
- What would others say is your PVP? What do they say about this PVP?
- Would the PVP be more powerful if you narrowed the field?
- Does the PVP have a good shot at becoming your calling?

If thinking through these questions supports the course you've set, you have grounds for confidence and aggressive implementation. If not, take a return trip back through the logic you've followed, explore reasons for any discrepancies, and reconsider.

Finish with quality. Prepare *a full written description of the PVP and the reasoning that led to it.* Be explicit. You'll use this written document again and again as your career proceeds.

Your aspirational PVP completes the work of Chapter 5. More broadly, it completes Part I. The PVP is your long-term career direction if you're ready to make that kind of commitment. If you're not ready to commit, your PVP identifies promising possibilities and what's needed to succeed in each one. Either way, this aspirational PVP becomes the goal of your long-term action plan—what you'll see next in Part II.

Part II

# LONG-TERM STRATEGY

I am tomorrow, or some future day, what I establish today. I am today what I established yesterday or some previous day.

JAMES JOYCE

You can always amend a big plan, but you can never expand a little one. I don't believe in little plans. I believe in plans big enough to meet a situation which we can't possibly foresee now.

HARRY S. TRUMAN

**BUSINESS STRATEGIES SOMETIMES RESULT** from near-term decisions on big commitments. Perhaps the decision is to build a new plant, launch a new product, or make an acquisition. Or perhaps it is not to do those things. These near-term decisions may accelerate the company's progress down its existing track. They may start something new. Or they may be misguided and lead to problems later. Big near-term decisions often come with big long-term implications.

There are risks to deriving long-term strategy from near-term decisions. The urgency to make a near-term decision may lead people to decide without fully understanding the issues at hand. And the opportunities that leaders consider may be limited to the ones that come up in the course of events rather than opportunities

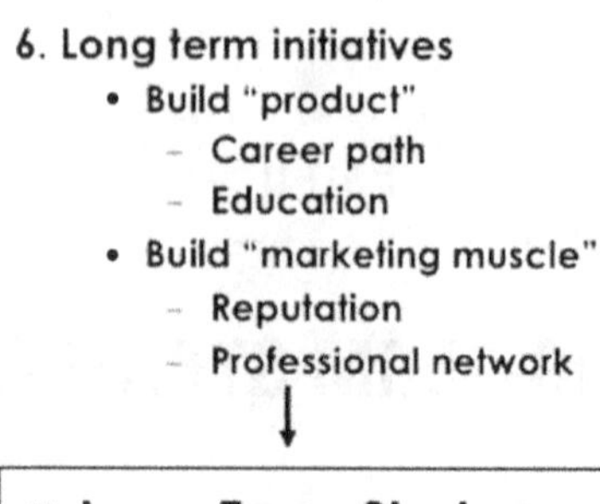


**FIGURE PII.1** Develop Your Long-Term Career Strategy

they deliberately create over time. Not necessarily bad, but they may not be playing at the top of the game.

Executives with their eyes on the future have a better shot at true leadership. They anticipate threats before the situation becomes urgent. They create opportunities to position their institutions for the future. They get ahead of the game.

Career strategies also can come when they're required—when a surprising new opportunity appears, when there's a setback, or when there's a change in personal circumstances. Just as in business, however, the best time to set career strategy is not when you must. It's earlier, before the opportunities and challenges arrive at your doorstep.

Without the time pressure generated by the need for an immediate decision, you can think big about what you'd like to accomplish over the next decade and where you'd hope to be then. You can plan for the uncertainty in that. How to set aspirations and the PVP you hope to build over your work life was the subject of Part I. That aspirational PVP is the cornerstone of your long-term strategy, but it's not the strategy. The strategy is the action plan to build that PVP to realize those aspirations.

In Part II, you'll see how to convert the aspirational PVP you just developed into a long-term strategy, following the steps shown in Figure PII.1.

In Chapter 6, you'll read about the initiatives that can constitute your long-term strategy: career path planning, education, reputation building, and network building.

Chapter 7 completes the long-term strategy program. It shows how to assemble the right portfolio of initiatives and turn them into a dynamic implementation plan—the strategic road map.

Chapter 6

# LONG-TERM STRATEGY INITIATIVES

**WITH YOUR LONG-TERM PVP** in hand, you'll need to decide what to do about it. You'll be like a product development team that's just determined the target value proposition for a new product. They have a great idea. Their action plan comes next. From the lab to the plant to the market, they imagine the many activities that are needed to bring that new product to life. Is it time to go all in? If so, the company's leaders will take a series of big and expensive actions. Sometimes they decide to take smaller steps to try things out first. Maybe they'll begin the development projects that have long lead times while delaying others, conduct hands-on customer trials with prototypes, or do a full-scale market test in an isolated market. If those tests go well, then they're off to the races; if not, it's back to the drawing board.

In the same way, moving from an aspirational PVP to an action plan requires a new level of imagination. How to bring that PVP to life? Some career initiatives will require considerable time and resources, others much less. You'll do best if you develop a full menu of potential actions. From that full menu, you can decide what to do, knowing that you considered everything that might make sense.

Whether they're big commitments or small, career initiatives fall into four categories.

The first two classes of initiatives are career path planning and education. They develop the product you hope to become by building the record of accomplishment and the skills you need to move ahead.

The other two classes of initiatives are about creating reputation and a professional network. They lay the groundwork to locate opportunities when you need them. Better yet, they make it more likely that great opportunities will come to you. Similar to advertising and advance professional selling, they're essential assets to market your product.

This chapter investigates these initiatives one by one and shows how to use them to formulate your long-term action program. I start with career path planning.

## Career Path Planning

Seek a career path that can take you through positions that build the skills and record of accomplishment required to reach your long-term targets.

Some fields absolutely require a sequence of assignments. No one becomes a general officer without moving up through the officer ranks. At McKinsey & Company, almost every senior partner worked his or her way up the apprenticeship system from associate to engagement manager to associate principal to principal to director—typically over twelve to fourteen years. There are good reasons for requirements like these. The experience can build the skills needed to be effective at higher ranks. It also allows the institution to judge qualifications for advancement.

Some institutions' HR processes lead that kind of progressive career development. People viewed as high performers gain experiences across divisions, functions, or countries to strengthen the talent pool. Some companies are called "career academies" because they do this well. People also move from company to company seeking that growth.

Whether you're emphasizing advancement inside your current institution or you're looking outside, think through your career path. With one or, better yet, several paths toward your long-term aspirations, you'll increase the prospect of meeting those aspirations.

Here's an example. Imagine you left college with an engineering degree and began working in a large paper mill. Over five years, you worked in quality assurance, scheduling, and then as a shift supervisor. At that point, you'd know a lot about paper manufacturing. Let's assume you liked this line of work and hoped to lead a paper company or perhaps another kind of manufacturing company. What assignments might make that possible?

One obvious path would be to move up the line within that mill or other mills with the same company. You'd hope to become a mill manager and then lead the company's overall manufacturing function. Or you might follow a path through similar roles at another paper company. There might be good alternatives in related process manufacturing industries, such as steel or cement. These moves would make you a stronger and stronger operations leader.

A different route to the top might be through assignments in different functions. For example, you might move to corporate engineering, where you'd lead capital projects across the company. Or perhaps you'd move farther afield to sales or to finance, a decision based on the logic that your operations experience would equip you for those roles in an unconventional way and that those experiences would make you a better general manager later. In considering step-outs like these, you'd be thinking about how well you'd do in those roles and how well your new skills would prepare you for cross-functional leadership.

Let's look at a career path in action, corporate executive John's. Even back in college, John knew he wanted to become a CEO. He consistently pursued that aspiration through thick and thin, gained the required experiences and skills, and ultimately made it happen.

### How John Followed His Vision through Ups and Downs

I'll begin John's story when he was in his mid-forties and was a staff SVP at a large consumer goods company. He'd been viewed as an up-and-comer, but fell off the fast track. He declined a proposed international transfer that posed personal challenges. He then was asked to move laterally to another headquarters position, but with no interest in that function, he declined that too. No new transfers were suggested over the next year, and John concluded that he no longer was on the high-potential list. He began looking outside.

A search firm presented John a CEO possibility in a midsized company. He liked the product. He liked the people. It absolutely would have met his long-term aspiration. But after he and his wife visited the headquarters in a small town out on the prairie, they concluded they wouldn't be happy living there.

John then became SVP in another sizeable consumer business. His role was to lead a turnaround in sales. Returning to line management was exactly what he wanted, but the role came with challenges. "It was huge and bureaucratic," he said. "It wasn't performance based. If you kept your nose clean, you could stay for a career and get a nice pension even if your sales were far below what was expected." Despite the many assurances he got when being recruited, John was surprised by the lack of support from his boss, by the resistance from other officers, and therefore by his lack of progress turning things around. These relationships deteriorated when John terminated several blockers. He threw in the towel after three years, with few lasting accomplishments.

John began another search. He was surprised to learn that his experience leading a five-thousand-person sales and marketing group made him a strong candidate for another senior position. Maybe his recent experience wouldn't harm his future.

After more than a year of living off of his severance payment and dipping into savings, John became staff SVP in a large consumer electronics company. That role offered another opportunity to build expertise and make things happen. This time, John got off to an excellent start and was having obvious positive impact. Toward the end of his second year, however, the lab missed two product development releases. That meant the company wasn't competitive in this fast-moving industry. Sales fell dramatically, cash was burning at a fast rate, and the company failed.

John spent several years investing in start-ups and serving on small company boards. He enjoyed the board perspective, but wanted to get back to hands-on management.

The CEO opportunity that turned up from John's network was to lead a midsized retail chain. John was a good match. His experience in sales and marketing, his work with corporate functions, and his board experience set him up to get the offer. Under John's leadership, the company grew, and profits increased. John built a strong team, and he had fun. He finished his career on a high note.

John's route to the corner office had detours and disappointments, but throughout he kept his leadership aspiration front and center. Every time John considered a new position, he thought about whether it would prepare him to lead a company. Not everything went as he'd wished, but his growing capability and accomplishments were the ticket.

John also provides a lesson in resilience. He believed in himself. Facing similar events, others might have assumed their careers were dead. I suspect John had those thoughts, but they stayed in the background, and he kept to his purpose. That steadiness in the face of disappointments was essential to his ultimate success.

•

How to plan your career path? Take these steps.

### 1. Roll Back the Future

Follow a technique we used to help business clients develop long-term strategies. We'd work together with the clients to imagine the desired future for the business. Then we'd step back toward the present time to determine what to do year by year to create that desired future. Beginning with the end in mind, we worked backward. We called it "rolling back the future."

To apply this technique to your career, take the target you've set in your long-term PVP. Roll back the future from that time to identify what you need to be doing right before you secure that position. Take another step backward and imagine what you'd need to be doing just before that. And so on, back to today.

Be ambitious and advance as rapidly as your capabilities allow, but pace yourself, like a long-distance runner. Challenging but doable is a good standard.

This is the time to consider the collective impact of your different positions. Which assignments will build the PVP needed to deliver those aspirations? Which ones will prepare you for the next step? Pull this thinking together to determine the overall architecture of a good career path.

Direct, linear plans can make sense. So can indirect paths. One of the best metaphors I've seen for career planning was coined by Facebook COO Sheryl Sandberg.[1] As she put it, "There's only one way to get to the top of a ladder, but there are many ways to get to the top of a jungle gym." She recommends that everyone have a "long-term dream," along with an "eighteen-month plan." And that eighteen-month plan includes both accomplishments and personal growth. I've seen the truth in that. A record of accomplishment and capability growth are required to move up the career ladder, and they also create opportunities to move around the jungle gym.

Because you can't know if your direct career path will actually unfold as you intend it to, it's smart to imagine one or two or other plausible routes up the jungle gym. Less direct ways may turn out to be better, and they can be good fallback options if the preferred path doesn't develop as you hope it will.

Pay special attention to the first steps on the path. They're the ones you can take now. They're by far the most important. If you don't take those steps, you may never reach the later ones.

## 2. Consider Job Crafting

It may be inadvisable to leave your current position to get started on the path you just identified. If so, perhaps you can achieve some of the goals of the early steps on that path through what Amy Wrzesniewski, Justin Berg, and Jane Dutton call "job crafting." The central idea behind job crafting is that if you'd like to shift responsibilities while remaining in your current position, you may be able to redesign the content of your work. Perhaps you can shift your role to add the potential for different accomplishments or to build new skills. Maybe you can expand your internal network by working with new people. Or maybe you'll benefit from enlarging your own perceptions of your work. These authors have written a lot about this concept, so I won't go further here, but if you'd like to learn more about job crafting, a good place to start is their *Harvard Business Review* article.[2] Job crafting can be the first step on your career path.

## 3. Execute Flexibly

I doubt that you'll follow the plan exactly as you laid it out. There's too much uncertainty. Some steps on the path may work out well; others may not. Steps on the path may set up opportunities you like better than the end points you had in mind when you prepared the plan.

General Eisenhower's comments on war plans are applicable to careers: "In preparing for battle I have always found that plans are useless, but planning is indispensable." The massive planning before D-Day was absolutely necessary. It targeted Normandy's beaches, along with the deception plan that appeared to target Calais. It established the locations, the sequence of deployments, and logistics support. Once the invasion was under way, however, many things changed, and plans were revised again and again and again.

Career path planning is one way to develop the product you hope to become. The other is education.

## Education

Some fields have absolute, literal educational requirements. If you wish to be a physician, you must graduate from medical school, complete the follow-up specialty training, and pass the appropriate exams. To be a real estate broker, you must pass certification exams. You'll have no choice if you pursue fields like these. There can be good reasons for requirements. I doubt, for example, that you'd select a surgeon who lacked that training or who failed those exams.

Advanced degrees aren't required in other fields, though they can accelerate progress. The master of fine arts degree is an example. It can help the artist grow and find galleries to promote his or her work, but it's not necessary.

Nondegreed training programs and certifications—programs in human resources management, environmental management, and software development, for example—also can help build careers.

There are less intense ways to keep up or sharpen expertise—for example, reading journals related to your medical specialty or attending continuing legal education classes. Everyone should take advantage of these lower-commitment activities. They may be all that's needed for some people. In this section, however, I'm going beyond that. I'm encouraging you to consider the role of significant commitments of time and energy to education as part of your long-term strategy.

Sixty-two-year-old physician George shows the power of midcareer education. His master's degree helped him find the role he wanted.

### Dr. George's Master's Degree

After two years as a physician with the Peace Corps in Africa, George began private practice back in the United States. He enjoyed the diagnostic challenges and the visible differences he made in patients' lives. His was not the most highly compensated medical specialty, but he felt adequately paid. For most of this time, George also spent four to eight hours a week teaching or advising residents from the local medical school. He liked the university environment.

Twenty years later, however, George was burning out. His work felt no different than it had five years before or even ten. He'd stopped learning, and school politics affected his teaching. He resented the growing power of health insurance companies. Although he'd never been served with a lawsuit, he didn't like practicing defensive medicine just to be safe. He'd also come to resent patients with rich insurance policies who demanded expensive treatments that he didn't think were needed.

George took two initiatives that he enjoyed and that he hoped would lead somewhere good.

Enrolling in evening classes, he got a master's degree in public health (MPH). It was a two-year commitment that left him with few free nights and weekends on top of everything else he was doing, but the learning he did in that program and the credential he earned equipped him for management roles.

George also volunteered for short medical trips, supporting the work of US NGOs operating in less developed countries. He took personal satisfaction from those trips, and they fed his interest in that work.

He almost died the year after he got the degree. After a first operation and then a second, he was back to normal with a good prognosis. This experience and his general dissatisfaction led him to think actively about a change. He wanted to help disadvantaged people.

George got lucky. He's one of two midcareer people I've known in my research who found a new position through a recruiting advertisement or job posting. (The best source of opportunities is networking, as I'll discuss in depth later in this chapter.) The ad was in a medical journal—to lead the medical division of a Europe-based organization operating in developing countries. He'd never have thought of this position without the ad.

One reason I'd wanted to talk to George in the first place was to learn about his decision to move across the ocean at age sixty-three. I'd assumed that it was complicated and that he'd done a big assessment of pros and cons. I was wrong. George accepted the offer the day after he got it. Three months later, he and his wife sold their house, their car, and most of their possessions and moved. He described it in a colorful way:

> We were jumping off a cliff. We didn't think about it much. I was ready to leave. I was tired of what I was doing. This may have been more of a fleeing than a calling. The act of walking away, selling our car, and so on, was gratifying. I'd wanted to get back into international health and to make a difference ever since my time in the Peace Corps. But I had needed to make my mark professionally and raise a family first. I'd had two life-threatening illnesses. I knew that if I got sick again there, I'd be done. But I still was prepared to do it.

This was the first time George had been excited about work in a decade. His medical practice and his professor role had been a calling or close to a calling, but he lost it. Returning to his earlier international experience, he found a new calling.

Not many people George's age invest the effort he did to reset career direction. He certainly didn't predict how the public health degree would affect his opportunities, but the education and the volunteering led exactly to where he wanted to go.

Education, learning, and certification can enhance your PVP. They can create a new PVP. Think it through this way.

### 1. Decide Whether to Apply

Learn about the benefits of the educational program you're considering—what you'd learn, how inspiring it would be, how it might affect professional acquaintances and reputation, what opportunities it might unlock, and what else it might do for you.

I'll illustrate the value of education with the program I know best: the MBA degree. I sometimes ask the students who take my class why they decided to get an MBA. Most think back to their logic two years earlier and mention one or more of three goals: to accelerate their career in a function or field, to move from a technical or functional discipline into management, or to find a new and different line of work. Those goals are sensible, but vague.

I also ask how their MBA experience has affected their PVP. This question opens a different door, and they're much clearer. They see themselves as reshaping their PVP in one or more of these ways.

- Business knowledge: Why attend B-school if it doesn't deliver business knowledge? Students mention familiarity with functions where they had little prior experience, deeper expertise in functions where they already had experience, and perspective on the big picture, including organization and strategy.

- Problem-solving skills: more rigorous students mentioned more rigorous approaches, including analytical frameworks and quantitative methodologies.
- Working with others: productive teamwork, communications skills, and network building were on several lists.
- Personal productivity: better time management, absorbing new material rapidly, and making no-excuses commitments to do hard things.
- Personal reflection and direction setting: exposure to different academic disciplines and industries, a diverse group of students and professors, and the career office all enlarged the range of fields and roles students considered.

Whatever educational experience you're considering, talk to people who've completed the program and assemble a list something like this one to help judge its importance to you.

Compare those benefits to what you'd be giving up if you continue working—the accomplishments and learning you'd realize there. Calculate the financial cost (both lost earnings if that's relevant and out-of-pocket cost). Taking all these factors into account, what role might education play in your overall career plan? Is it helpful? Is it essential?

Investigate individual programs. Learn how well they'd serve your goals, along with their implications on the cost side and whether they'd require a move. Determine whether to apply and, if so, where. If you do apply, leverage what you've learned from the thinking you've done about aspirations and your PVP to write admission essays and prepare for interviews.

### 2. Decide Whether to Attend

Deciding to apply is one thing. Deciding whether to attend is another. The decision-making methodologies you'll see in Part

IV of this book very much apply here, and there are special considerations related to education.

If you're admitted, three things are different than they were when you applied. You'll now evaluate a specific program or programs where you've been admitted, not the general idea of entering a program. You may know more than you did before about the outlook if you stay where you are. You may know more about yourself. The thinking you did to prepare the application essays and your reflections since then may have solidified your rationale for applying or raised questions about it.

If you can't commit to a big education program, might there be smaller steps toward the same goals? Perhaps you can audit courses at a local university without being a in a formal degree program. There may be certification programs that add to your knowledge in important (and perhaps more specific) ways than degree programs. What can you learn on your own?

Let's now shift from building your record and your capabilities to the marketing side—how to get ready to present yourself to find and secure the right opportunities. One part of this is reputation.

## Reputation Building

A positive product reputation can lead to a trial purchase. If customers have good experiences, those products can become brands. People aren't brands like those you see in business, or at least the great majority aren't. But something similar comes to mind—reputation.

Your reputation with colleagues comes first. It directly speaks to what you've accomplished, what you might accomplish in the future, and what it's like to work with you. People who consider you for a new role will want to learn about that work experience. There's no GPA or SAT score for that. They'll ask about that experience in job interviews. They'll contact past coworkers—both bosses and peers—for references. A reputation for being an authentically good person to work with is most important. (How to be such a person is a huge subject, but doing well at work is not the subject of this book.)

A second source of reputation results from the reputations of the institutions where you've worked and the schools you've attended. It's a secondary implication of the earlier discussion of career paths and education. The more prestigious the institution, the greater will be the impact.

What I address here is a third facet of reputation building. It's like product branding and marketing. Commit some time to this, but don't let it interfere with the reputation you're building at work. Here are ways to get the word out about you.

### Professional Organizations

Join professional associations related to your field—for example, a local business organization, a national organization related to your profession, or an alumni organization. If you'd like to create reputation in the electronics industry, join the relevant electronics association. If you're focusing on human resources, join an HR association.

Attend meetings and conferences. Become known as a contributor. Seek opportunities to organize events and lead sessions. You will also meet people and build your network, a topic we'll get to soon.

### Community Service

Voluntary contributions of time or service in nonprofit board of director roles also can build reputation. Volunteering works best if you're truly interested in the institution's purpose, so that comes first. Make that your primary reason and the reputational or networking benefits secondary. You need to make a meaningful contribution to build reputation, and without that interest, you may not accomplish anything important.

## Publishing

Your name in print or other media is a third avenue to reputation, as long as you have something meaningful to say. Readers may think of you when seeking someone for a particular position. You can bring publications to meetings to help build networks or when interviewing for a job. One good path is to submit an article to an association publication, tied to conferencing activities.

## Strategic Focus

Reputation building is competitive. Others may be doing something similar. Whatever initiatives you take need to be high quality.

Don't expect to develop a reputation as a generally good person. People won't get it. Determine a substantive theme that's tied to your PVP (perhaps a function, an industry, or a trend in the environment). Let that theme determine your subject, your conferences, your groups, or perhaps your blog.

An excellent example of reputation building and its career impact is the personal website developed by MBA student Cara.

## The Unexpected Result from Cara's Website

Cara hoped to find a position in a part of the entertainment industry related to her other academic work and work experience before school. She pursued the traditional avenues: interviewing when relevant companies visited campus, contacting them directly where she had no other introduction, and talking to people she already knew in the field. Her problem was that few of those institutions sought MBAs.

Cara was getting nowhere and needed a different approach. In August before her second MBA year, she created a website about entertainment business management. She regularly posted short papers showing connections between what she was learning in B-school and entertainment. It wasn't an advertisement that said "I am capable." It was content that *showed* she was capable. It showed her insight and ability to relate what she was learning in school to the entertainment industry. It showed she knew how to write. It showed she'd go out of the box.

Cara also attended industry conferences, met people, and gave out business cards that encouraged visits to her website. She followed up with site visitors.

She got two offers from people she met through this activity. That was good, but both were positions she might have gotten without the MBA. That made no sense to her.

Cara was surprised to see that her blog was creating a reputation for her in social media. She was invited to speak at conferences about social media in entertainment and to talk about building personal reputations through social media. She ended up with an attractive position with a social media consulting firm, helping client companies set up websites, marketing through the websites, and teaching social media strategies to employees. She'd begun by using social media to pursue the entertainment industry. She found a new career in social media.

Throughout the book, you're seeing how to develop plans to pursue an aspiration. You're also seeing how those plans sometimes lead to appealing surprises. Cara not only provides an excellent example of the impact of reputation building, but also shows how well-executed plans can lead to unexpected and appealing opportunities.

The other source of marketing muscle is professional network.

## Network Building

There are three sources of opportunity: public sources, such as job postings; affiliations; and professional networks. Networks are by far the most important.

Anyone can respond to Internet job sites, print ads, and the career sections of company websites. For some positions, sources like these are the only route. For example, you can't enter the career foreign service without taking the exam and going through other required steps. If that kind of institution is your target, follow the application process rigorously. For other situations, use public sources but contain the time spent. Absolutely don't rely on them.

I say this acknowledging that job postings feel concrete to someone in a search. There's likely to be a real opportunity there, though hundreds of others may respond too. I also recognize that postings may be a greater part of the market for people with less experience. Nonetheless, there usually are better places for everyone to go.

Affiliations often are better. University career offices encourage companies to visit campus to meet student job candidates. Some also help alumni. Professional associations may sponsor job fairs or have member-only Internet job sites. There are career workshops for former military officers. Employers view the affiliation as a screen, a way to ensure that the applicant has a certain background and quality. Take full advantage of affiliations, but don't rely on them either.

The best source of opportunities is other people. Professional networks are enormously helpful in every aspect of career strategy—identifying opportunities, evaluating opportunities, and thinking through objectives and PVPs. The great majority of attractive jobs begin with professional acquaintances, as attested to by three-quarters of the people I've spoken to who found new positions. That's true for people who leave their companies. That's true for people who advance in their companies. Without a strong network, you're operating at a disadvantage. And, of course, some professional acquaintances may become personal friends.

Here are two people who built powerful, but very different, networks. Steve's network is tiny and tight, whereas Baxter's is enormous and loose. Steve's reflects substantive value added, Baxter's the benefits of acquaintanceship.

### Steve's Tiny Network

You read about manufacturing CEO Steve in Chapter 5 when I described his narrow but formidable PVP. Viewed through the lens of this chapter, Steve is also an outstanding networker. He's outstanding even though the only effort he puts into it is the way he handles phone calls.

As I've noted, Steve's network includes three people—two from investment firms who sometimes need leaders for the industrial companies in their portfolios, and one search firm consultant who specializes in those positions. Steve gets calls about CEO or COO positions three or four times a year from these people. When I've spoken to other executives about Steve's experience, some have been astonished to hear that figure—three or four real possibilities a year from a network of three people!

Steve's success results from three things. Most important, these acquaintances stay in touch because he's a good candidate. They know he almost always declines to consider the jobs they call about, but at some point he might be interested.

This relates closely to the second reason: Steve's PVP. Steve focuses narrowly on a certain kind of position. It's easy to understand him and what he wants to do.

Finally, Steve always tries to help. He doesn't just say "No thanks" and hang up. He described it this way: "I take their calls and am helpful. I refer people I know, but I also ask them to refer me. That mutual back scratching extends my network by quite a bit. I speak to each of them once every two months or so."

This is different than being pleasant. Steve may share a perspective on the position or the company they call about. Other times, he suggests someone else to call about the job. When he has no immediate reactions on the phone, he'll call back if he has an idea. These three people make up a powerful career-shaping network. One of them brought Steve his current CEO position. Another brought him his previous job. Steve adds value, so they call again. Talking to Steve is time well spent.

Steve put together a powerful network by helping a few people in a significant way. Others emphasize staying in touch with a wide circle of people. Corporate attorney Baxter is the best I've found at this.

## Baxter's Aggressive Stay-in-Touch Networking

If you met Baxter, one of the first things you'd notice is that he pays close attention to what you're saying. His natural talent at paying attention contributed to his success as an attorney. It's also built his network.

Baxter served companies in the electronics and telecom industries as a partner at an international law firm. He left the firm to become chief legal officer at a telecom equipment manufacturer. After several good years there, he became general counsel of a high-tech start-up. Although this position began as a legal one, his role broadened. After a year, this became a part-time commitment so that he could become temporary CEO of another start-up. He moved through similar companies. Several were acquired, one at a high price. In all of this, Baxter's emphasis was on high-level executive tasks such as defining the business's value proposition, initial business and intellectual property strategy, fundraising, office setup, and hiring a full-time CEO. During the dot-com boom, he estimated he was getting a call about a job almost every week, close to fifty a year!

These opportunities came from Baxter's vast professional network. He first realized the importance of networking as a law firm partner. That's where clients came from. He also had seen networking's critical role for high-tech companies that depend on each other. He made professional networking a high personal priority and put more than a little time and effort into it. Baxter described his approach this way:

> I had literally thousands of contacts and relationships. I was known as a fine lawyer with experience in cutting-edge deals and a strong service orientation. Not in a rapacious sense, but I would make it a point to keep up with people. I had a talent at remembering names, what people were interested in, and their faces. I was really good at it. Definitely a competitive advantage. And I made it a point to diligently follow up with notes, birthdays, and so on. I always gave without any expectation of a definite return, but also with the belief that what goes around comes around.

Baxter also was a small angel investor in start-ups, so people contacted him about that too. These investments sometimes led to job opportunities, and his network helped him add value in these roles.

Financial success has given Baxter the freedom to design an unusual portfolio of career activities in his fifties. He now splits his time among nonprofit leadership roles, some continued board and advisory work for businesses, and teaching. An adjunct professor appointment resulted from Baxter's reputation: he'd become known on the conference circuit as an expert in corporate citizenship; the dean was aware of this and invited him to create the school's first course on business and human rights.

Although Baxter told me about his networking approach, I didn't have to rely only on the way he described it. I'd had a front-row seat. Of all the people I've interviewed about career strategy, no one has gotten back to me more promptly on follow-up questions than Baxter. Nor has anyone been more attentive to ensuring

I understood his perspective. I saw his networking strength first-hand as I was writing about that strength!

Despite the obvious differences in scale and process, Steve and Baxter share essential characteristics. Both of them do more than just meet people. They connect. They pay attention and help others. Steve adds insight and ideas. Baxter is memorable, and creates networks not only for himself but for others, too. The network he created in the 1990s was a bit like today's Facebook or LinkedIn. Finally, both Steve and Baxter are completely genuine. What they do is effective because they're comfortable and honest. What they do is good for everyone involved.

Maybe you're one of the lucky people whose natural charm attracts others. That can get you to first base, but acquaintances don't make a network. Meeting people isn't so easy for most of us, but everyone can create network. Take the steps I describe here.

### 1. Think of People You Know Well

People you already know well are a good place to start—whether they're from current or past work, school, a community organization, or even the neighborhood. Some people might be trusted advisers and confidants, like members of a personal board of directors. Close connections like this can be very important to career strategy. They'll come first to mind. That's natural.

### 2. Add Others Tied to Aspirations

Although it makes sense to start with people you know, if that's all you do, you're greatly limiting your opportunity. In my experience, the most productive network contacts have been people known professionally, not personally. Many were distant acquaintances.

Stanford professor Mark Granovetter has led thinking and research into what he calls "weak ties."[3] In one survey, for example, he sampled professional, technical, and managerial job changers in a Boston suburb. He asked how often they saw the person whose information led to a new position. People responded as follows: about 17 percent saw their contact at least twice a week, 56 percent less often than that but more than once a year, and 28 percent once a year or less. The less connected people were more important. Weak ties may have information you and your tight circle don't have. Weak ties mean that the person who mentions you for a job won't feel uncomfortable about her objectivity, the way she might if recommending a friend. Weak ties also can connect you to different groups of people who broaden your network for the long term.

How to grow these weak ties?

- Join civic or professional organizations, meet people as you participate, and volunteer to help on programs. Do some of this in a targeted way related to professional goals.
- Join career-oriented social networks. Create a profile that reflects your aspirations and PVP, and add acquaintances that relate to those aspirations.
- Include people inside your current employer. Identify people you'd like to know and perhaps work with at some point. Meet them. Learn about what they do.

### 3. Get to Know People

Cultivate both strong ties and weak ties. Stay in touch after you no longer work together. Get to know social acquaintances professionally. Learn about their work. Remember names, faces, and something about them. Keep a rich list with contact information and details. Do more than just meet people: pay attention to them.

### 4. Be Helpful

When the opportunity presents itself, contribute meaningfully to what people are doing. If they ask you to react to a substantive issue, that's a fine opportunity. If they ask you for career advice or for help in a job search, that's better. Add value. The only reliable way to build a powerful network is to be helpful.

### 5. Be Genuine

I'm absolutely not suggesting scheming to find ways to create advantage. That won't feel natural, and if it's not natural, it may not be effective anyway. Nor am I suggesting doing anything heroic or outside your normal personal style. People will notice if you're uncomfortable. You're not using contacts; you're creating contacts by adding to their acquaintances in a way they find pleasant and helpful. The mind-set of helping others is the high road.

Adam Grant of Wharton has researched relationships at work, including networks.[4] He shows the benefits of being a "giver" and how to do that most effectively, along with the results of being a "taker." I'm suggesting that you be a giver, that you be helpful to other people. Not everyone will react as you hope they will, but many will value a relationship with you, and that relationship can pay dividends year after year. Do well by doing good.

A professional network is critical to long-term career success. I'll now describe a special class of networking—with search consultants.

## Building Search Consultant Relationships

I encourage search firm relationships, but I'm certainly not saying you always should be open to a new position. That's the path to failure. By the time they're forty or fifty, however, most successful business leaders will benefit from positive relationships with two or three quality search consultants, who are the closest thing to the market for people like them.

In a search, the employer is the client, not you, but that doesn't mean mutually beneficial relationships aren't possible. Just as you may need search consultants, the consultants may need you. You may be an attractive candidate for one of their client's positions. You also may become their client on the hiring side.

Here's what two different search firm partners told me about building a search consultant network. The first one mentioned ways to help him.

> For me to spend time, you need to be valuable in one of two ways. You're valuable if you're someone who will spend time identifying others, to be what we call a "source." Not to recommend your colleagues, but others you know. It may not take a lot of time. You're also valuable if you're good and sometime may think about moving jobs. If I know you're really good at something, it's valuable to me to get to know you.

The second one discussed how to be helpful without spending much time on it.

> Return headhunter's calls, but dispatch them as fast as possible. Ask three or four questions. If it's not for you, offer to help, and if you can help, do. Spend as little time as possible to engage the person who calls, but help them so they'll call again. If you do well at this over a career, there should be five or ten reasonably responsible recruiters that'll respond if you send a note.

Your record of professional success is required if you're to be on their radar. Otherwise, consultants won't be interested. Once you're well down that path, take these steps.

### 1. Develop Search Relationships before You Need Them

Return phone calls or proactively meet consultants when you're not in play. It's much harder if you really need them—when you've just been laid off or when you've just resigned. If the consultant already knows and respects you when those things happen, it may not feel risky to suggest you for openings.

### 2. Be Selective

Look for someone working in your field. Boutiques serve particular industries, functions, or regions. Large firms serve a broad clientele, but within large firms, individuals often focus on an industry, function, or region.

Look for a relationship-oriented consultant. Ask colleagues or others in your industry for advice on the best search people. One test is whether he or she will talk to you beyond populating a candidate database or filling an immediate job.

Interview the consultant, much as you would if you were hiring him or her to advise you on your career. Ask questions like these: "What's your role in the firm and your practice focus?" "What are examples of your clients and positions filled?" and "What are examples of placing someone similar to me?" You'll learn from questions like these, and they'll show the right consultant that you're serious and thoughtful.

### 3. If You're Interested in a Job, Help the Consultant Help You

Prepare a resume that supports a compelling PVP and shows where you're a good fit. Don't ask to be proposed for a position if you're not qualified.

Let the consultant manage your pursuit of an offer. "The number-one mistake," one consultant said, "is to try to go around the recruiter, pinging the CEO you met with emails. If you're not comfortable trusting the recruiter, don't work with that person."

### 4. If You're Not Interested, Be Helpful

Make the consultant's call worthwhile even if you're not interested in the job.

Provide feedback—perhaps reasons why you're not interested in the job or how it might be more appealing. Provide feedback on the client's reputation. Help the consultant keep up with nonconfidential developments in the industry or function.

Suggest others to call, but not just anyone. Choose people you think are high quality and who match the job specifications. According to another search consultant, "Anyone referred is a reflection on you. If not an 'A' player, it demeans your value." And finally, be cautious about referring people from your current employer.

Look across all four classes of initiatives—career path planning, education, reputation building, and network building—and imagine how to move toward your long-term aspirations and build that aspirational PVP. They are the menu of possible actions that could become your long-term strategy. What remains is to determine which of those initiatives matter most, combine those initiatives into a productive portfolio, and develop an action plan to guide implementation. That's what I'll describe in Chapter 7.

Chapter 7

# INTEGRATED LONG-TERM STRATEGY

**YOUR ASPIRATIONAL PVP** is in place, and you've developed a list of initiatives that can build that PVP. Three steps remain to complete your long-term strategy: determining the best portfolio of initiatives and committing yourself to implementing them, turning that portfolio into an implementation plan in the form of a strategic road map, and preparing for on-the-go learning.

## Committing to a Portfolio of Initiatives

Investment advisers construct portfolios of securities with different characteristics. Some of these investments may do well, others not so well. With a balanced portfolio, however, investors can expect a better risk-return relationship than if they made a few big bets on individual companies or on a single class of assets. Long-term career plans also need portfolios of initiatives to maximize the return on effort and reduce the risk.

Investment advisers also talk with clients about their long-term goals and the associated financial requirements. They encourage people to save enough money to permit investments so that within a range of projected investment returns, they'll be able to fund those long-term goals. Again, there's a parallel to careers. People must set aside enough time and resources to accomplish the initiatives that will set their future course.

How to transform your list of potential initiatives into this kind of portfolio? Take these steps.

### 1. Evaluate the Initiatives

The first step is to understand the initiatives from a strategic perspective. Rate each initiative on these criteria:

- Impact: some initiatives may offer lots of upside, others less. That benefit may come soon for some; for others, it will be far out in the future.
- Scale: multiple activities may be needed to get in position to land the right opportunities.
- Uncertainty: some initiatives may have the results you'd hoped for; others won't.
- Time and effort: some initiatives may naturally flow from other aspects of your life and require little extra time or effort; others, such as a major educational program or a job change, will require a fundamental shift in your life. Some initiatives, such as reading into an interesting field, can be accomplished on nights and weekends; others, such as some network meetings, must fit into the workweek.

Looking at initiatives through this lens will make their benefits, uncertainties, and costs clear. This exercise also may lead you to think of new initiatives that better balance these considerations.

### 2. Decide to Commit

It's one thing to come up with a list of initiatives. It's another to find the time and resources to implement them. That requires commitment. This is where the rubber meets the road. Now that you see what you'll need to do to pursue your long-term aspirations, it's time for the big question: *Are you really going to do it?*

Even if you're sure you're going to do it, I encourage you to take a moment and make this a conscious decision. Ask yourself how important those aspirations are to you. Judge the prospect that the initiatives will launch you toward those aspirations. If the aspirations are very important and if you're confident that the initiatives will build momentum, then I hope you'll follow through on all of them. That will give you the best chance of creating the future you want.

The first result of Chapter 7, then, is your commitment to implement the initiatives. That's your long-term strategy. Record *your portfolio and your rationale.* Return to it in three months or in six. Recognize what you've accomplished, how you're doing compared to what you'd intended, and what to do next.

I'll make one final comment on commitment. If even a scaled-down version of your initiatives seems too hard, then I suspect one of two things has happened: either you haven't found an exciting long-term direction, or the aspiration you've set is unrealistic. I hope that's not your situation. But if it is, I suggest that you pause, return to the material in Part I when you're ready, and reengage with the direction-setting process.

I'll now explain how to establish a productive implementation plan to guide all these initiatives: the strategic road map.

## The Strategic Road Map

Disappointment in business can be the consequence of failed execution, not the wrong strategy. Effective leaders develop implementation plans to drive the change they hope to see and avoid that failed execution. There's no substitute for a good implementation plan—what to do, by whom, and on what schedule.

I saw this firsthand as a management consultant. The assessment required to help a client determine the best strategy was front of mind and usually took up the lion's share of my team's efforts. Once the client adopted a strategy, we helped prepare an overall implementation plan and often helped on individual implementation projects. When I returned a few months later for what we called a "5,000 mile check-up," the client frequently pulled out that overall plan and talked from that. Although market and competitive assessments took center stage when strategy choices were being made, what became important now was the step-by-step plan and what had happened. The company had been living with that. It had affected everyone's lives.

Sophisticated implementation planning can also have a strategic purpose. Leaders develop provisional plans to test the organization. If execution requires capabilities that the institution lacks, they determine how to add the needed capability. If that's not practical, they may have to change the strategy.

Sophisticated plans incorporate important contingencies. If the decision makes sense only if certain things outside the company's control happen or only if initial steps go well, effective plans bring those contingencies out into the open. They specify gates that must be passed before later steps are taken. For example, planning a new product launch that requires regulatory approval would include thinking about what to do under different regulatory scenarios.

Business strategists pull all this together with a strategic road map. The road map both prepares for implementation and provides a last check on the strategy and the logic behind it.

Individuals face a similar task. I'm sometimes surprised when people conceive a sensible career strategy and then nothing happens. Inertia and more urgent priorities crowded out the long-term initiatives. They needed a device to create accountability. They needed a push. A strategic road map can make the difference between getting off to a good start and wasting time. It can turn your strategic intentions into real action.

The contingencies in a well-crafted strategic road map explicitly build in learning and flexibility. Your course isn't welded in place. Once you complete the first steps, you may take the next ones in the plan, or you may learn things that cause you to reevaluate the plan or parts of it. Combining aggressive execution with periodic reassessment and adaptation is the hallmark of a first-class career strategist.

Finally, you can use the road map to help conceive strategy. Provisionally pick one alternative, plan how you'd implement it, and test how that feels. Do the same for other alternatives. Seeing these all together may show you the best approach.

Let's look at the power of this style of implementation planning when used as a strategy development stimulus, through the story of how corporate SVP Keith determined his long-term strategy.

### How Keith's Road Map Led to His Plan

Keith, forty, leads marketing, business development, and partnerships at a high-tech business unit of a multibillion-dollar company. Before that, he worked at two start-ups, a consulting boutique, and a marketing company. He knows high-tech businesses and B2B marketing.

Keith was at an early stage when we talked. Nothing was urgent, but he wanted to be proactive about his future—just as he managed his teams at work. He had three visions of his future.

First, he might advance with his company. He'd been told he was a candidate to succeed the current business unit president in two to four years, and he thought he had a better than even chance. He liked the business, but it required a great deal of international travel. A promotion might increase that travel; it certainly wouldn't reduce it. He wasn't sure he was "willing to give up the next five to ten years of kids' activities but for the weekends. With my wife's business scaling, I'm interested in finding the right model for me."

Keith understood this first opportunity well. The other two were sketchy.

He might start a high-tech company. He'd need an actionable idea to do that, and didn't have that idea. If he had a good idea, he was confident he could make the business happen. Or at least he was confident if he were to get the funding. Fundraising was a question for Keith—both his ability to do that and whether he'd like it.

The third idea was to join a high-tech VC firm. Keith thought he'd be good at screening applicants and helping funded businesses succeed. However, he'd never been in that arena, wasn't sure what the work would be like, and therefore wasn't sure he'd like it.

How a start-up or a VC firm affected travel would depend greatly on the particulars.

In the context of this book, Keith was at the end of Part I. He had three targets and a sense of the PVP he'd need for each. He hadn't consciously prioritized among them, nor had he a real plan. Once he got the possibilities clearly in mind, Keith's first conclusion was an easy call: to pursue the promotion to run his business. He knew how to make that happen and was well under way. If he got the promotion, great; then he could reconsider the travel issue or try to contain it. If he left after being promoted, his more senior position would better support the other ideas.

The start-up and VC alternatives weren't new. He'd mused about them before, but never gained traction. He wasn't in a better position to pursue them than he'd been three years earlier. He didn't want to be in the same place after another three years.

Keith used the strategic road map concept to exercise his thinking. If he were absolutely sure he wanted to pursue each of those two ideas, what would he need to do in the next year to create that opportunity? By assuming he was absolutely sure (even though he wasn't), Keith forced himself to be concrete.

For the start-up, he'd need to conduct a full-scale market study for several months, interviewing perhaps a hundred potential customers and determining exactly what market to attack. Given enough time and effort, he was confident he could come up with a winning idea. He'd also need to build relationships to get in position to raise the money required.

To improve his prospects for joining a VC firm, he'd need to get acquainted with VCs, beef up his investment skills, and get closer to the start-up world. He might volunteer with a new business incubator or invest in one or two companies where he could take an advisory board role.

Seeing these long-term initiatives was clarifying. Keith had a lot to learn; it was clear what he needed to do to learn; and once those ideas were out in the open, he had to decide how serious he really was. I hadn't thought of the term yet, but he was assembling his portfolio of strategy initiatives.

Doing this also led Keith to imagine other alternatives. Quitting his job to pursue a new venture full-time was an alternative he'd never considered. It certainly would get the ball rolling, but he wasn't close to ready for that. Committing nights and weekends to that venture was another possibility, but it came with drawbacks. It might affect his performance in his current position, and it would definitely affect his family time. He had to balance conflicting objectives.

Keith decided to start in a low-key way. He'd grow his network related to funding—an activity that would help with either alternative. He'd also commit a little time to imagining start-up ideas, but not conduct the thorough research of a full market study. That was manageable.

He planned to return to this question in a couple of years. At that point, he would know more about his prospects with his current company. He'd know more about the two alternatives to that. That became his long-term plan: to learn enough now to be in a good position to decide later, while also pursuing advancement with his current company.

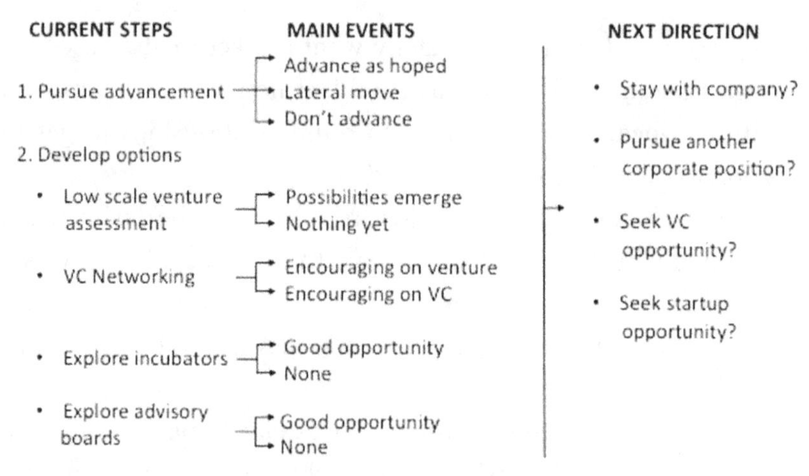


**FIGURE 7.1** Logic of Keith's Strategic Road Map

Although we talked through Keith's strategic road map and put some notes on paper, he never actually wrote it down in a formal way—but I did (see Figure 7-1).

The two alternatives to Keith's current work weren't new, but he'd made zero progress. By assuming that he was sure he wanted to pursue each idea aggressively and imagining provisional road maps for each one, Keith clarified his choices. Doing that led him to a balanced plan to get started on the new possibilities in a productive way while focusing on his top priority: doing well in his current position. The strategic road map concept normally comes at the end of strategy development. In Keith's case, it kicked off strategic thinking.

## Preparing Your Strategic Road Map

How do you go about preparing your strategic road map? Construct a diagram that looks like Keith's chart. Think of it as a tree branch on its side. Three kinds of entries are on this chart.

### 1. Initial Activities

At the left, show each step you're taking at the outset. If activities will start at different times, show the later ones toward the center of the page. If one activity leads directly to another one, connect them with the later one to the right.

### 2. Events

The next column of the road map lists what could happen following each activity. For example, if you plan to change positions, that might happen quickly or it might not. Or if you plan to get involved in a particular community organization, you might or you might not accomplish that.

### 3. Next Activities and Decisions

List what you'd do as a result of each possible event if it's obvious. Or portray the choice you'd face then.

For example, let's assume you were seeking an offer and expected to accept it. If you actually got that offer, however, you'd still need to step back for a moment and decide whether to accept. You'd know more about the new situation, about your current course, and about yourself than you knew when you started. It's possible that you might come to a different view. And if you didn't get that offer or if you decided not to accept, there might be other avenues toward your aspirations.

Although it's logically possible to spread the road map out over multiple iterations (from activity to event to activity to event and so on), doing that seldom makes sense. Go to the second tier of activities and then stop, or perhaps develop only one or two of the branches beyond that.

Record *your strategic road map.* You'll return to it repeatedly. It sets up continued engagement with how your initiatives are developing and what decisions those developments suggest. That learning attitude merits additional attention.

## On-the-Go Learning

The step-by-step process you're seeing in this book is a proven path. Follow that path up to this point, and you'll have aspirations you believe in, a PVP that can meet those aspirations, and a plan to build that PVP (or at least to try it out in earnest). However, there's no guarantee that you'll end up where you plan to be. Because there's so much inherent uncertainty in careers, an experimental and learning attitude is indispensable. Learning from how well your plans are working is a big part of a strategic career.

This isn't the first time I've discussed learning in this book. Learning was the subject of Chapter 4: research of public sources, speaking with people in the know, and experiments. Learning also is important *during* strategy execution.

I recall from my days in the army hearing about a "Ready, aim, fire" approach to decisions and how that differed from "Ready, fire, aim." People sometimes make similar comparisons in business.[1] That distinction is important, but I'm suggesting something slightly different here: "Ready, aim, fire, learn, adjust." Parts I and II show you how to get ready and how to aim. They prepare you to fire by implementing the strategic road map. As you do that, pay attention to what's happening, learn from those results, and adjust as appropriate. You'll like some of the results, others not so much. Maybe you can increase your bet on the initiatives that are working best. New possibilities may emerge that look better than what you'd hoped to find. Or you may discover that you aren't excited by that aspiration once you get near it. Well-thought-out planning, aggressive execution of the plan, and continued learning and adjustment as things happen are the surest route to success.

Let's now look at a man who put the concepts from Parts I and II together to prepare and then pursue a new strategy. Senior government executive Zach wanted to create new career options. His rigorous assessment helped him determine where to point himself and how to get started. He followed a deliberate process. Nothing was urgent. He turned over every rock.

## Zach's Thorough Long-Term Strategy Development Process

Zach followed a pre-med curriculum in college, along with majoring in political science and history. He'd long been interested in emergency services. "I grew up watching reruns of the television show *Emergency*," he told me. Volunteer work with his college's ambulance squad was a big part of his college experience. Shortly after getting a medical school acceptance letter, he received a call in the early morning from his ambulance company. A massive fire was under way in an apartment building, and everyone needed to come quickly. His dorm was only twelve blocks from the hospital, so he was among the first to arrive and set up the temporary triage facility in the hospital lobby. He was in the thick of it for sixteen hours straight, making visible impact in a very important way. As he recalled to me with enthusiasm, "It was the most dramatic day of my life."

The last two months of school were unsettling. Zach remained charged up about his EMT role, but he wasn't sure he wanted to be a doctor. He deferred admission, worked full-time for a year as an EMT, and had a fabulous experience. He knew a physician on site could have made a difference in a couple of the accidents he saw. His experience that year led him to decide to enroll in medical school the next fall. Then, when it came time to pick a specialty, Zach chose emergency medicine. No surprise there. The emergency field also offered the prospect of relatively stable hours, something his new wife would appreciate. He finished emergency care training and settled into what he assumed would be a career at a hospital in his hometown.

Several years in, however, Zach grew restless. He saw firsthand the uneven quality of the city's different emergency management services, and the more general challenges facing emergency services after 9/11. He became a guest lecturer at the local university and wrote articles on emergency preparedness. One article caught the attention of a senior person at a federal agency. She asked Zach to visit, and three months later Zach was running emergency preparedness policy for that agency.

Zach's move went well. He brought new ideas, and some were sticking. He was learning a lot—from emergency preparedness to operating effectively in the federal government to management in general. He continued to have a foot in the academic world as a university lecturer. He was promoted, and transitioned into the career senior executive service. That meant he could stay in government through retirement if he wanted to do that. Zach liked his work, but he also knew that responsibilities can change when more senior people change. He also wanted to see if he could get onto a higher compensation path. At forty-three, Zach was unsure what course of action would be best. That's why he decided to investigate career strategy.

The career strategy methodology I was developing was similar to Zach's experience with a rigorous public policy development process. He was like a sponge.

Zach first thought about his long-term aspirations and objectives. Over six weeks, he drafted his list, reflected on how it felt, and then redrafted. He put a lot of thought into that.

Next he imagined sixteen possible careers. Working from that list, he centered on four good possibilities. He decided that the other twelve were less appealing, or he incorporated elements of them into the remaining four. He then formally evaluated those ideas—weighting the objectives, assigning scores to the alternatives, and then tallying the weighted averages for each alternative. This assessment gave Zach confidence that any of the four ideas would be good. Their scores weren't much different, and that matched his intuition.

He then imagined how to enhance his prospects for each one and came up with this list:

1. Federal government emergency preparedness executive
   - Fully implement current policy initiatives; encourage discussion in the academic and consulting communities
   - Fully develop the agency's policy development process
   - Obtain a promotion in place or begin rotational assignments to other agencies or the Executive Office of the President
2. Professor with associated consulting
   - Fully implement current policy initiatives; encourage discussion of these initiatives in the academic and consulting communities
   - Fully develop the agency's policy development process; publish the process and encourage discussion in the academic community
   - Continue volunteer university lecturing
   - Serve on the advisory committee developing the training curriculum for the agency and for the government more broadly
   - Obtain a promotion in place or begin rotational assignments to other agencies or the Executive Office of the President
3. Consultant in emergency preparedness
   - Fully implement current policy initiatives; encourage discussion of those initiatives in the academic and consulting communities
   - Fully develop the agency's policy development process; publish the process and encourage discussion in the academic community
   - Continue volunteer university lecturing

- Obtain a promotion in place or begin rotational assignments to other agencies or the Executive Office of the President

4. Executive in a hospital or health system
   - Unknown

Because he didn't have good ideas for how to get started on the health system executive route, Zach concluded that it was a long shot and de-emphasized it.

The initiatives for the other three ideas were similar to each other. They'd contribute to success in his current position. They'd improve his prospects in all three. They were "no-regrets moves." He didn't have to prioritize one over the others. He'd pursue all three at the same time. Those overlapping initiatives became Zach's strategy.

The one difference among the three career directions was in the associated networking. The acquaintances would be somewhat different for each idea. Because nongovernment acquaintances were more distant from his current work, he put them at the top of the list.

Zach models the formal long-term strategy approach. He spent more than six months on his assessment, a period that allowed for thoroughness and personal reflection while staying fully engaged in his current work. This plan is under way, with some initiatives going well and others not leading anywhere. His recent government promotion is a good thing. The jury's out on the ultimate result, but he's doing all he can to direct his career.

If you're developing long-term strategy, recall Zach's initiatives, how they tied to specific opportunities, and the fact that most of the initiatives supported multiple new directions and continued success in his current position. That's a fine result.

Part II turns the long-term aspirations you identified in Part I into actions. Those actions usually include a search for the right opportunity to get started—the topic we address in Part III.

Part III

# OPPORTUNITY SEARCH STRATEGY

To find out what one is fitted to do, and to secure
an opportunity to do it, is the key to happiness.
—JOHN DEWEY

**MARKETERS IDENTIFY CUSTOMERS** in their product's target market; learn about their behavior, needs, and desires related to the product; and then communicate the value proposition to persuade them to buy. Before filming an ad to be shown on TV, for example, they conduct market research on consumers in their top market segment to learn what shows they watch. They may then test different ways to express the value proposition in an appealing and persuasive way. Strong industrial sellers use similar tactics. They identify the best prospects for their products, get to know them, and determine how their products meet needs that aren't well served by other products. In other words, they too deploy a value proposition to get the sale.

Most people who've contacted me for career advice are conducting a job search. Many are in a hurry. From students getting started to people who are dissatisfied with their jobs to people out of work, they all need job search skills immediately. Similar to what I said about long-term strategy, however, the best time to develop job search skills is not when a search is under way. The best time is before those skills are needed.

Job search comes up in a very different way as part of a new long-term strategy. People seek new opportunities under the radar,

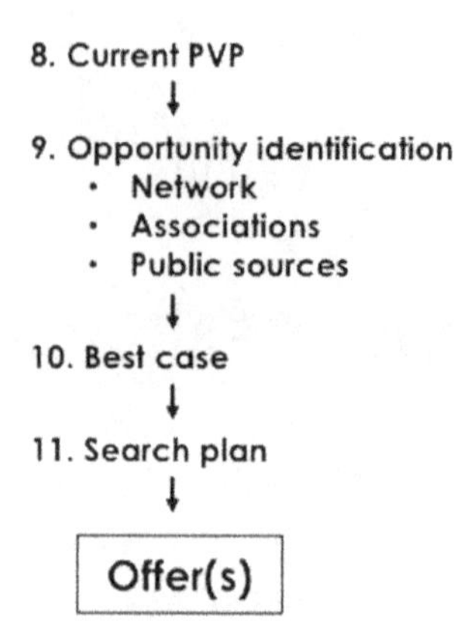


**FIGURE PIII.1** Part III: Develop Opportunity Search Strategy

either in their company or outside. Even the fully satisfied must react if something exciting appears.

Seek career opportunities the way excellent business marketers and sellers do. Take the four steps presented in Figure PIII.1.

Chapter 8 takes the PVP concept introduced in Part I and shows you how to use that concept in opportunity search—what I call current PVP.

Chapter 9 shows you how to identify opportunities where your PVP is a good match. Networking is by far the best source of opportunity. You'll need effective processes to network productively.

Once you identify appealing opportunities, you must get the offer. Chapter 10 shows how to make your best case—how to prepare to communicate your PVP and get ready for the interviewers' questions.

To conclude Part III, Chapter 11 shows you how to design an opportunity search plan. It pulls all these concepts together with the story of an enormously successful search.

This sequence is logical—set PVP, find opportunities, and make your best case—but it's not a rigid blueprint. In practice, you'll interweave activities with each other. For example, it will be hard to learn all you need to know to set a confident PVP (Chapter 8) without first meeting people in your network who know potential employers (Chapter 9); those meetings, however, may not generate much insight if you don't already know something about those employers and have some ideas about your PVP. View these chapters as a logical progression, but move back and forth among activities as you learn.

Also bear in mind that I describe these principles in the context of job search. That's a critical task. It's why many people will read a book like this one. These principles aren't only applicable to job searches, however. They work in many other situations—for example, applying to graduate school or getting into the right professional association. Master these activities in job search and you'll be prepared for other searches too.

Chapter 8

# CURRENT PERSONAL VALUE PROPOSITION

**HOW TO PLAN** a marketing campaign for a new product? How to sell it? The question isn't what product design would be best. The product already exists. The question isn't where the market may be in a few years. The time is now. Fruitful marketing and sales campaigns are founded on the product's current value proposition.

It's the same in a job search. What matters is your current PVP—the PVP you can deliver today. It's your fundamental product strategy—the kind of position you're seeking now and the reasons you're the right choice. If you get your PVP right, then your marketing and sales activities to identify opportunities and secure offers will come naturally. Without a good PVP, even highly effective search activities may not lead anywhere.

Your aspirational PVP was the principal result of Part I. There, the emphasis was on the PVP to develop over time. Follow the same logic to set your current PVP, but shift the time frame to today. Just as you did before, you need a target. You must understand the target's needs and how you meet those needs. What's different here is that your attention is on today's plausible targets, where your current strengths match the requirements of those positions or are close.

I've noticed how easy it is for people to skip over the PVP or to treat it casually. They want to discuss interview preparation, networking, and other activities to find and get offers, without first taking the time to establish a strategic connection to their values, interests, and strengths. They want to take action, but what they're taking is unnecessary risk. They may fail to pursue opportunities that will lead where they hope to go over the long term, they may not present themselves where they're most competitive, and they may waste time seeking positions where they don't fit. I can't overstress the importance of beginning an opportunity search strategically. Invest the time needed to understand your PVP. Slow down a bit at the outset, so that you can move faster down the road.

In this chapter, I'll describe how to build that PVP, and then tell the story of a woman whose situation dictated that she do some long-term thinking and then immediately shift to short-term strategy.

## Constructing Your Current PVP

The career path plan from your long-term strategy is the natural jumping-off place for your current PVP. Take it out, observe where you are on that path, and let that suggest your current target. Or at least start with that plan to help imagine the best current target. That's an excellent starting point for opportunity search.

If you've started the strategic process but haven't gotten as far, you still may have a lot to work with. Perhaps you have a long-term career direction (the result of Part I), but haven't yet prepared the plan to reach that aspiration (the result of Part II). If that's the case, you already understand your values and strengths, you've targeted a field or a role, and you've set an aspirational PVP to get there. That too can be a fine starting point.

Either way, you'll tune up your prior thinking in light of what may have changed about you or changed in the external world.

You'll also shift your gaze to the current time frame by applying some of the methods from Part I in the current context. You'll be updating your earlier work rather than discovering new insights for the first time. You'll naturally emphasize current strengths more and long-term interests less than you did when setting long-term aspirations. Follow the line of attack I provide here to work out your current PVP.

## 1. Know Your Strengths

Your know-how today is the reason someone would hire you.

Most powerful will be your knowledge and strengths that tie tightly to a position. For example, an oil exploration company's business development analyst must be able to determine which projects to fund and which projects to decline. A nonprofit development officer will need the experience and ability to locate potential donors, cultivate them, and lead them to become long-term supporters. Someone seeking positions like these for the first time will need to show that he or she can get up to speed in a reasonable time.

The more specific you can be, the better. For example, IT strengths are not just IT strengths. Perhaps it's IT in the retail industry. And even retail IT can emphasize subskills. Perhaps you're looking at IT solutions to support markdowns, productive shelf stocking, or seasonal employee staffing. Or your strengths may be on the more technical side of IT, such as network integration across multiple retail sites and formats. More senior retail IT people may incorporate all these skills to one degree or another, but they too will need to understand themselves in this way.

In thinking about their strengths, people sometimes list personal characteristics that make them proud—for example, diligence, putting in the hours needed, and team building. Characteristics like these can matter greatly, but employers may find it hard to distinguish people based on them. They can be part of your PVP, but if you're thinking of putting them at the top of the list, think again. Do that only if you can demonstrate job-specific distinctiveness.

Return to Chapter 2 and complete the strength assessment activities described there: your self-assessment, past performance reviews, strength surveys, input from others, "hiring" yourself, and pulling together a ranked list of your signature strengths. There are no good shortcuts, though your earlier list of strengths gives you a leg up. Your updated ranked list is the foundation for what follows.

### 2. Imagine Appealing Fields and Roles

Whether or not you're already looking at a job description, ask yourself where your current strengths are naturally taking you within your current field or role. Ask what other fields or roles need strengths like yours. Perhaps you're too modest. To stimulate your imagination, ask which ones might be possible now if your current strengths were absolutely at the top of the game for someone with your level of experience.

Test these fields or roles against three standards: whether they'd be areas you'd enjoy, whether they'd put you on track to reaching your aspirations, and whether they're feasible or close. Those that pass are your first list of potential targets. If you're looking at a specific position, consider the question, "Does that role in that field meet these three tests?"

### 3. Know Prospective Employers

Don't leave it up to the employer to figure out how your strengths relate to what she needs. Connect the dots. Taking her perspective, why should she hire you or promote you?

Learn what she was thinking about when creating the job opening ("I need to find someone who can do x and y."). Look at job specs from posted positions. They may be exactly what the employer needs, expressed in strengths. Or they may be about achievements and record, reasonable but imperfect first-round proxies for those strengths. Or sometimes the job specs aren't well thought through.

Make this a goal of networking, especially at the outset of your search when you're still working on your PVP. Talk to people who know employers that you find interesting. Get their view of what those employers are like and from that, what kind of people fit best. Learn what they're looking for and how they might view someone like you.

Chapter 4 described how to learn about a field of work. Follow those same approaches to learn about particular companies and positions. Read all you can about prospective employers. Meet people from those institutions; they're natural experts. Meet people outside the field who know it—customers, suppliers, partners, and ex-employees.

All that will help evaluate how well you're prepared for a particular field or a particular employer, and will therefore help set your job search target. It will make networking meetings productive. You'll do best with prospective employers if you're already familiar with their field, institution, and the position you've come to discuss.

## 4. Consider Your Expectations

You may have expectations about money, lifestyle, location, and other features of a job. Separate the features that matter most to you from the ones that are nice to have. The top expectations will help you target positions with a good prospect of meeting them and avoid spending time on positions that don't. If you're not prepared to move, for example, only target employers in town. Or you might consider an offer that doesn't meet your financial objectives if it offered something else you wanted, such as the perfect training ground. These aren't final decisions about what offers you would or wouldn't accept, but they do influence targeting and prioritization.

## 5. Incorporate Timing

Maybe a great opportunity will appear just when you're ready, but you can't count on that. You may find yourself torn between sensible (or perhaps expedient) goals that you're confident you can reach and goals that are both less likely and more appealing. You must judge how long you're prepared to wait before accepting an offer. You may decide to prioritize among targets in that light.

One side of the equation is your personal situation. Ideally, you can take the time needed to pursue the opportunity you like best. You won't feel pressure to accept the first offer that comes along or an offer that doesn't point to long-term goals. That's one benefit of looking for a new position when you're already employed and are reasonably content with work. But that may not be your situation. You'll set a short timetable if you're unemployed or about to be, or if you're very unhappy at work. Financial position also influences timing. A financial reserve can provide you the time to be discerning in your job search. Managing personal spending to build that financial reserve over your work life can enable you to take your time when you need to.

The other consideration is how hard it may be to secure different kinds of offers. Segment your hiring market to help make that appraisal.

What's called a good-better-best segmentation can lead to insight in business, and that's what I suggest here. Within the range of possibilities you're considering, judge which acceptable but not ideal positions you'd be highly likely to get if you pursued them (the good results), which more appealing positions would be good though not easy fits (the better), and which highly desirable targets would be a stretch at this stage of your work life (the best). This opportunity grouping represents the market segmentation for you at this time.

These could be different employers in the same field (some more selective, others less), they could be different roles within the same company or the same field (some higher in the organization, others down the line), or they could be entirely different fields or roles. If time is short, you may choose to emphasize opportunities that are close to where you already are. With lots of time, you can begin with stretch targets and good fits and seek the easier possibilities only if you need to.

### 6. Test Possible PVPs and Decide

Outline a current PVP for each target you're considering. Remember: your PVP includes your target, what the target requires, and what makes you a good match (better yet, the best match). Ask yourself whether you'd expect to be hired for that position and why or why not. Meet with people you know well and ask for reactions. Then test each alternative with these questions:

- Does the PVP tightly connect your current skills and knowledge to the target position?
- What would others say is your PVP today? What would they say about this PVP?
- Is the PVP part of a path to your long-term aspirations?
- Would the PVP be more powerful if you narrowed the field?

Step back and judge whether the PVP you like best is feasible. If it is, that's your choice. If not, then sort through the other possibilities in a similar way. After you've addressed these questions, modify the PVP as necessary. Write down *your current PVP and the reasons why you picked it* rather than picking something else. You'll consult it repeatedly during the actual search, and it will be a helpful compass to keep you on course.

I'll talk in Chapter 10 about how to make your best case. That includes your resume and your elevator speech. Those two things are the culmination of your current PVP. As you're finishing your PVP, it's a good time to get started on them.

I'll illustrate these principles with a story of one of the toughest job search challenges: coming back to work after a long absence. Your expertise is rusty. Your network is stale. People wonder whether you're committed. That was Shannon's challenge.

## Shannon Returns to Work

At thirty-two, Shannon had advanced professionally from health care consulting to investment management, with an MBA in the middle. Then she had children, moved overseas with her husband, stopped working, and returned to the United States. At fifty, Shannon was a divorced mother of teenagers, and she hadn't had a job for eleven years. She needed to restart her career.

Not an easy task, that's for sure. Shannon needed to reconceptualize herself and determine her long-term aspirations, set a fresh PVP to get that started in the near term, do what's required to put that PVP in place, create a new professional network, and present her total package in a convincing way. She needed both a long-term strategy and a short-term strategy. She didn't have the luxury of an extended period of assessment and reflection. As she put it:

> When I got kicked in the butt, I needed to get my old self back. That was working and trying to change the health care world—to make health care work better, to have a better model helping people with their health. Actually, I like to fix stuff. I'm the person who brings order to doctors. The passion has to do with knowing we do a horrible job in this country managing health care.

Shannon had been successful before, and she reflected on what had caused that. Where she had stood out, she concluded, was in helping executives understand issues, listen to each other, and decide. She knew executives would value that strength if they thought she had it.

But Shannon wasn't sure how to get ready. "I was afraid. The one piece I knew I was really behind on was technology. I didn't want to go into technology. I'd never before worked in health care IT." Even if IT wouldn't be a specific part of her purview, she needed to upgrade in two areas—how IT was shaping health care and how IT was changing the way people worked together.

She remembers where she was when she decided what to do.

> I was sitting in the sun room. There was a cup of coffee next to me, and I was debating it. I saw an article in the newspaper about a health care IT study program. It hit me that was what I was going to do. I need a plan to be working towards. Like in driving a motorcycle, I need to see where I'm going. If you look where you are, you'll get in an accident. The course gave me a short-term goal. Wow! It was six months, a reachable goal. I knew it would launch me.

Few were on top of the regulatory and reporting changes that were under way, and the IT program covered those in depth. It also met her other IT need—that she become facile with basic tools such as Outlook, PowerPoint, and online shared meetings.

Good things began to happen. Her Internet research revealed that the new government body responsible for health care information reporting in her region was located five minutes from her home. She visited, briefly introduced herself to the person in charge, and returned for a meeting to find out what they were doing. As she recalls, "We hit it off. He had a position open. He needed help. It became a little consulting project." She later realized that the job had a second benefit: "It meant somebody else had vetted me." That made it easier for others to consider hiring her.

The IT program and the consulting project led to her new short-term PVP. I'd like to say that she wrote the PVP down just as I encourage you to do. Although Shannon embodies the PVP concept, she never recorded it. Instead, she prepared elevator speeches that collectively made her case:

> My PVP was a series of elevator speeches. It was about my desire to change health care, not about my job. A lot of stuff is broken. I'd love to be part of an organization whose position is to improve health care. I'm going to make you successful. I figured out what their need was and showed them how I matched what they needed to accomplish.

She devised stories about herself to demonstrate her commitment: "I was making sure I relayed what my passions were, and that's why people were able to fit a job around me. When I applied for the jobs I saw, I wasn't necessarily having the specs for a particular role."

Other elevator speeches were what she called "name dropping." Shannon's study program required her to meet health care leaders in the community, and she talked about how those enterprises were affected by industry changes. She also prepared to describe her work years before—most important, her consulting to a hospital where she believes she developed the concept of integrated care management.

Shannon resolved to show her personal style in interviews. She hoped to demonstrate listening skills with good follow-up questions—allowing people to see firsthand that she could facilitate tough meetings. If she did that right, it would be obvious she'd be a good colleague.

Shannon also knew that she needed to combat doubts about why she dropped out of the work world and whether she really was ready to return. The IT certification course and the consulting assignment helped with that, but she wanted to do more. At the start of conversations, she raised the subject of her absence and described why she was excited about returning to work. She said: "I wanted to set the record straight quickly. I moved internationally and came back. I had kids in school. My quick elevator speech was about the gap of time right off the bat. Then they didn't feel they had to pry into it."

Doing this also demonstrated confidence, honesty, and determination. People liked her transparency, her story made sense, and they wanted to help.

She prepared to make her case persuasively: "I practiced the stories in my brain in the shower or when I was driving."

Shannon needed a new professional network to help locate possibilities. She began with social acquaintances and then moved out to people they suggested in local health care companies.

In three months, Shannon landed two strong offers. Although her IT preparation had retuned her and demonstrated that she was serious, neither offer was primarily about IT. As she told me: "What got me my current job was my old background. I didn't look at IT at all, but at health care where everyone needs to understand the technology. My goal was strategy and projects. It was their gap that the CEO realized during our meeting and created the role I am in."

She got what she wanted: a new special projects position. The man who made that offer told her that he was persuaded to hire her because of her passion.

I spoke with Shannon when she was shaping her opportunity search, but at that time I hadn't yet developed the list of steps that I shared earlier in this chapter to construct a PVP. Two years later, I showed her the list and asked whether she'd used them. Here's her response:

> Oh, I absolutely went through these steps, just not in the deliberate fashion and order you suggest. It was pretty methodical in my head, and I created a notebook that I have since tossed. I even had bullet points written of my value added, also known as PVP, for different jobs—consulting, research, hospital operations improvement,

> strategy/change management, health info technology, and medical staff relations. Time frame for me was a pretty short goal of three to six months. I needed to get back in the game for a few years and then worry about longer term. My strengths I worked through with you, and we developed a "cover letter" elevator speech. I had one or two sentences to explain away the gap and moved on to value added.

Shannon didn't do a big formal assessment. She operated more on the intuitive side, but her activities were the ones I'm recommending to you. Most important was recognizing that health care was the right long-term field and identifying the PVP she could deliver in the near term. She then rebuilt the expertise required to deliver that PVP, recreated a network, and presented herself in a way that demonstrated her capability in a compelling way. We reconstructed her PVP a couple of years later (see Table 8.1):

Shannon conceptualized a new strategy, moved smartly to execute that strategy, and conducted a successful job search. She'll explore her long-term purpose as her experience grows. I find her inspiring.

There are benefits to be gained from having a single PVP like Shannon's, but it may not be simple to get to that single PVP. I'll cover that topic now.

## Benefits of a Single PVP

A single PVP streamlines opportunity search. You can become expert in that field or role and in how to present yourself for that. You can concentrate your research, outreach, and interview preparations. That's best practice. It will give you the best chance of success with the target.

I asked a search consultant about PVP. Although he'd never heard the term before, he immediately recognized what I was talking about, liked it, and encouraged this kind of focus:

**TABLE 8.1** Shannon's Current PVP

| TARGET | INSTITUTIONAL NEEDS / SHANNON'S STRENGTHS | SHANNON'S EXPECTATIONS |
|---|---|---|
| • Important healthcare providers located in her city<br>• Need change and improvement<br>• Prefers cross enterprise roles<br>• Focus on clinical strategy and operations | • Spot improvement opportunities<br>• Work within organization to realize opportunities<br>- Ability to work up and down organization<br>- Listening skill<br>- Facilitation skill<br>- Project management skill<br>• Passion and drive<br>• Contemporary healthcare management knowledge around risk and use of technology | • Reach conclusion in 3 to 6 months<br>• Platform for personal and career growth<br>• Competitive compensation, accepting that she's reentering workforce after hiatus for family |

If you're in a job and want to change, figure out what you want to do. Just coming in and saying you want to move on is not helpful. You don't go high on the list. What get's people high on the list is someone who gives me a thoughtful idea of what they want. Not general ideas about where they want to go, but "I'd love to be with a company like XXX and here's why." It's not just XXX, but it says a lot. You're not running from something but looking for something. If people want to move soon, they'll want to cast a broad net. But if it's more like they're looking for a needle in a haystack, it's much more persuasive.

You might think that the more possibilities you have, the more likely you are to receive attractive offers. Not so fast.[1] If more possibilities mean you're not well prepared for any of them, they may reduce your chances of getting offers. Even if it doesn't do that, you may be perpetually dissatisfied, wondering if something else would have been better.

Even though a wider playing field means there'll be more possibilities, it's harder to do two searches with quality because you must divide your time. If you're considering two unrelated or loosely related fields, that'll require two different PVPs, two different resumes, and two streams of activities. In some broadcast formats like social media, you may be making a generic statement about yourself rather than a statement that targets a particular field; that generic statement is less likely to attract attention from any of your targets.

All that said, having different targets will sometimes make sense. Perhaps there are few opportunities in your target area—for example, a tenure-track professor's position in a small area of art history. Perhaps the opportunities you're seeking are highly competitive. Or what if you're simply unsure of what you'd like to do?

If your situation is like these, follow separate, distinct strategies rather than a generalized, mushy strategy. Pick a first target, prepare to pursue it, and begin executing that strategy. As time permits, pick a second target and do the same, and so on. If you find an opportunity you like, that's a terrific result. There's another benefit: as you conceive and begin executing separate strategies, you may discover that these different fields or roles share one or more important characteristics. That insight might be the key to unlock a new and more coherent opportunity search strategy.

I have some sympathy for people who can't narrow things down. I've been there too, and I've seen people change targets for good reason. Target switching is more frequent when people are pursuing very small employer markets, or fields very different from their past experience. As they begin meeting people, they learn more about what target employers need, get feedback on how well they match those needs, and shift PVPs on the basis of what they've learned. That kind of flexible learning is an essential ingredient in a successful job search.

I'll mention one issue I've occasionally heard people raise about the PVP. A few have assumed that the PVP is a sales concept that's largely about appealing to a hiring market. In this view, what's right for the person developing his or her strategy is secondary. Also secondary is the PVP's promise that the person truly fills the hiring person's gap. Ouch! Let me be clear about this: the PVP is authentically about you. In job search, it's the position you're ready for at the current time. If you follow a so-called market-driven strategy and define yourself in a way that meets prospective employers' needs with only a limited connection to your strengths, you might end up in a place where you don't really fit, you may not succeed, and your chance for finding a calling may have fallen dramatically.

A final thought: if your current PVP falls short of your aspirations, you may have to pursue opportunities now that aren't exciting. Let that disappointment drive innovation. Recognizing the gap between where you are and where you'd like to be can be a valuable insight. It can set you up to prepare a new long-term strategy by following the suggestions in Part II.

With a current PVP in hand, you're ready to use it. That starts with finding potential opportunities, the topic of the next chapter.

Chapter 9

# OPPORTUNITY IDENTIFICATION

**VALUE PROPOSITIONS POWER** sophisticated marketing and sales strategies. For products that are sold to businesses, this means sales coverage for target businesses (not all businesses) and actions to create the right reputation among those targets. For products that are sold to retailers and then to consumers, this means sales coverage to retailers who reach target consumers (not all retailers) together with positioning and media programs to reach target consumers (not all consumers).

Even if you have a strong PVP, attractive opportunities won't land on your doorstep. Just as in business, you must go out and find them. That's the hard part.

In Chapter 6, you read about the three sources of opportunity: job postings, affiliations, and professional networks. Networks are by far the most important. As I mentioned in that chapter, of the people I've counseled about careers, more than three out of four who found new positions did so through networking. Take full advantage of job postings and affiliations, but commit the great majority of time to networking.

Having a strong professional network is indispensable. In this chapter, you'll see how to make the most out of that network to identify potential opportunities. And if you turn up something interesting through public sources or affiliations, you'll talk with people to confirm the possibilities and, you hope, be invited to interview. Use many of the same networking practices I'll describe in this chapter to do that well.

Business executive Frederick provides a world-class example of leveraging a network.

## Frederick's Astonishing Outreach

Frederick rose through the ranks to become a partner in a management consulting firm, but then events intervened. His wife died, and he had to raise two small children. The pace and travel of consulting were too demanding, so Frederick left to became head of the North American division of his European client. The business grew from $100 million to $500 million during his four-year tenure. That success had its own consequences. The business hit a plateau, and Frederick's opportunities were limited unless he moved to corporate offices across the ocean. He decided not to move his children and joined a different consulting firm in the same industry practice area. That position offered less travel, but then the company was sold, and Frederick decided to move on. He and a friend then raised a small venture fund focused on the industry he knew best. That business launched nicely in 2007, but the recession slowed the flow of possible deals and investor commitments. They dissolved the fund.

Frederick's job search led him to become COO of an industry start-up. Not only did that job search turn into an offer, but Frederick also saw how active the hiring market was for this kind of position and that he was competitive in that market. It was a good thing that he became optimistic about his prospects, because after a year and a half, a disagreement with the company's founder led him to leave the company. He was back in job search mode.

Frederick concentrated on discovering good opportunities through his network. From his twenty years of working in and consulting to the industry, Frederick had developed close professional friends and many contacts. He started in a strong position, but it's almost astonishing how he made the most out of that network. He established a highly productive method to turn up appealing opportunities, much like the way he ran sales campaigns at work. Here's how he described it:

> How to manage the pipeline to keep multiple opportunities open? I see three yellow lights, chugging along, and I'm managing the process. I see four red lights and can't get a response. It's the process engineering. It's a question of how many people I'm touching each week. It takes wide outreach. Discussions to possibilities to offers. I keep an Excel spreadsheet: name, location, industry, prior career, and intensity of relationship. Each week I touch fifty people and score the quality of touch from 1 to 7. Is it an email or a meeting? If I touch fifty a week and score 150 a week, then I was going to get a job whether it's three months or six months. For the majority of people, they're not touching enough.

No kidding. Frederick was communicating with fifty people a week through a large number of emails, a smaller number of phone calls, and a few in-person meetings. Each week! Frederick asked broad questions about industry outlook and what parts of the industry might offer the best prospects. He asked about possibilities at his contact's company and whom else to meet. Multiple opportunities appeared.

The other element of Frederick's process management was timing and sequencing. He hoped for offers, but he didn't want to have to decide whether to say yes while waiting for an offer he'd prefer. As he said: "It's very hard if you have an offer. Are you going to give up an offer with X dollars in hope another one shows up in January? Once a piece of paper is in hand, you've got three weeks.

Otherwise, you poison the offer. The offer I got the first week of October retracts on November 1."

There's no magic way to avoid dilemmas like this, but Frederick gave some thought to this when scheduling meetings and making calls. He described it this way: "One guy is busy enough so that if I cancelled a meeting it'd be three weeks before it occurred to him we haven't talked." Once he had an offer in hand, he could use that as a reason to call others and see if they could accelerate their decision. That would be a smart move if he really was prepared to accept the offer in hand. It would be risky if he wasn't. The people he called might simply wish him the best and say good-bye.

Frederick thought about timing. He hustled to make something happen in six months or sooner. Having talked to search firm friends, he concluded that "as long as you're back to work in six months, no one's going to care."

Frederick also was philosophical about any particular situation: "It's like a marathon. So much can go right or wrong. If you start the race and are confident you trained well, how you do that day doesn't matter."

The result of all this was very good: a new position at a similar level of responsibility and compensation four months after his job search began. Most people like Frederick who were seeking senior positions would be pleased with this time frame. Frederick's networking is the best I've seen.

## Massive, Structured Outreach

Massive, structured outreach is the best way to identify opportunities, and I've drawn lessons from Frederick and other strong networkers about how to do that well. I've grouped networking principles into four categories—whom to contact, when to contact them, how to conduct the discussion, and what to do after meetings:

## Whom to Contact

### *1. Broadly Define Your Network*

As I noted, the way to win is through massive, structured outreach. The way to lose is to limit contacts to the few people you know well and to let things happen in a hit-or-miss way. When people only approach close friends, they don't realize the power of the "weak ties" I discussed in Chapter 6. Consider former classmates, colleagues from earlier employers, business relationships outside your institution, and civic acquaintances. Be expansive.

### *2. Create New Network Along the Way*

Ask people you already know whom else to see, and ask for introductions.

Imagine people you don't know who are relevant to your search. Various company lists may yield ideas in your target area—for example, lists of good places to work, fast-growing companies, best CEOs, and so on. Online sources of information about individuals can be a source of people who might be able to provide advice about your search.

If you find a connection to one of these people (such as a common friend, a tie to the same school, or a shared former employer), you may be able to make a "cool call" with a greater prospect that the person will find time to speak to you. If you don't find that connection, go ahead and cold-call them. Although it's harder to meet people you don't already know, most people are flattered to be asked for advice.

If your search is out in the open (not under the radar), you may want to broadcast your plans and ask for help. Social media will get the word out quickly, but announce a search only when the time's right. Recalling his search, Frederick said: "I can post something on Facebook or LinkedIn and tell three hundred people something has changed in my life. I wasn't ready at first. I didn't want twenty people calling and saying they have a great offer for me. I've got to do this and this first." He wanted to resolve any issues related to leaving his employer and to think through his new plan. If he'd gone out too soon, he'd have used up these contacts before he was ready to ask for help. He might not get their attention again.

How to use social media in job search or more broadly in careers is a topic big enough for a whole book. In fact, there are many. When I queried Amazon.com and Barnesandnoble.com for books related to "job search social media," I got 226 hits on one site and 483 on the other. If you'd like to go deeper into this topic, there are numerous opportunities to do that.

### When to Contact Them

#### *3. Get Started*

A mental block may keep you from writing an email or picking up the phone. Perhaps you're uncomfortable asking for help. Or maybe you're waiting until you're highly confident that you're prepared. You may be surprised to find that a month has gone by and little has happened.

Everything will take longer than you might first assume. You're asking busy people to fit you into their schedules. Go ahead and contact the first one or two or three. Get started. Nothing like a meeting on the calendar to lead your own closure on your provisional PVP!

#### *4. Start with People You Know Best*

Although it's unwise to limit yourself to close colleagues, beginning with them is natural. They're the easiest to meet. It also makes sense from a learning perspective. At the outset, you're trialing your PVP—getting their reactions to target jobs and how well you fit those targets and perhaps hearing ideas for what else to consider. Try for wide-open, exploratory conversations. People who know something about you have a basis for making suggestions. They may know others to call.

As your plan develops, you'll have more conviction about your direction. That's when to cast a wider net and see people you don't know well. It's when to meet people for the first time.

Contact people in different ways. Contact close friends in the most comfortable way. For distant acquaintances and certainly for people you're trying to meet, the best path usually will be an email or a letter, followed up with a phone call, and then, one hopes, a meeting. Buy coffee or lunch.

### *5. Determine Whether to Begin with Higher-Priority or Lower-Priority Employers*

Because job search can be hard, people sometimes hope to do as little as possible but still land the perfect job. They begin with the possibilities they think they'd like most. That approach may make sense, but give some thought to sequence before laying out your plan.

If you approach top priorities first, you'll have more time for possibilities to develop there. If instead your early meetings are with lower-priority prospects, those meetings can hone your PVP and interviewing skills. You may then do better in interviews at the higher-priority employers. And you may be surprised to find that some lower priorities look appealing.

### *6. Sequence Follow-Up Meetings*

Ideally, you'll turn up two or more good offers at the same time. You'll compare them and determine the one you like best. You won't have to decide whether to say yes to an acceptable bird in the hand when a bird in the bush may be better—a situation you want to avoid.

Once conversations are under way, you may be able to influence timing. Some people may not notice if you're slowing things down. Or you might try to speed up another situation or at least learn where that prospective employer stands. If you can, time meetings so that you don't have to decide before you're ready.

## How to Conduct the Discussions

### *7. View Conversations as Learning Opportunities*

Ask about more than jobs. Ask about the industry, how to succeed, and how to position yourself. What you learn can be valuable. It may lead you to shift tar`gets or change how you present yourself. Approaching these meetings as conversations breaks the ice. It's disarming.

### *8. Let Your Strengths and PVP Be Your Calling Card*

As I noted in an earlier chapter, most people, even the people you know well, will find it easier to react to your thinking than to come up with ideas on their own. Let your view of your strengths and your PVP drive the content of conversations. Describe your strengths, ask for reactions if appropriate, and seek ideas about how to deploy those strengths. Tell people why you believe you can win with the target embedded in your PVP. Ask for reactions and for other ideas. Use the conversations both to deploy your PVP and to test it.

## What to Do after Meetings

### *9. Be Systematic with Good Record Keeping*

Staying on top of broad outreach is complicated. There are many moving parts. After each meeting, write down when it was, what you learned, and what you'll do as a result. Set up a database or a filing system to help keep on top of everything. Frederick's spreadsheet and scoring methodology to gauge progress are one excellent example of an effective system.

### *10. Follow Up*

After a substantive discussion, send a thank-you email or letter. As time passes, go back to people with an update on what you're learning and with follow-up questions.

### *11. Periodically Evaluate Progress and Strategy*

View your job search as conducting a study. Review your notes from different meetings and look for patterns. Are there better ways to move in the direction you've selected? Are there reasons to shift direction, to change your PVP? Are you putting in enough time? You may benefit from confiding in a friend or a spouse. Even if you don't have the right discussion partner, "meet" with yourself.

Management consultant Isabel decided to leave her firm and look for something else. Where her networking stands out is on the learning side.

## Isabel's Learning through Outreach

While Isabel was still working part-time, her job search targeted three fields connected to her past client work. She built a contact list related to those fields through current and former colleagues and from university alumni records. She added relevant search consultants. She worked a spreadsheet like Frederick's.

When Isabel met people, she asked questions about the different parts of her target industries and different kinds of careers. She didn't highlight job openings. She described it this way: "I had forty or fifty conversations. Thirty-five were informational. I was talking to anyone who seemed close to being relevant. What do you do? What do you like? I was willing to explore any option in my target areas, in some cases if only to learn."

What she learned guided her search. She recalled four insights.

Isabel was looking for a new position to better align the conflicting demands of family and work. Through her networking, she gained new perspectives on how to achieve personal balance. One mother who was president of a small company reported that she had one group of people to lead and one boss, the board chair. Two sets of relationships sounded much less complex than Isabel's current work environment. This woman's life wasn't stressful. She could define her scope of work. Her life sounded manageable. Isabel called this an "ah-ha moment."

Another person helped her think about incoming roles. If she came in as a company's strategy leader or something else similar to consulting, Isabel risked being stuck in a position with a ceiling. The people who ran the big functions of large companies usually worked up through one of those functions; seldom was an outsider promoted into those roles. It dawned on her that most people who had suggested jobs for her were thinking about something like consulting, and that only would make sense for Isabel's career if she transferred into a key function after learning the company. Long-term-scenario thinking and attention to a career path became critical. As she recalled it: "I recognized different criteria over the six months. One was the long-term implications of any job. Early on, I thought about what's cool about a given role; but I became more disciplined to ensure I thought about the role over time. I was trying to figure out what's next."

These meetings also provided ideas about how to "do the due diligence" on a role. One man told her about having taken a new position with enthusiasm. But "he'd never had an explicit up-front conversation about his authority to fire someone. When he felt he needed to replace someone, he learned he couldn't." Another person helped Isabel think about how to question a board member who was interviewing her. It's hard to ask directly, but "questions about how they made some decisions in the past can help determine whether they are an operational board or a governance board."

From several people, she learned about life in her three target fields. She realized that positions with a big future in one of her provisional targets would require too much travel for her at this point in her life, whereas the other two were manageable. That same field was less likely to have a place for her to make a lateral move from her current position; she'd probably have to take a step down. She pruned the list.

The process was progressive. The more people she met, the more she learned. Insights from earlier meetings helped her ask better questions later. People suggested others to contact. Momentum grew. Isabel found two good opportunities in three months.

Targeting was critical. As she put it:

> There's a step zero before step one—what things matter. I wasn't going to call someone to ask him to open his Rolodex. I had forty meetings. I might have had two hundred if I hadn't known early on what matters. I doubt people would have reacted as well to me if I hadn't been focused. And if I'd needed two hundred meetings, they might already have filled the job I took with someone else.

Everyone's heard about networking. People know they need it, but many find it hard to get started. My blog posts about networking in hbr.org received many comments. I especially remember comments from professional career counselors. Some were frustrated. Their biggest challenge, they thought, was to convince clients to reach out.

If you're starting a job search, first establish your target and know why you're a good fit. That's your PVP. Next, identify good possibilities. That's largely about networking. Neither Frederick nor Isabel had the list of networking principles from earlier in this chapter, but they both were naturals. Now you have those principles. Follow them, and you too will gain important information and identify potential opportunities.

Once you find those opportunities, you must be ready to meet people and get the offer. That's the subject of Chapter 10.

## Chapter 10

# THE BEST CASE

**EXCELLENT PROFESSIONAL SELLERS** tightly link their product's value proposition to the prospective customer's needs. They stand in the shoes of potential customers, sense their needs, and think about how their products can meet those needs. The best diplomats and attorneys bring the same mind-set to negotiations. The best at this are intuitive game theorists. They picture what the other side wants to accomplish, and imagine win-win solutions.

A winning near-term PVP and the associated networking can surface attractive opportunities, but you still need to get the offer. That's when interview preparation comes in. You'll have the best chance to turn interviews into offers if you can operate like excellent sellers, diplomats, and attorneys. Take the employer's perspective, understand what's needed, and show you're the right fit.

Prepare in two ways. Draw on your current PVP to prepare to explain how you match the employer's needs. And get ready to respond to questions. That's how to turn interviews into offers.

## Developing Your Case

Your goal is to communicate your PVP—what's needed to succeed in the job and why you're an excellent fit. It's possible your PVP will come out naturally in the discussion, but you can't count on that. The conversation may be confused, and even in the best of circumstances, it may not be as clear as you need it to be. Here are the steps to making your best case.

### 1. Prepare Your Resume

Translate the PVP into your resume, the top of your LinkedIn profile, and other similar portraits of you. Your summary statement states your target and why you're a good fit. The activities under that statement present a full view of your background, but you want to emphasize the ones that best support your PVP. Keep it up-to-date. Online information means you're always out there. You want to look your best all the time.

### 2. Conceive a Compelling "Elevator Speech"

Your PVP also translates into your elevator speech. Prepare a thirty-second elevator speech, a two-minute version, and a five-minute version. They all say the same thing, just at different levels of depth. With those pitches, you're ready for every situation. Write them down.

### 3. Devise Engaging Stories

Interviewers may remember and trust vivid stories as much or more than the direct claims in the elevator speech. Prepare stories about yourself to illustrate different aspects of your PVP and to show how the PVP ties to your personal history.[1]

### 4. Determine the Right Style

Rather than just describing yourself, conduct your side of interviews to display aspects of your PVP (as creative writing instructors say, "Show, don't tell"). For example, you can demonstrate listening or leadership skills by the way you communicate. Or you can show a more analytical style in your interviews, a more practical get-things-done style, or whatever else you're hoping people will recognize in you.

### 5. Imagine Thoughtful Questions

Prepare questions to ask if given the right opportunity. Thoughtful questions make your case. They show you've invested time to prepare and that you're interested. They demonstrate insight. They show that you're a serious person.

Ask questions that display more than just basic knowledge. If you're interviewing for a job at a company known for consumer marketing, for example, don't ask: "Do you do much market research here?" If they're known for marketing, you can be sure they do lots of research. Instead, perhaps you would ask, "How do market research findings connect to product design and pricing decisions?" or "What are the differences in careers up through the market research function compared to careers in brand management?" Questions like those indicate that you're thinking deeply about the job. They're impressive lines of inquiry.

Another good angle is to ask about a topic you know the interviewer's dealing with in her work. As is true of so many things in this book, the more specific you can be, the better. And be sure to have follow-ups in mind. The way to win with questions is to create an interesting conversation.

### 6. Design Your Plan for Success

Come prepared to describe how you'd win in the job. That requires understanding what's needed beyond conventional job specifications.

The way to show you can get off to a strong start is to develop the plan to do just that. Start by acknowledging that you have a lot to learn and that you'd need to confirm the plan once you were on board. But after that qualification, be confident. Do this well, and they'll be thinking more about what it'd be like to work with you than whether to make you an offer.

This line of discussion is important for everyone, but it's essential for senior roles. CEOs and boards expect new senior leaders to hit the ground running. Think back to the way Ian prepared his plan to turn around the financial services company, described in Chapter 4. That both got him the offer and prepared him for his first months as CEO.

### 7. Marshall the Evidence

Achievements are evidence of the PVP, not the PVP itself. If you're an engineer pursuing a position designing bridges, for example, the PVP is what you know and are able to do. Then the evidence comes into play. For recent graduates, it might emphasize your civil engineering class standing and university reputation. For the more experienced, it would emphasize your work experience and perhaps include your professional engineer certification.

Review past achievements and prepare to deploy them in interviews to illustrate your PVP. Weave key facts into your elevator speeches. If possible, assemble a nonconfidential portfolio of your work—for example, reports you wrote that had impact, or facts on measurable achievements such as sales growth or cost reduction. Concrete results with numbers usually will have the greatest impact. You may or may not use this material in interviews, but you'll have it ready if you need it.

### 8. Help References Get Ready

You're not the only one who needs to know your PVP. Your references do. They'll be most helpful to you if they understand what's required to succeed in the job. If you feel comfortable doing so, share your thinking about how you'd bring the needed skills and talents. If they want to support you, they can make your case more effectively than you can.

Take advantage of these ideas, and you'll be ready to showcase your PVP. That's critical, but it's only half of the preparations. You're also making your case as you respond to interviewers' questions. Priming yourself for that is harder, of course, because you can't know what they'll ask.

## Preparing for Interviewers' Questions

Take their perspective. Imagine what you'd ask if you were them.[2] If I were advising interviewers (not you), I'd suggest they pick some of the following topics (divided here into five categories). When you're preparing for an interview, look at this list, tailor it to match the particulars of the institution and the position, and think about how you'd respond if questions like them come up.

### Knowledge, Capability, and Record

Your past: Tell me about your education, work experiences, and any other activities. Tell me about anything on the resume or in the public record. Tell me about your biggest success. What made it happen? Describe a big disappointment. What caused that? What have you learned from these situations?

Tests: [Depending on the hiring company, you may be asked to take tests of knowledge and capability—for example, skills at quantitative analysis, writing, and industry or functional knowledge.]

### Intrinsic Talents and Interests

Problem solving and thinking: Describe a hard problem, how you approached it, and what happened. [You may be given various problem-solving tests, such as cases (often a real business situation)[3] or imaginary problems (such as how many marbles could fit in a jar). If you expect interviewers to use special interviewing formats like these, practice ahead of time.]

Creativity and curiosity: Tell me about your hobbies or other things you do outside work, the most interesting course in school outside your major, or your reaction to a big topic in public discussion this month.

Things that excite: What do you enjoy most (both in and out of work) and why? What do you dislike and why? Describe the times when you've absolutely loved what you were doing at work and what caused that. Describe an accomplishment you're especially proud of and why.

Objectivity and self-insight: In what areas are you much stronger than peers? What are your shortcomings, and what are you doing to work on them? How would another person describe you? How would someone you worked with who's not on your reference list describe you? What was your best personal learning experience in the last year? Who mentored you, and what did you get from that? What mistakes have you made, how did you deal with them, and what did you learn?

## Values, Aspirations, and Personality

Personality tests: [Some employers require that candidates take these tests.]

Independence: Tell me about an instance where you refused to budge on an issue and why. Tell me about one where you compromised and why.

Dealing with hard challenges: What are the toughest things you've had to do at work, and what happened (for example: firing someone, reporting an ethics violation, or disagreeing with a supervisor)?

Personal confidence and resilience: What risks have you taken, why did you take them, and what happened? Describe a decision when you avoided risk, why, and what happened. What is your greatest disappointment, and how did you deal with it?

Aspirations: Tell me about a decision you made to leave a job and why. Tell me about your rationale for accepting the new job.

What would be your ideal work environment and why? What would be a horrible environment (though some of your peers might accept it) and why? How important is your current work relative to other things in your life? What are your goals related to money, prestige, power, service, craft, and institution?

Long-term plan: Where do you expect to be in five years and in ten, how important is this direction to you, and what are you doing to pursue it? How ambitious are you? What would you most want to accomplish over your career? How's your current work going, and how do you feel about that? How does the job we're discussing fit into your long-term plan?

Clues from your background: Where did you grow up, and how does that affect you today? What were your favorite things in high school? Why did you pick one college or another? Why did you pick your first job? Your current job?

## Style of Working with Others

Leadership: Of the people you've led, whom did you like best and why? Whom do you feel you developed most effectively? Whom did you fail to develop and why? Whom did you hire and why?

Working with others: Describe a situation when you worked with peers and needed to influence them, and what happened. Describe a situation when you worked with senior people and needed to influence them, and what happened. Describe a conflict situation, what you did, and what happened. Tell me about an occasion when you got your hands dirty on the front line and what happened.

Insight into organization culture: Describe your current institution's culture—its strengths and weaknesses and how you fit. Tell me about purpose, teamwork, colleagues, people practices, communications, performance, and productivity. [In answering these questions, be sure to keep confidential things confidential.] What have you learned about our culture from the people you've met, and how well do you think it serves our strategy?

The Institution, the Position, and How You Fit

PVP for this position: What's needed for success in this position? How would you prioritize the requirements? Why would you be good at it? [Although they may not have heard of the PVP concept, they're implicitly testing for it throughout the interview.]

How well you understand our institution: Tell me about our institution, its organization, its strategy, its biggest challenges, and so on. What's required for the institution to be successful? How are we doing?

Why you want this job: What would you expect to accomplish, and what would you expect to learn? What do you like about the culture, and why do you think you'd be excited to be part of the institution?

Preparing for the kinds of questions you've seen here is critical. Write down the most important points you hope to make to ensure you have them clearly in mind. What remains is to practice. Practice in front of a mirror. Practice in the shower. Practice with friends. Pay attention to their reactions.

There often will be two or more rounds of meetings. Learn from the first interviews, and return for round two with follow-up insights and questions.

Make your best case, but don't try to imagine the answer the interviewers want to hear and then how you could say that. People can see through that tactic. Be yourself. One search firm partner emphasized the advantages of being straightforward:

> Be authentic, transparent, and honest. You'll never fool the recruiters. Be authentically interested in the job. Show that by being authentically interested in the people you're talking to. There's a big difference between proving how much you know because you're so smart, and personal connection. If you've gone through most of the process, they believe you can do it. They want to relate to

> you personally. Gaming it out is a mistake. It's very much about personality. It's the plane ride test. They might take a trip to St. Louis with you, but there's no way they could go to Europe with you. Eighty percent of the time, we know who'll be the winner when we send in three people. It's more about chemistry than skills.

Finally, postpone the meeting if you're not prepared. You want to give it your best.

Chapter 11

# OPPORTUNITY SEARCH PLAN

**YOU'VE SEEN HOW** to set your PVP for opportunity search, how to identify opportunities, and how to prepare for interviews. We'll now cover the last step in Part III: the opportunity search plan. I'll first discuss that plan and then share a story of a young man's opportunity search that incorporated all these activities.

## Search Plan

In Chapter 7, you read about the long-term strategic road map. It helps busy people convert good intentions into action. By building in contingencies, you revisit your strategy and the logic behind it. And it can start the strategy process by creating a vivid picture of what alternative strategies would mean.

The opportunity search plan is a similar idea, but it's all about execution. Because you may be making fifty or a hundred or more contacts in your search and because you can't know where any particular contact will lead, it's seldom practical to use the strategic road map for explicit contingency planning. The opportunity search plan is a sequenced to-do list. It can speed your search and make it productive.

Recall Shannon from Chapter 8, returning to work after eleven years. Here's how she described her plan:

> It was seat of the pants. Meet someone and get a better understanding of needs in that company and maybe someone they know to contact. It's the branch-out method. You can't make a list of all you'll do, because you branch from each meeting. It becomes a tree. You have a series of short-term plans to extend each branch. A fixed list limits you.

If you've followed the suggestions from the three preceding chapters, you'll mostly be assembling materials you've already created and letting them serve as your plan. A complete plan includes these steps.

### 1. Record Your PVP

Write down what you've decided to do, if you haven't already done that. That's your PVP and the rationale behind it. Your PVP helps you imagine whom to contact about opportunities and how to describe yourself. It provides the baseline when you're ready to check progress and reevaluate the approach. It's the point of departure when you're deciding whether to accept an offer.

### 2. List Actions to Surface Opportunities

List the steps you intend to take to identify opportunity, from public sources to affiliations to your professional network. List whom in your network you plan to contact and in what sequence. Modify this list, perhaps weekly, as you learn from initial activities and as you identify new contacts.

### 3. Prepare to Make Your Best Case

List the substantive preparations you'll carry out in parallel to network outreach. That includes four kinds of activity: conducting the research on target industries and institutions; designing elevator speeches, stories, and other actions to describe your PVP in a persuasive way; getting ready for questions you may be asked; and practicing. Don't forget to build in time to practice.

### 4. Prioritize Preparations

The more you prepare for a networking conversation, the more you'll learn. The more you prepare for the first meeting with a potential employer, the better impression you'll make. And if there's a follow-up meeting, people will expect you to have absorbed the previous meeting's discussion and be prepared for a deeper discussion.

Recall Pallab from Chapter 2, who prepared extensively for each meeting with the CEO. He listened to that corporation's conference calls with investors each quarter, kept up with news about the company, and thought about what he had learned. Meeting after meeting, Pallab was up-to-date and brought topical questions with him. That preparation contributed importantly to the impression he made, and led to the offer.

You'll always be better off with more preparation. The more you prepare for one meeting in a given week, however, the less time you have to prepare for other meetings. So you'll need to allocate meeting preparation time to where you expect the greatest impact.

The prioritization embedded in your PVP is input to your time allocation decision. Meetings in the target field—and, within that field, the institutions you like best—generally are important. Other factors also come into play in allocating time—for example, what you hope to learn in the meeting and how important that is to your search, whether there's an open position at the company, the expectations of the person you're meeting about how well prepared you'll be for the meeting, and whether preparation for one meeting might help in other meetings at that institution or somewhere else.

### 5. Plan Progress Reviews

Schedule assessment and decision points. Review your search tactics weekly—what's happened, whether the previously mentioned activities are on schedule, how well they're working, and whether to adjust tactics. Put strategic checkpoints on the schedule—probably every three or four weeks. Review whether your target and your PVP seem to be working and whether to shift your plan or continue. Or if you start with mostly stretch target employers (what I called the "best" in Chapter 8), reevaluate whether that path looks productive or whether to downshift for now.

Many things can happen during job searches. It's hard to predict exactly how events will develop. An opportunity search plan like this will both prepare you to execute a productive search and set you up to review progress and react as the search proceeds.

MBA student Anthony was beginning his job search three months short of graduation. Starting so late, Anthony needed to execute world-class application of all these job search ideas to come out a winner.

## Anthony's Last-Minute Job Search

Anthony, twenty-six, was beginning his last semester in business school. Many classmates already knew where they'd be in June. Others were well under way on job searches. Not Anthony. When I first heard about this, I saw the makings of a disaster.

The barrier was that Anthony couldn't settle on a target. Younger than the majority, he'd had less time to explore different roles and fields of work. He'd worked two years in real estate and had had two short internships in that field. He had no other work experience. His family was in real estate. When he began his MBA studies sixteen months earlier, he'd assumed he'd return to real estate after graduation.

When school started, however, Anthony met classmates with diverse experiences, and noticed companies on recruiting visits to campus. It was exciting. Many fields seemed possible—from high-tech to energy to finance. As he put it, "I felt like a kid in a candy store. Every time I learned of a new industry, I became intrigued. I spent most of my first year trying to become interested in other things, only to realize that I had no real interest." After flirting with those fields, he returned to real estate for his summer job, liked the experience, but remained in exploration mode.

It's not unreasonable to enter an MBA program and investigate diverse possibilities. Most students do that to at least some extent. But they all want to find the right positions when they graduate, and they need targets to have the best chance of success.

As the final semester began, it dawned on Anthony that he'd better decide. Over three weeks, he went through most of the exercises from Chapters 1, 2, and 3 and decided to return to real estate. That was where he'd be most competitive. It might or might not become his calling, but it was a good place to start.

Three months later, Anthony had six different offers and was choosing between the two he found most exciting. I'm not making this up—six acceptable offers in three months! This wildly successful job search reflected Anthony's solid background in the industry, his natural analytical and logical bent, an engaging personal style, and the quantitative skills he'd sharpened in school. He was a good product for that market. But he also made the most of his capability by deploying a winning job search strategy. That's what we explore here.

Four features of Anthony's job search stand out.

First, the different direction-setting exercises helped him not only decide to target real estate in general but also discern which parts of the industry to target and which to avoid.

He got a lot out of imagining perfect and horrible jobs. When he did that, he realized he was very interested in conceiving new real estate development possibilities and getting them up and running. He also realized that he had no interest in the developer's "never ending" operational activities. That was pivotal: "This was such a great exercise for me. It helped me decipher which particular day-to-day functions I would most enjoy and which activities would seem monotonous and boring. Connecting these activities to potential jobs helped me identify the two potential careers to target."

He decided on either of two parts of the industry: real estate investment funds or real estate development companies. Although they'd differ in terms of daily tasks and the skills developed, they'd both begin to enable the fulfillment of Anthony's ultimate goal: running his own real estate portfolio.

Second, Anthony constructed a PVP for each role—what he called "a marriage between my inherent understanding of real estate as a result of my upbringing and the financial skills acquired during my academic and professional career."

Third, he worked on his "pitch" to explain these PVPs. The more people he met, the better he did: "The interviews went better and better. I was smoother and more comfortable. I had the story down well. It didn't matter what question was asked." He didn't literally script himself, but he did craft a persuasive and entertaining way to tell people about his resume, why he was pursuing real estate, and why he'd do well there. As Anthony recounts it, it went something like this:

> I think I bring something to the table that many other candidates don't or can't. Because I grew up in the industry, I like to think I have developed an intrinsic understanding for real estate as an investment. And to supplement this fundamental understanding of the real estate industry, I have spent considerable time and effort refining my financial understanding, capabilities, and acumen during my academic and professional career. My internships

> with Company A and Company B both had a heavy focus on finance and developing Excel modeling skills, as well as gaining an understanding for what makes a real estate investment successful.

Because the two target roles required similar skills, the same PVP and the same pitch prepared Anthony for each. He brought three examples of his nonconfidential work to interviews: a financial model that he helped develop at Company B to help structure partnerships and projects, one of his university competition reports (which had won "Best Report"), and a pitch book he put together for a fictitious real estate development project in a different class. Bringing different materials allowed him to choose the one that was most appropriate for different situations.

Finally, Anthony aggressively networked and researched prospective employers. He prepared a comprehensive list of all the companies that might have the opportunities he was targeting. He used LinkedIn, his university's alumni databases (both graduate and undergraduate), people he knew from two industry associations, and his personal network.

He was well organized, with a folder on each contact and what had happened there. His database was structured by city, listing all the companies in that city where he found contacts. If he sent an email on Monday, he set a reminder in his calendar to follow up the following Monday. If he sent two emails and never got a response, he moved on. He made reaching out efficient by building individual emails off of several different draft introductions. He paid attention to the responses to different emails and learned what type of language was most likely to elicit a response.

All six offers came from this kind of networking. Four of the six weren't as interesting. They weren't exactly the type of work he wanted, they focused on a single category of real estate, they addressed a smaller geographic area, and/or the firms didn't have as strong a reputation. He liked the other two offers best.

One was from a national developer with an office in Anthony's city. His manager from his summer job referred him. After two rounds of interviews, Anthony was offered a role that largely had to do with getting development projects under way.

The second offer was in another city with the real estate arm of an international investment firm. The opportunity came after Anthony cold-called an alumnus of his university who had a leadership role there. Anthony knew it would be hard to land this offer, and he waited until after he had his "ducks in a row" to make that contact. There followed a telephone interview with the company's HR department, a two-hour online test on Excel, and then a one-day visit for seven hours of interviews.

Anthony faced a tough choice. Both offers were strong and pointed to his aspiration. He had a week to decide. He was surprised that he felt more stress about this choice than when he had no offer. As he put it, "At least before, I was able to sleep at night."

Anthony did three things to help him make a decision.

First, he went through a scenario exercise. He imagined where he might be in five or ten years if he took each position. Both positions would put him on his way to his long-term aspiration. The local position would set him up with a strong industry network in his city, with a path to opportunities there. The investment fund in the new city offered a broader learning platform, the potential for opportunities in other regions of the United States and in other countries, and potentially the option (which he wasn't sure he wanted) to move into other investment classes outside real estate.

Second, he prepared a payoff matrix to compare each alternative in a rigorous way. He set seven objectives, weighted each objective, and scored each alternative against each objective. The result was a close call, but tilted in favor of the financial role in the other city. That led Anthony to double-check by looking back at his ratings and revisit why he'd scored the two positions differently.

Third, he assembled the "case" for each alternative—how he would justify each decision. Doing that made his decision clear. In his view, the investment firm offered greater personal growth and better long-term prospects. It was less like his past experiences, it was global, and it offered exposure to a wider range of products. It might be a stronger culture to be part of, and he expected it to lead to more opportunities. The drawbacks included longer hours, similar pay in a city with a higher cost of living, and the move. After some reflection, he concluded that the move could be an adventure. Once he did that, he had no doubt it was the better choice.

Anthony started his search late, but was wildly successful. He was an excellent fit for either of the real estate roles he pursued. That was essential. But it was his highly productive job search strategy that allowed him to showcase his skills to a large market. He went by the book—from aspirations and skills to targets to PVP to aggressive networking to a compelling description of how he matched the targets. He knew why he was right for those positions, and he knew how to tell the story to make it credible. Anthony's a far cry from a role model in terms of when he got started, but once he began, he showcases the strategic approach to opportunity search.

That's not all. Anthony also models a rigorous offer evaluation process. How to decide whether to say yes is where I'll take you next. That's the subject of Part IV.

Part IV

# DECISIONS ON ALTERNATIVES

> There comes a time when you ought to start doing what you want. Take a job that you love. You will jump out of bed in the morning. I think you are out of your mind if you keep taking jobs that you don't like because you think it will look good on your resume. Isn't that a little like saving up sex for your old age?
>
> **WARREN BUFFETT**

> It's not hard to make decisions when you know what your values are.
>
> **ROY DISNEY**

> Prediction is very difficult, especially if it's about the future.
>
> **NIELS BOHR**

**SOME BUSINESS DECISIONS** are straightforward. Approving an investment project with a 40 percent return can be a "no-brainer," whereas it almost never makes sense to approve a project with a 0 percent return. Management decides and moves on. Yet many business strategy decisions are close calls. Objectives are in conflict. There's uncertainty. Strategically mature leaders meet these challenges head-on. They deploy structured processes to help judge what's best.

Likewise, some career decisions will be obvious. Let's imagine you've received a job offer that excites you and holds the promise of setting up attractive opportunities for a later time. It's a once-in-a-lifetime opportunity. If that's the case, then go ahead and say yes. Just as in the business world, however, your choice may not be that easy. The offer might meet some objectives, but short-change others. You're unsure what will happen if you accept that offer or, for that matter, what will happen if you stay in your current position. There's risk either way. When you're facing a tough career decision, follow the example of world-class business strategists: establish a rational process to help you make up your mind.

Both in business and in careers, a sound judgment rests on a thorough understanding of the situation. How to get those facts was the subject of Chapter 4. Those methods are indispensable. A lot is at stake. You owe it to yourself to know the situation.

Once you know the lay of the land, you're ready to use those facts to evaluate alternatives. That's what we cover in Part IV, as you see in Figure PIV.1: two analytical methodologies to help you reach a wise decision.

Many career decisions require tough trade-offs among objectives. The first alternative meets some objectives best; the second meets other objectives best. What to do? Chapter 12 shows how to evaluate alternatives against objectives.

At the fork in the road, you can't be absolutely sure what will happen if you take one path or the other. In some cases, the results will be highly ambiguous. Chapter 13 shows how to make sensible decisions when facing uncertainty.

In Part IV, I emphasize one kind of choice to illustrate these methodologies—whether to accept a job offer. The stakes are high, and it can be hard to know what's best. These methodologies aren't solely about job offers, however. They apply to other commitments, such as whether to accept admission to graduate school or another training program, to volunteer a

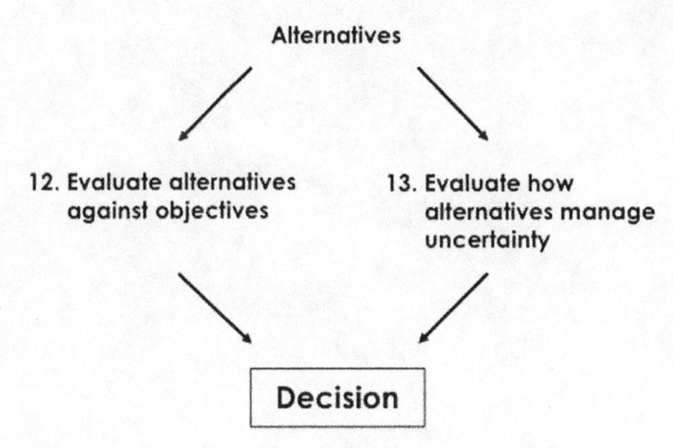


**FIGURE PIV.1** Part IV: Determine Which Alternative to Accept

significant block of time, or to prioritize one long-term career-building initiative over others. Let the concepts from Part IV be your guide in all these decisions.

## Chapter 12

# ALTERNATIVES AND OBJECTIVES

**BECAUSE ALL BUSINESSES** have an economic purpose, financial objectives like cash flow and profitability always affect strategy decisions. Nonfinancial objectives also come into play. Some are internal, such as passing product development gates or strengthening the organization. Other objectives reach outside the enterprise, such as setting an industry standard or becoming market leader.

Strategy gets interesting when objectives collide. What should the CEO do if some of the company's objectives point one way, while others point in a different direction? If that happens, strategists assemble the pros and cons and collect the facts required to compare them rigorously. That's when structured decision models can help in business.

Career decisions also become uncomfortable when different objectives suggest different answers. One alternative introduces you to the field you hope to try out, but it's a step down with a pay cut. Or an otherwise desirable promotion requires a move, but you have roots in your community. You need a rigorous way to compare how well alternatives meet objectives. Set up your assessment to apply a professional mentality to yourself.

I'll begin with Michael's story. It first demonstrates the absolute opposite of best practice—*what not to do.* Three years down the road, he'll show *what to do*: how the strategic mind-set led to his calling.

## The Ugly and Then the Good—Michael's Evaluations

When I first began researching career choices, I was surprised to hear about people who were highly successful in their work but who bungled their own career decisions. I've come to learn that this happens all too frequently. People can be in a different mind-set when thinking about themselves—more inward looking and less objective.

Michael's a prime example. The first time he faced a career strategy decision, he blew it. That's when, without much thought, he left consulting to take a job with a new venture. He knew the founders. He could be part of the dot-com boom and change the world. He thought the business opportunity was exciting, though he relied largely on the founders' assessment rather than his own. His stock options provided financial upside. The company was in town. The job was easy to accept.

He paid no attention to culture. None. As he recalled, "That was a big miss. I asked a few questions, but not enough to really understand what it was like. I didn't know enough to ask."

The other reason Michael left was his fear of failure. Looking back, he wondered why he'd been insecure: "I didn't have any confidence I'd succeed, zero confidence I'd get elected a partner. I assumed I'd be figured out at some point and that I really didn't belong. The mental anguish of fearing I might fail was overwhelming. It was better to take myself out before they did it." This made no sense. Each year, Michael had been told he was rated at or near the top of his class. He just didn't believe it.

Michael's main responsibility in the start-up was complex sales, the company's top priority. To convince someone to buy the company's products, Michael showed how to modify business processes to cut costs. These were big decisions with intricate trade-offs, so sales proposals were something like consulting assignments. This work was right down Michael's power alley, but he "disliked it pretty immensely." The analysis was intended to point to a predetermined answer—to purchase the company's product. He never recommended a solution that he believed wouldn't benefit the customer, but he wasn't comfortable with the self-interested purpose of the work. A second problem was that the results couldn't be 90 or 95 percent right, as is the case for most business decisions. Process errors could be serious, so processes had to be right 100 percent of the time. "We couldn't do an overall drawing of the tree," he said. "We had to draw every leaf and every vein in each leaf." It was tedious.

What bothered Michael most was the unpleasant way people communicated. As he saw it, "People didn't treat each other right. There was a lot of yelling and aggressive emails. The environment wasn't a match for me at all." Michael felt that people were blunt, rude, and far too critical. Apparently, others found that style acceptable, but it was a bad fit for Michael.

After three years, Michael had had it. He recalled that unhappy time:

> I spent the last year trying to figure out what I wanted to do. I was borderline depressed. I always went in to work, but I quit setting my alarm in the mornings. I didn't know what I wanted. I would have left sooner had I found something I thought was a fit. In truth, I also was hanging on a bit for the possibility of wealth creation.

Michael had taken the position thinking like a careerist—and a poorly informed careerist at that. Over time, he migrated to a job mentality. He hated it.

But what to do? He was told he could return to his former consulting firm in his old role. He was close to an offer with a

VC firm. He could pursue another start-up. He didn't want to make another mistake, so he avoided concrete discussions. The possibilities churned around in his head for most of a year.

One day, it all came together in what he says took four minutes. Michael wrote down six objectives. He scored the three possible careers against each objective on a matrix and multiplied the results to get a total value for each alternative. It looked like the matrix in Table 12.1.

The numbers suggested that consulting was best for Michael, largely due to his view of how it scored on cultural factors. That was his big insight, and it felt intuitively right. Had he listed objectives in this way three years earlier, he might not have thought to list pride and people. He'd taken them for granted. The numbers weren't the answer, but they helped him decide. He put the old anxiety behind him. As he said, "I'd matured and could say to myself that if I don't make it, it'll be a good experience. I was sick of being scared of failing. I was ready to give the firm all I had."

Ten years later, Michael was highly satisfied with consulting and expected to stay with it throughout his work life.

That's quite a shift in approach! This rigorous thinker left his problem-solving skill on the sideline and blundered into the start-up without knowing what he was getting into. Four years later, he intuited a structured evaluation process that led to a good decision.

That's not the only shift. Michael left university in a "career" mind-set that took him to consulting and then to the start-up. His new evaluation process directed his attention to the fundamentals, and he recognized a calling several years into his second consulting tour.

A last feature of Michael's story concerns money. One reason he stayed in a situation he disliked was to allow his stock options to vest. The options encouraged employee retention just as they were designed to do. Michael's options did vest, but the company failed after he left, and those options turned out to be worthless.

**TABLE 12.1** Michael's Matrix

| | ALTERNATIVES (1 TO 5 SCALE) | | |
|---|---|---|---|
| **OBJECTIVE** | **STARTUP** | **VENTURE CAPTIAL** | **CONSULTING** |
| Pride | 3 | 3 | 5 |
| Tasks | 4 | 3 | 3 |
| People | 3 | 4 | 5 |
| Learning | 3 | 4 | 5 |
| Lifestyle | 4 | 3 | 3 |
| Financial Reward | 1 to 5 | 5 | 4 |
| **Total** | **18 to 22** | **22** | **25** |

The big lesson from Michael's second time around is the way a thorough evaluation model can clarify tough choices and lead to confident decisions. I'll now explain how to do that kind of assessment.

## Conducting Your Evaluation

Put yourself in a good position to reconcile objectives and make thoughtful decisions. Structure your thinking in a matrix like Michael's by following these steps.

### 1. Specify the Alternatives

Get the alternatives clear. Alternatives certainly include the offer as you understand it. Other versions of that offer may be possible—for example, a new way to set up the position to increase the likelihood of success or to better meet your needs.

Don't forget that you can decline the offer and stay where you are—whether that's your current position, your current full-time job search, or something else. Staying is an alternative. When you carefully describe the staying alternative, you may discover that it has multiple versions and that they're different enough that each one needs its own evaluation. You'll make the best-informed decision if you assess them separately.

And, as is true of so many things in career strategy, putting all this on paper may lead you to realize that you need to learn more.

## 2. Specify Objectives

Aspirations for the long-term shape long-term decisions. Those long-term aspirations also set the stage for near-term decisions, such as whether to accept a job offer, but you'll need something else. I use another term to capture what you're seeking in this more immediate situation: *objectives.* Here's how to specify objectives.

List the alternatives' pros and cons as you first think of them. They'll imply some (maybe most) of the objectives that are important to you.

Return to the material in Part I on setting direction, and the thinking you did to set your current PVP. Think about your immediate objectives related to the following topics:

- Aspirations: how the opportunity fits with your priorities about the content of the work (service, craftsmanship, and institution) and what's taken from work (money and prestige)
- Strengths: how the opportunity lines up against your signature strengths
- The four big topics: the culture, role, sacrifices, and outlook for the future
- PVP: whether the opportunity delivers your current PVP as you intended

To help with your decision, objectives must relate directly to the alternatives. If some fundamental aspirations are unimportant to the choice among your current alternatives, simplify and discard them for now.

Consider time frames. You may want certain things in the coming year, other things further out in the future. Incorporate these timing differences into your estimation of relative importance. A prominent example of an unusual time is when you're out of work. Several people who commented on my blog posts argued that although values-centered decisions would be nice, during the Great Recession people should take any offer they get, whatever the fit with objectives. That may be right in some cases, but for the most part I disagree.

Structured decision modeling can be especially helpful in tough situations like that. The objectives or their weightings may be different than at other times in your life. Reasons to accept an offer that doesn't meet your long-term goals can include the unusual role of money at the time, the way you feel about being out of work, and the job's potential to enhance your PVP and lead to another opportunity later. But be cautious. The wrong role, field, or culture may make you unproductive and put you at a disadvantage in looking for something else. Taking the job usually means you won't have time to pursue the opportunity you most want. If you're tempted by a company you suspect might be unethical, get to the bottom of that. Working in a bad environment may be a horrible experience, and that employer will be on your resume forever. Objectives aren't equally important. When you're comfortable with your list of objectives, rank them.

### 3. Evaluate Alternatives Against Objectives

Construct a matrix to structure your thinking. List objectives down the vertical axis of the matrix on the left side, and put alternatives across the top. Fill in the boxes of the matrix with written judgments about how well each alternative meets each objective, along with the reason why. For example, Alternative #1 may introduce you directly to a new function, which is one of your objectives, whereas that function is a sideline for Alternative #2, and Alternative #3 doesn't help with that function at all. Write "High," "Medium," or "Low" in each box to begin to scale the judgments.

You'll realize many benefits from using the matrix in this way.

The matrix makes the assessment thorough and rigorous. By explicitly showing how alternatives perform on objectives, the matrix requires completeness. All alternatives are evaluated against all objectives. The trade-offs will be unmistakable.

The matrix brings issues out in the open. A potential job may look very good, but just not feel right. Filling out the matrix can spotlight what was implicit and unstated.

The matrix focuses attention on objectives. People may assume they already know what they want, that they don't need to think about what they wish to achieve. The matrix makes it hard to do that. You'll give fresh thought to objectives when preparing the matrix. You may imagine a new objective you hadn't thought about before. Or you may determine that your prioritization of objectives needs to change.

In the same way, the matrix focuses attention on alternatives. When you're filling in the boxes of the matrix, you may imagine a different alternative that relieves the tension among objectives.

The matrix focuses your inquiry on what's most important about an alternative, not what's easy to learn. People can gather information on a new job, but learn only the easy facts about it (for example, the company's size and details about its product line). Those facts seldom swing decisions. What usually matters most is a deep understanding of what the job would be like (for example, the culture or the personal growth opportunities). With the matrix, you'll be more likely to think about how alternatives measure up against the criteria you most care about. You'll know what questions to ask and what else you need to learn.

And last, the matrix puts you in the role of observer. It briefly takes you out of the decision. You see the choice more objectively. For some people, that's its biggest benefit.

### 4. Quantify the Outcomes

So far, so good. With your matrix drawn up and the boxes filled in with words, you'll have a rational assessment. That may be all you need. There is, however, an additional way to sharpen insight: subjective quantification. The matrix is most powerful when quantified.

I suggest you do it this way: (1) weight the objectives by dividing one hundred points among them, (2) score how well each alternative meets each objective on a 1–10 scale, and (3) calculate a weighted average total score for each alternative. The alternative with the highest score comes out on top. Quantification takes more time, though rarely much more. If it's worth doing a full assessment and if you can get comfortable with the idea of subjective math, then quantify the matrix. It integrates all the considerations.

I like subjective quantification, but I don't recommend basing your decision solely on the numbers. In many cases, people look at the weighted averages and something doesn't click. They rethink. They may adjust the weighting of the objectives or the alternatives' scores. They may change an objective or add an objective they hadn't thought about. They may realize they'd missed an important alternative that they find is a valid input to their decision.

If you're tempted to skip the quantification, know that you're doing something like it in an offhand way. You're weighting your criteria in the back of your mind either by assuming that all the criteria are equally important (virtually certain to be wrong) or by informally according some criteria more importance than others. Putting quantitative weights on the different criteria brings these assumptions out into the light where you can test what you really believe. Similarly, when you think about how alternatives stack up against criteria, you're implicitly scoring them. Actually doing the scoring makes you compare the alternatives objectively.

Everyone I've talked to about careers has easily adopted the thought process embedded in the matrix. It's easy because people already do something like this. It's not rocket science. One friend told me that he'd just quantified a matrix like this one to evaluate which kitchen appliance to buy. Doing rigorously what comes naturally can lead to better decisions.

### 5. Make the Case for Each Alternative

Translate what you've learned into words. Make the argument for each alternative, emphasizing the reasons to do it while also acknowledging the drawbacks. What does the assessment mean to you? How to interpret the different ratings and the overall numbers? If you pick the first alternative, why would that be? What if you pick the second or the third?

In practice, people generally follow this progression while also moving fluidly among the steps. That's a sign of productive learning. When you first do the trade-off analysis, for example, you may realize you missed an objective. As you're scoring alternatives, perhaps you'll see you need to learn more before deciding. Or you may spot a way to modify an alternative to make it more appealing.

Let's now look at another story. You read about management consultant Isabel's job search in Chapter 9 on networking. Here, I'll take you back six months before that job search to Isabel's decision to leave her firm and find something new. She followed an approach like Michael's, but arrived at a completely different conclusion.

## Isabel's Surprising Insights

It was a year before I decided to write this book. I needed good case material for my first career strategy course, and I got lucky.

Thirty-three-year-old Isabel called me. We'd known each other for most of a decade. She wanted my reactions to the surprising job offer she'd just received. When we met, I told her about the course I was creating. If we worked together to evaluate the offer, that would both help her determine the best decision and help me develop teaching material. She was enthusiastic. We met several times over the next four months.

Isabel's consulting career began when she was twenty-two. She did well as a junior analyst, was rated highly, and received an MBA scholarship. Isabel liked the problems, her principal industry, and her pro bono assignments for nonprofits. Her success wasn't the result only of her high IQ but also of her high EQ. She enjoyed her team members. Several clients had become personal friends. Junior consultants viewed her as a mentor, and junior women saw her as a role model.

It never was easy. The hours were long, the deadlines short. Her business travel had averaged around two nights a week away from home, some months more and others less. Her husband was moving up in another company. The birth of their daughter had been exhilarating, but the stress level went up. The stress went up more when their son came eighteen months later, even after a liberal amount of maternity leave and moving to a 75 percent program. Two nannies made their two careers possible, becoming almost like family members.

Isabel's end-of-year performance feedback was positive. Advancement depended on the vote of an arms-length election committee, so there could be no promises. But it looked likely in a year. She had many things to do to make that happen, but most of them were under way. Becoming a partner had been her objective for over a decade.

Then, for the first time in her life, Isabel was presented with an appealing alternative.

Isabel's client SVP asked her to join his staff as the VP of new business development. This was a high priority, an outgrowth of her ongoing assignment there. He needed someone to start very soon. Who'd be better than Isabel, who'd helped him see the need for the new role? Over time, the job would open up other options at the company, perhaps a route to the executive suite.

Isabel's initial instinct was to say no thanks. However, she wasn't sure she wasn't interested, and she didn't want to be rude. So she said she'd think about it. Only the day before, she'd been content—even excited—about consulting. Now she wasn't sure. It dawned on her that she'd just completed her first job interview in twelve years.

Isabel approached her career decision with a skill most people don't have. She was a professional strategist. Over the next few days, she used her business strategy expertise to begin assessing this choice.

Isabel knew that fundamental visions guide most successful institutions, and she thought through her objectives as some of her corporate clients had done. She wrote down a first draft of her objectives, tested them, and then revised them. She prepared a page of the pros and cons of each alternative and used them to test that first draft.

Although she didn't know enough to decide, she knew she'd benefit by pushing her initial thinking to provisional conclusions. To help do this, she constructed a matrix similar to ones she'd used with clients and subjectively quantified it, as shown in Table 12-2.

Isabel made a few adjustments to the relative weightings and the scores, but even when she did that, the calculated "values" of the alternatives remained about where they'd been. How to interpret this?

Isabel first noticed how much she'd changed. She still valued colleagues, the professional culture, and client relationships, but the thrill from the intellectual side was not where it had been a few years earlier. She felt the difficulty of tamping down the intensity of her work and of having to spend so much time away from her

**TABLE 12.2** Isabel's Matrix

| | | ALTERNATIVES | |
|---|---|---|---|
| OBJECTIVE | WEIGHTING | CONSULTING | NEW OFFER |
| Colleagues/mentoring | 20% | 5 | 3 |
| Intellectual excitement/ learning | 10% | 4 | 3 |
| Personal growth | 10% | 3 | 5 |
| Really run something | 20% | 2 | 4 |
| Flexibility/control over life | 20% | 2 | 4 |
| Stress/intensity | 10% | 3 | 4 |
| Family/moves | 10% | 5 | 2 |
| **Weighted Average** | | **3.3** | **3.6** |

children. She'd assigned 40 percent of the total value to objectives related to lifestyle and personal sacrifice.

Second, neither position looked exciting. This was unsettling.

Isabel fully understood the need for this new position, but her matrix represented only initial thinking. She needed to learn more to decide whether she wanted the position with her client. Especially important was to learn what would lead to success (and to failure) in the position and how career paths typically developed at the company. The client SVP quickly arranged meetings for her, including with the CEO. She also met with outsiders who knew the company.

Isabel took what she'd learned from these meetings, looked ahead five years, and imagined different ways her career path might develop. She saw the risk that an outsider like her might be rejected by the organization. She learned that career paths to the top of the company included at least two and possibly three moves to other cities. After three or four years, she'd likely need to relocate, accept limited upside, or leave; and then she'd probably need to move again to stay on the fast track.

Isabel made two decisions.

First, she declined the offer. The future moves were unacceptable. She couldn't accept the impact they would have on her husband's career. Looking back at the matrix she'd done before investigating the offer, she realized that she'd underweighted the importance of moves. The impact of future moves, it turned out, was huge—almost a knockout factor by itself.

There remained a fundamental question: Did Isabel want to be a consultant? What had seemed close to ideal only a month before no longer seemed right for her. She knew she couldn't work toward partner election and conduct a high-quality job search at the same time. She was proud of being decisive. As I mentioned in the book's introduction, she put it this way: "Call me crazy, but in a year when jobs were scarce, I decided to quit and look for a job!"

There'd need to be a good reason to leave with partner election so close. Isabel's assessment gave her the conviction she needed to act: "Putting it on paper made everything transparent and easy. I had been there for nine years. It was the only place I ever had worked. It was like leaving home. It was a very emotional thing. Without the framework and the structure, it would have dragged out. The assessment took the emotions out."

I'm not saying that a decision like Isabel's is right for everyone. The financial side was easier for her, because she was part of a two-income family and because she and her husband lived below their means. And Isabel's work experience was marketable, even in a soft economy.

Isabel provides an excellent example of the strategic approach. Her story also offers a second lesson. What if the bolt-from-the-blue offer hadn't come? Isabel might have continued in a role where she had fundamental though largely unrecognized issues. Even without the offer, she could have thought about her objectives and reached a similar decision. That would have been even more strategic. In Chapter 14, I'll describe a process you can follow to stimulate that kind of forward thinking.

This kind of integrated thinking across objectives is at the core of intelligent career choice. Isabel and Michael had experience with analysis, but you don't have to invent an assessment methodology as each of them did. Follow the process described here, and you'll find similar rigor and insight. If there are no important uncertainties, you'll have covered the waterfront. If uncertainties matter, the next chapter will help.

Chapter 13

# ALTERNATIVES AND UNCERTAINTY

**THE TOUGHEST BUSINESS DECISIONS** often are tough because no one can be sure what will happen. New product development commitments often are like that. The product's actual performance and costs aren't known, what other players will do isn't known, and customer reactions aren't known. The only thing that is known is the up-front commitment of engineering resources to that product (rather than to another product). New ventures typically get the chance to make only one of these big bets. Large companies manage portfolios of bets.

Sophisticated business leaders consciously manage that uncertainty. They forecast what may happen if they go one way or the other. They investigate the market, look into regulatory and macroeconomic developments, and evaluate potential competitive moves. They estimate the likelihood that their team will execute the plan as intended (such as whether those engineers really do develop the target product). Decisions can be straightforward if forecasting yields a single highly likely future. That single future, however, seldom matches reality. Several outcomes are plausible. Decisions that don't take those possibilities into account can turn into blunders.

When I was leading McKinsey & Company's Strategy Practice, one of our initiatives was to develop methodologies to help clients manage uncertainty in situations like that.[1] I've especially enjoyed working out how to apply the same concepts to careers.

Uncertainty in careers already has come up in several places in this book—from career path planning to job search to not being sure about aspirations. Managing uncertainty is central in career strategy.

I've seen three kinds of irrational reactions to uncertainty in careers. Uncertainty can paralyze. Some people put off decisions, hoping to avoid risk, but delay actually becomes a decision when their opportunity expires.

Uncertainty makes other people uncomfortable, so they ignore it. They decide, sometimes quickly, but their decision is based on a single view of the future. They don't see themselves as taking much risk, but in reality they're putting all their chips on a single outcome. They can win with that bet, but only if the future they expect is the one that arrives.

Still others see themselves as courageous risk takers. They go full speed ahead knowing they don't have a good road map. They think they'll enjoy the risk. They might succeed. They might fail.

Don't let uncertainty blind you. Although no one can know the future, good forecasting can reduce uncertainty. And then the right intellectual structure can help you understand the risks and opportunities facing different alternatives. Make near-term career strategy choices with an eye on the long term. This chapter provides a rigorous way to do that.

## Forecasting

Wise decisions begin with good forecasts. Even though they'll never know the future, sophisticated people clear out as much uncertainty as possible. Look at this story of first-class forecasting.

You read about Sean in Chapter 4. After thoroughly evaluating organization culture, role, the prospect of moving, and company outlook, he turned down what he'd first thought was an attractive offer. He stayed in consulting and was elected a senior partner. But Sean had almost quit six months before election. The forecasting he did at that point made all the difference.

### How Sean's Forecasting Led to a Renewed Commitment

Sean was in turmoil as he neared an up-or-out decision point. In the next six months, he expected to be elected a senior partner or to be asked to leave. Christmas and New Year vacations came along. Sean used that time off to consider his future. The long-range forecasting he did helped overcome the emotions he was feeling and led him to decide to stay. Here's Sean's account:

> I was worn out and emotional. Little things were bothering me. I was caught up in the uncertainty. At one point, I'd more or less decided to resign. My election wasn't a sure thing, even though the signals were positive. No one's a sure thing. It's an up-or-out place. I certainly didn't want to be told that I hadn't been elected.
>
> I read about other people making hard personal decisions.[2] I wrote down all the things I'd done over the years. By looking backwards, I was better able to think about my future. I thought about where my current trajectory would take me over the next five years, where I'd be when I was forty-five. Just like we do with clients, I rolled back the future. I thought about if I wanted a particular world in five years, what did I need to be doing over the next year to make that longer-term vision happen.
>
> All of this was calming. I asked myself, "If they fire me, would I really be upset?" My answer was "Probably, but mostly from an ego point of view. If it forced me to rethink my career, I'd probably end up in a fine place too." So in effect, I decided to reenlist, like in the army. I doubled down and recommitted to my clients, and I found a new practice role.

Forecasting let Sean step back and realize that he was likely to advance. And if he didn't, he'd be competitive for other things. Either way, he saw a bright future. Forecasting calmed Sean, overcame the emotions, and let him decide to stay rather than go.

## How to Do Career Forecasting

Although you'll never know what will happen if you make one decision or the other, you can get a good sense of the possibilities and their likelihood. Drawn from the experiences of Sean and others, the following are steps for productive brainstorming to stimulate your thinking about where different choices may lead.

### 1. Specify the Alternatives

Describe the alternatives, following the approach in Chapter 12.

### 2. Imagine Possible Scenarios That May Result from Each Alternative

When I use the term *scenario,* I mean a plausible set of assumptions about the future if you select an alternative. That's one scenario. Because you don't know what will happen, there may be two, three, or more plausible scenarios for that alternative.

If you accept an offer that's a move into a very different function, for example, you might imagine one scenario where you do well, learn a lot, and advance to a more senior position. Another scenario might assume you do well but then get stuck with no role to advance into. In still another scenario, you might not be happy with your progress, but your broader familiarity with this new function would be preparing you for a new function. Or something else. What you're doing is describing the different possibilities so that you can assess them. Of course, these are just examples to illustrate the idea. You'll need to work out your own scenarios.

Now you have a first list of the scenarios that may result from your first alternative. Imagine similar multipronged scenarios for the other alternatives. They aren't the same, because different alternatives will lead to different events.

### 3. Test the Scenarios

Let your history suggest possible futures. Estimate where the momentum from your past and current activities may take you. What does the arc of your career to date tell you about the possible results of your current decision?

You've already seen how a draft article about your future can stimulate aspirational thinking. So too can an article help you imagine the result of a decision. Draft an article about yourself as though you picked the first alternative. Write a second article (or at least imagine how it would be different) as though you made a different choice. Articles can enrich the scenarios for each alternative that you're already developing. They may surprise you and suggest a different way the future may unfold.

Do a business assessment. You saw how to assess industry outlook in Chapter 4. Follow the same approach. Evaluate whether the institution or the overall field is likely to do well or poorly and how that might affect you.

### 4. Prepare an Integrated Forecast

Combine the results from these activities to create the scenarios you'll use to guide your decision. Starting with your initial scenarios, modify them as suggested by the different testing methodologies, and prepare a set of internally consistent scenarios for each alternative you're considering. Write them down in the form of the diagram shown in Figure 13.1.

When you see the alternatives and the scenarios together in this way, you can judge whether you've captured the plausible future. You may imagine other plausible scenarios that you don't want to

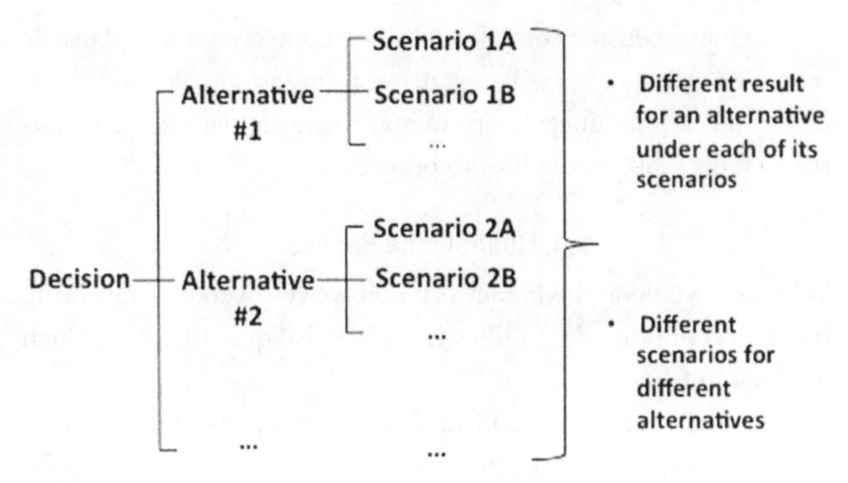


**FIGURE 13.1** Structuring the Evaluation: Alternatives and Scenarios

ignore. Possible though unlikely scenarios also may merit attention, but unless they're very important to you, they'll play a secondary role in your assessment.

In long-term planning, the forecast must go far out into the future. Some of those long-term details will be vague. In the short term, you can specify immediate scenarios with more precision, but you then must reflect on the more nebulous question of what happens next. If the forecast looks only a few years out, you are assuming everything will continue as is after that. That's almost certainly wrong.

I'll now share a productive way to use forecasts to manage uncertainty.

## Uncertainty Management Model

If you're working with a single highly likely forecast and you're stretching to imagine other reasonable scenarios, what to do may be obvious. Or, better said, ambiguity about the future may not affect your decision. It'll be determined by the alternatives/objectives assessment from Chapter 12. But few of the big career decisions that I've witnessed were like this.

Decisions become complicated when there are several plausible scenarios. Alternatives will look better from some angles and worse from others. The uncertainty management model often suggests the best decision. Here's how to proceed.

## 1. Quantify the Results

When you've done the homework that we've covered so far, bring the uncertainty model to life with subjective quantification much like that in Chapter 12.

Score the *attractiveness* of each alternative under each of its scenarios, using a 1–100 scale. Use the same scoring standards for all alternatives under all the different scenarios so that you can compare alternatives on an apples-to-apples basis.

Here's an example. Imagine that you have two alternatives, that the first alternative has two plausible scenarios, and that the second has four. In total, that's six alternative/scenario pairs. You'll score each of these six results. Let's assume that you conclude that Alternative #1 on its Scenario A is a good but not ideal result, and therefore you decide to give it a score of 80 out of 100. Let's also assume that you believe that this result is a lot better than how you feel about Alternative #1 on its Scenario B and that it's a little better than Alternative #2 on its Scenario D. Their respective scores should reflect the magnitude of these differences. After reflecting on this, you might decide to give Alternative #1/Scenario B a 25 and Alternative #2/Scenario D a 70. Obviously, I'm making up these numbers to show how this works. You'd also need to score the other three alternative/scenario pairs.

The scenarios associated with each alternative aren't equally likely. So the next part of the quantification is to estimate each scenario's *probability*. Here you're rating the probabilities separately for each alternative. In the illustration from the previous paragraph, that will total 100 percent probability for the two scenarios that come with Alternative #1 and a separate 100 percent total for Alternative #2's four scenarios.

You now have the score and the probability for each alternative/scenario pair. Take that information and multiply the score of each alternative/scenario pair by the probability of each scenario. When you do that and add up the results for each alternative, you'll have calculated what statisticians call the "expected value" of each alternative.

You've reached pay dirt when you compare the alternatives' expected values. When you do that, one alternative may obviously look best. That's a good result. Or if expected values are similar, you'll be able to discern what differences among the alternatives (as reflected in your scoring and probabilities) are making your close call close. That's also a good result, though the best decision won't be obvious. Or when you look at the numbers, you may see that you've left out something important, need to rethink how it fits in the picture, and perhaps redo the assessment.

The numbers are valuable. The further you go down this path to specificity and quantification, the greater insight you'll uncover. Bringing your thinking out into the open in a countable fashion clarifies nuances that lead to more confident conclusions.

### 2. Make the Case for Each Alternative

Draw on your assessment to state the rationale for each alternative. Include the reasons for the alternative while also acknowledging the drawbacks. That completes the assessment and prepares you to decide.

Twenty-eight-year-old attorney Blair was stuck because she didn't know the future. By deploying this uncertainty model and doing the quantification, she found the right course.

## How Uncertainty Management Unfroze Blair

Blair finished law school three years before her encounter with uncertainty management. She was a law review editor, graduated high in her class, and published three scholarly articles. She worked a year with a large law firm, but then took a two-year leave of absence to clerk with a federal district judge. She liked this experience a lot—the intellectual stimulation, the sense that she was influencing the course of law, and the acquaintances she made there. As the clerkship was ending, she wasn't sure whether to return to her firm or do something else.

Blair's first idea had been to apply for an appellate court clerkship. She'd enjoy clerking in a higher court, and the experience might lead to other opportunities. It was a no-brainer. However, there were few positions in town; she applied for them and was turned down.

The end of her clerkship no longer was in the distant future, and she asked me how I'd approach the decision. I suggested scenario planning and imagining the options each path might create for her. Once she got going, the process came naturally.

Blair knew more about the law than she had when she left her firm. She couldn't be sure, of course, but she felt confident she'd do well if she returned, with a good shot at partnership in eight to ten years. That could be a good future. It also might create other options, such as moving to another law firm, joining a client's general counsel office, or starting her own firm. But she was concerned about the work environment and hours. Three-quarters of the law school classmates she'd kept up with had changed jobs in the three years since graduation.

There also was a prospect that Blair could become a law school professor. She lacked the practice and intellectual track record that most law professors have, but her ace in the hole was relationships. A close acquaintance was about to become head of a law school nearby. She also knew the person who would be his deputy. She expected she'd enjoy teaching and research and might stay for the long term. It was a natural extension of her time in the judge's office. Future opportunities made possible by taking such a position might include moving to another school, becoming a judge, adding legal consulting to her professor's role, and perhaps engaging in high-level public policy work. This wasn't the only time in her life when a professorial appointment might be possible; it wasn't "now or never." However, the new school and Blair's relationships there made this a special opportunity. The one drawback she saw was that with little experience as a junior attorney, it might be hard to reenter full-time legal practice later.

The diverse scenarios were complicated, so after a good bit of reflection, Blair simplified the uncertainties to two dimensions: how much she would like the work and how well she would do at it. That created four scenarios for each alternative. She thought about how likely each of these scenarios would be and, in that case, how she'd rate the different results. She subjectively quantified the probabilities and scored the outcomes, as you can see in Figure 13-2.

Structuring the decision like this helped Blair perceive the uncertainty and judge how she felt about it. The way she'd assigned the numbers suggested that becoming a professor offered a higher upside (greater likelihood she'd like it, do well, and advance, along with the opportunities that might result). Becoming a professor also risked a greater downside (not becoming a tenured professor and then not being well prepared to be a practicing attorney). Returning to the firm was practical and safer. It was more predictable. From a risk-reward standpoint, her two alternatives were quite different. She'd vaguely sensed this difference before, but the assessment clarified the profile of each alternative and how she'd feel about them. She gained fresh insight.

The other reason Blair had been stuck was relationship risk. It would be awkward to seek the law school position, get it, and

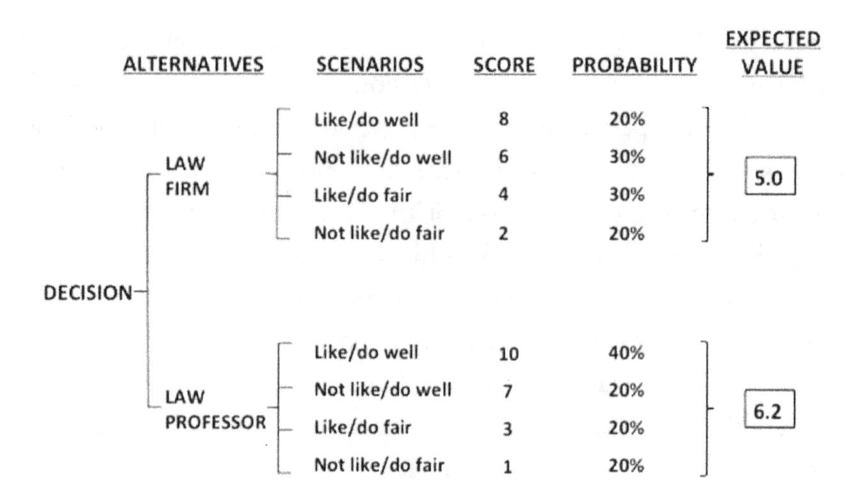


**FIGURE 13.2** Blair's Expected Values

decline. Her friends would have to do too much to make that offer happen. So she needed to be sure that was her top choice before moving ahead. In the end, she decided to try for the professor's appointment. The way that she structured her thinking turned a complicated decision into a simple one and took relationship risk off the table.

Blair raised the question with the incoming dean. Although he understood why she was interested, and he thought a professor role ultimately might be the right thing for her, it was a hands-on school, and all his professors would be coming with significant hands-on experience. So the position wasn't possible for Blair at that time.

So Blair ended up back at her firm, developing skills as a practicing attorney and preparing the record she'll need to advance there. So far, so good. She's enjoying the experience. It's more likely that she'll end up in the "like/do well" box from her quantitative evaluation illustrated in Figure 13.2, a fine result.

In the meantime, Blair is taking initiatives to shape her future—adding to her credentials, reputation, and network. She assembled publishable material from her clerkship, drafted two articles, and is submitting them for publication. In addition, she's constructing a professional network. She's a volunteer moot court coach at her old law school, she's joined a panel for her bar committee, and she's staying in touch with people at court. She's going out of her way to create options for the future.

Deploying forecasts in the uncertainty management model is a productive way to determine the best course of action. You also can gain insight into the future by thinking through strategic intent. That's where I'll take you now.

## Strategic Intent

When I use the term *strategic intent,* I'm thinking of five classes of strategy to manage uncertainty. Three of these reflect choices about the amount of risk to accept. The other two are add-on steps to create the possibility of additional upside or to contain risk. Classify each alternative into one of these categories. When you do that, the implications of the alternatives will become clearer, and you may recognize how best to steer your future.

### Taking Risk or Playing It Safe

The first three strategy categories are big bets, adapting to the future, and no-regrets moves.

*Big bets* in business can include acquisitions, capital projects, or product development programs. Big, hard-to-change commitments like these put a lot on the line. They can lead to big wins, sometimes because the move itself shaped the environment and increased the prospects for success. They also can fail spectacularly.

A second strategy is to *adapt to the future* as events develop. A business example would be pursuing low-scale R&D programs in several areas to see what's most promising before making a big commitment to any one of them.

Third is a *no-regrets move*—an action with positive payoff no matter what happens. In business, no-regrets moves can include straightforward actions to reduce cost or to improve organizational effectiveness. The upside comes with little cost and risk. I like no-regrets moves. I always looked for them in my business consulting practice. No-regrets moves always make sense unless they take time and resources from something more important.

Let's now explore how big bets and adapting moves can work in careers. Facing significant uncertainty, Brian and James chose very different strategies that reflected their respective situations and attitudes toward risk.

## Brian's Big Bet

You read about Brian in Chapter 1. He left his secure, well-paying job to found a food company whose new branded food products would improve diets. He hoped to improve the world and build an institution.

Brian knew the hours would be challenging and that he'd be living off of savings. The money in his bank account was what he called "the first investment in the company. That's what I paid myself the first year. I started out making a lot less money, but if it didn't work out, I was confident I could find a paying job. Then it got worse. I went from earning less money to having to put up personal guarantees on loans."

Brian couldn't really know what would happen at his new venture. And a second baby was on the way.

I asked Brian whether he ever considered starting the company on nights and weekends without giving up the regular paycheck. He could test the water before jumping in. He briefly considered that, he knew it was safer, but he was sure it wouldn't work. As he said:

> I had to take the full plunge. I wanted investors to commit. If I wanted them to write a check, I had to do it all the way. I couldn't bring on employees if I wasn't fully committed. And if I presented

> my product to a retailer's buyers, they'd be making a leap of faith too, so I needed to be fully committed for them.

Brian hoped to shape his future, and he judged that a full commitment was required to do that. If he'd started the company part-time, it might not have done well and would have taken energy away from his day job. Even though he knew this venture might fail, he spent no time dwelling on that. If the business didn't work out, Brian assumed he'd find another good job. He'd always done so.

Brian's big bet proved to be a wise choice. He created a new product category, built a successful company, and sold it at an attractive price a decade later.

### James, Playing It Safe

Big bets aren't for everyone. At thirty-seven, corporate SVP James was completing the two-year cost reduction project that would eliminate his position. He couldn't lead the company's new cost-driven philosophy and protect his own senior position when it was no longer needed. He was becoming surplus. As he put it, "I had no seat in the musical chairs game."

James considered his alternatives. He talked with private equity and consulting firms—the fields in which he'd worked a decade before. He talked with companies that competed with his current employer. In the end, he moved to a smaller VP role with his company.

James had three reasons to take that role, all having to do with containing risk.

He had doubts about the alternatives. He wondered whether he'd succeed back in the trenches with the day-to-day intensity and travel that private equity or consulting requires. At first, he'd looked forward to finding something new, but then he got worried about how well he'd do.

A second factor was the people: "knowing I stood with people who had my back." He wondered whether he'd work well with others in the industry and how he'd feel about competing against his current colleagues.

Finally, these other jobs all required a move. He'd divorced the year before, and his two children lived in town with their mother. He wasn't sure how his relationship with them would develop if he stayed in town. He was even less sure if he moved.

Thinking about risk led James to find a fresh way to stay where he already was. As he summed it up, "It's safest to stay. Even if I didn't want to, I'd be better off crafting my new message from there." He took a downgrade, but as a VP kept the associated pay and prestige. Things will change. He'll learn more about his relationship with his children. Maybe he'll return to an SVP position with his current company. He'll learn more about other possibilities. Perhaps he'll be ready for something bolder in a year or two.

These two people faced different situations, and they also had different attitudes toward risk and reward. Brian went all in. His strategy was to shape his career with a big bet. His bet had both large upside and large downside depending on how things developed. James, in contrast, hit the pause button and planned to react to events as they developed. His strategy reflected caution about his prospects if he left the company and about his personal situation. He'd become a risk avoider.

I like talking about Brian. I think I'd like talking about him even if the business hadn't been successful. I find Brian uplifting, exciting. But I can't say James was wrong. He was different. His situation was different. Everyone must make an individual choice. How to think this through?

If you see lots of upside and downside, ask these questions.

## 1. What Strategic Class Are the Alternatives?

Specify each alternative as a big bet, adapting to future events, or a no-regrets move. Just doing that will bring out what's at stake.

For each alternative, describe what could go well and what could go poorly. If you make the bet, how likely is success? If not full success, what else might happen? If you don't make the bet, what happens then? Maybe you're closing a door forever, or maybe something better will come along. Should you stay in place, develop capability, rethink your strategy, and prepare to take another shaping move in the future?

Come at it from the opposite direction. Take each strategy category and consider whether you might do something you hadn't thought of that fits within that category. Could you make a totally different bet? Are there other ways to adapt to an uncertain future?

Pay particular attention to no-regrets moves. They're seldom on the table at the outset. Examples of no-regrets moves in careers can include seeking a promotion at your company in your current area, keeping your bar membership active even if you're now in a business role, taking the test to be designated a professional engineer, enrolling in low-commitment education programs, and going out of your way to keep in touch with former colleagues. Remember that no-regrets moves always make sense unless they keep you from executing higher priorities.

Do all this, and you'll know your original alternatives better. You may uncover better ones.

## 2. Does the Opportunity Require the Commitment in a Big Bet?

Some do. Sink-or-swim situations are energizing and can create the mentality needed to succeed. And risk takers can attract support from others, support that's essential to success. When you are shooting for high aspirations, caution may be more risky than taking the plunge.

But that's not always the case. Maybe there's a less risky path to the same destination.

### 3. Can You Accept the Risk in a Big Bet?

People have different attitudes toward risk in general. And they can have different attitudes toward risk at different times in their lives. Consider the downside, how it would affect you, and how you'd feel about that.

### 4. Is It Best to Learn More?

When facing high uncertainty, corporate executives sometimes take small steps to learn—for example, market tests or technology research—and prepare to act decisively once they know more. Or they may wait for external events—for example, competitive moves, or changes in regulatory policy—to clarify the situation. They adopt a "reserve the right to play" posture.

You also can reserve the right to play, deferring a big commitment until you learn more about it or more about yourself. Rather than just putting things off, explicitly decide to defer. You're deciding to build understanding and make the big commitment later, or not to do that. Do this consciously, working with explicit learning objectives and time frames.

## Creating Options and Hedging Risks

The other two uncertainty management strategies are *options* on additional opportunities and *hedges* to recover if things aren't developing as you wished. Take another page from business strategy. A technology company, for example, may bet on its own R&D, while also securing a license to use a competitor's technology if it needs to. Or it may bet on an R&D program both for its intrinsic potential and how it may lead to other possibilities.

These hedges and options are analogous to the financial products with those names.

In careers, options exist if what you're doing may lead to appealing new opportunities, even though they're not assured or may not even be likely. You just read about how attorney Blair is creating options to enlarge her future. The mirror image of an option is a career hedge. It's an off-ramp—an acceptable way to change direction if you need to.

Smart career strategies include both options and hedges, often deployed on top of a big bet, an adapting move, or no-regrets moves. We'll look at two examples—Craig's options and Jessica's hedge.

### How Options Led to Craig's Decision

Craig was the VP of real estate in a privately held retail company, responsible for property acquisition and leasing. He enjoyed his work and his positive relationship with his boss, the CEO. He led board discussions when a real estate commitment was on the agenda. Craig was adding two senior people to his staff. When that was done, he expected an SVP title.

But all was not well. Although that promotion certainly would be good, Craig was worried.

When Craig joined the company, he'd hoped to have a chance to lead it. His rapid advance in real estate, however, meant he'd missed the operations experiences people normally have before becoming leaders. Success running an individual property or a group of them would be the surest way to get that experience, but he already was senior to the regional managers. And he had no interest in reporting to the operations SVP, who had a different style. Even mentioning this to the CEO was risky. If offered a move to a region, Craig might decline and in the process paint himself as someone who wasn't serious about broadening himself.

Craig saw no good way out. There were few outside opportunities in real estate in town, and moving was a barrier. His wife took considerable satisfaction and good income from her work as VP of another company, the children were settled in school, and both sets of grandparents were in town. He was worried about his prospects.

Craig thought some more about outside opportunities in town. He tried to imagine promising routes to the top of his company. Nothing interesting came to him at first, but then he remembered that the CFO was likely to retire next year. Although Craig's accounting degree and finance experience two jobs ago gave him familiarity with finance, he was rusty. He'd have a lot of catching up to do if he wanted to compete for that position. It wasn't the best way to the CEO's desk, but it was Craig's best chance. He put his hat in the CFO ring. What got him excited were the options that might flow from being CFO. As he said:

> This mostly came down to the options a new job might create. The CFO position is better because of its option value. If I stay in real estate, what else could I do? I could join a real estate fund or go into a real estate function in another industry. Maybe a real estate development company. All those industries follow the same business cycle, and they're all risky. If I can move into the CFO role and be there for a while, that'd open finance possibilities not only in real estate companies but also in different industries. I'd also have a better shot at the real estate positions my current job sets up.

Option thinking gave Craig the conviction he needed to take initiative. The CFO position, if he got it, would be a step up. That was good, but what got Craig excited was the potential it had to open other finance doors in town and what that might do for his CEO prospects then. That was this strategy's option value as Craig saw it. He decided to invest his time trying to make the CFO position happen rather than to begin looking outside the company. It was just what he needed to recharge his personal strategy.

Craig's strategy began working. He was promoted to SVP, he got encouraging signals that he was the lead CFO candidate, and he began preparing for that. Having a confident personal strategy also changed his overall outlook. He had a plan, there was a good chance it would work, and he was optimistic about the future. He looked different.

But it wasn't to happen. The company's owners sold the business. That was one uncertainty Craig hadn't considered. When he learned of the acquirer's plans, he saw there was no good role for him. Craig's job search strategy rested on his new understanding of himself and his new option-driven attitude toward his future. Within a few months, he ended up in a fine place with another company in town.

The options that came with a potential CFO role changed Craig's strategy. Let's now turn to hedges and the way they enabled Jessica to make a big shift when she needed to.

## How Hedges Reinforced Jessica's Strategy

Jessica, a National Science Foundation fellow, is deliberate and curious in conversations, reflecting the scientific researcher that she is. A natural uncertainty manager, she's intrigued by what she doesn't know, perhaps more than by what she does know.

Jessica benefited from a hedge, though at the time she wouldn't have thought to call it that. After completing her PhD coursework with top grades, she had to select a research program—a four-year or longer commitment leading to academic publications and completion of the degree. Selecting the right research program was difficult.

Jessica developed six good research possibilities. She was most excited about a project that would have great impact if successful, but one with great uncertainty as to whether she'd be successful. She told me:

> This might have been a little silly, but I had a vision of winning a Nobel Prize. I wanted to discover something new, something unique and valuable that no one else knew about. It could have been a huge breakthrough in how we think about curing two or maybe three types of cancer. I joined this lab because I wanted to do applied cancer research, and this project would have fulfilled that goal. But it was high risk.

The other alternatives were more likely to be the fast track out of school, but they were only incremental steps forward, and of course there was no guarantee that those experiments would work out either.

During her last semester of classwork, she discussed this decision several times with her thesis adviser. Whatever she did, her research would be in the adviser's lab. Jessica's adviser told her that the cancer research might lead to patents, a very good thing. But Jessica would largely be on her own, the lab had little expertise in that area, going down that path was risky, and it might delay her graduation. A more straightforward project would almost guarantee at least one and possibly two quick publications. The work might not end up on the cover of *Science,* but it was worth doing. The adviser recommended that alternative.

Jessica reflected on why she'd decided to do research in the first place and the excitement she felt about the potential for a breakthrough. Anything else felt like a compromise, and she didn't want to compromise at this stage in her life. She took the more risky project and secured her adviser's support. For a year and a half, she pursued that breakthrough by conducting experiments largely on her own. Small successes teased her, but she concluded that the outlook wasn't promising: "I watched some of the senior lab students do the same thing and not get the break they needed. Yet it wasn't easy to abandon that path. I had a lot of ego wrapped up in it, along with a lot of effort. This may have been sunk cost, but it still was hard to leave."

Jessica shifted to one of the earlier alternatives. Her work didn't end up on the cover of *Science*, but it did get into *Nature*. No one predicted that those relatively easy experiments would reveal a complex set of molecular interactions that changed the prevailing thinking in that area of bioscience.

Taking the risky path was easier than it might be in other circumstances, because there were good ways to shift her research if she needed to. Jessica had off-ramps—both because there were other good alternatives and because she maintained positive and active relationships with her adviser and with others in the lab. They liked her, wanted her to succeed, and supported her when she changed direction. She got back on track and finished her degree at almost the same time she'd have finished if her first research program had succeeded. Jessica had intuitively constructed a hedge. When things didn't develop as she'd wished, she took full advantage of it.

Take these steps to incorporate options and hedges into your strategy.

### 1. Identify the Natural Options and Hedges

Desirable options and hedges may come naturally with some alternatives. To imagine options, ask yourself: What will I have learned after a couple of years? What will I have accomplished? What new relationships—both in and outside the company—will I develop? What new directions might then be possible? Note when these same questions may suggest hedges. Also ask: What might I do if things aren't working out?

### 2. Try to Add or Enhance Options and Hedges

You also may be able to cultivate new options or hedges or to make an existing option or a hedge more accessible later. For example: What would you need to do to maintain former professional acquaintances? How might you enhance your knowledge and qualifications for other possibilities?

### 3. Determine How Options and Hedges Affect Offer Evaluation

Though frequently unstated, hedges and options are part of offers.

An offer that creates no options stands or falls entirely on its own intrinsic merits, whereas an alternative with options gets a higher rating. If you can't imagine an appealing off-ramp from one alternative, that's a disadvantage relative to a second alternative with good hedges.

I'll add another thought on hedging. Smart strategies often include a hedge, especially if results are highly uncertain. But once the hedge is in place, put it on the shelf. Don't let it detract from your main focus, your primary strategy. Do all you can to make that strategy successful.

Reflect on strategic intent, and you'll perceive the risks and opportunities more clearly. You may discover that an alternative you thought was risky can be pursued with little concern about downside. Or you may identify risks you'd missed. Categorization also can serve as a powerful brainstorming tool. Take the five categories as a starting point, and new alternatives may come to mind.

These forecasting and assessment techniques can guide you out of the uncertainty jungle. And remember, if you don't forecast and evaluate uncertainty, you're probably assuming that circumstances won't change much or that a single future scenario will play out. Making such an assumption is, in fact, the most risky choice of all.

Pull all the considerations in Chapters 12 and 13 together by *making the integrated case for each alternative.* State the reasons for each alternative, incorporating both the objectives assessment and the uncertainty assessment. Acknowledge the downside you'd be accepting with each alternative and how you'd deal with it. You'll benefit if you complete the cases on your own and put them in writing. You'll benefit still more if you review the cases with others.

Use these questions to test the answer you're coming to:

- Will the alternative meet your objectives?
- If you meet your objectives, will you be on track to achieving your long-term aspirations?
- Will the alternative manage uncertainty?
- Is there no better alternative?

Once you decide on your course of action, *record your decision and the reasons for it.* It's a good final test, and you'll be less likely to look back later and question why you did it. A search consultant described the benefit this way: "Write down the decisions and why. Keep it. Look back and reconstruct the logic. Otherwise, it's too easy at a later time to see other alternatives better."

After you've made your decision, update your strategic road map. If you accept a new position, the road map records your plans to succeed in the new position, the things you'll do beyond that to build your career, and where that might lead. You're resetting long-term strategy, with your new position as the starting point. If you're declining an offer and continuing to look, learn from your decision, refresh your opportunity search strategy, and then move forward on your search. And if you're staying with your current employer, prepare a new strategy to build your future from there.

I've described the evaluation methodologies in the context of helping you decide on a job offer. But as I mentioned before, the approach works for other career decisions. And be sure to use the alternatives/objectives decision matrix when buying a car!

## Part V

# STAYING POWER

Success is not final, failure is not fatal: it is the courage to continue that counts.

**WINSTON CHURCHILL**

There is only one way to happiness and that is to cease worrying about things which are beyond the power of our will.

**EPICTETUS**

**SOUND BUSINESS PRINCIPLES** can contribute to success at work in one more way. The best leaders stay on track when things change. They stay on top of developments in their businesses, often leveraging strategy updates and other processes to help them understand the situation, anticipate changes, and take action in that light. And they're personally resilient when events don't go their way. Without that toughness, they might succumb to the challenges all institutions encounter. Boards hire CEOs who they believe will stay on track. Those CEOs do the same when selecting leaders down the line.

In Part V, I describe two ways to build staying power through practices like these. If you can stay on track with the winning strategies you've developed as illustrated in Figure PV.1, you'll have moved from career strategy to The Strategic Career.

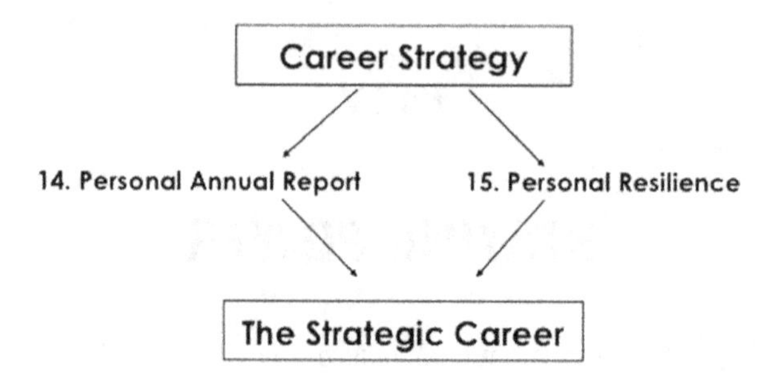


**FIGURE PV.1** Part V: Develop Staying Power

Just like most businesses, you'll benefit from a structured way to review progress and anticipate the future. Chapter 14 shows how to prepare your personal annual report to do just that.

Some disappointment is inevitable. Chapter 15 shows you ways to build the personal resilience you'll need to deal with those situations.

Chapter 14

# PERSONAL ANNUAL REPORT

**MANAGEMENT SHARES** lots of information with owners. Public companies report quarterly on financial performance, adhering to accounting standards and regulatory requirements (such as the annual reports and Form 10-K filings I mentioned earlier as a source of information for researching companies and industries). Most private company management teams provide similar reports to their owners and investors. These reports inform people outside management, but that's not all they do. They also can stimulate strategic thinking inside the company, because management won't be comfortable if early drafts of these public reports show problems but no plans to deal with those problems. And management teams sometimes conduct their own internal strategy reviews independent from these public reports.

It's essential to stay on top of events in your work life, but no reports are required except for your annual income tax return. You'll need to establish your own process to manage your career. For example, you can track developments in areas like these: your employer's prospects, how well you're doing there, whether you're enjoying the work, and whether your long-term plan still makes sense. No sleepwalking allowed!

I'll first describe the structured process Jackson developed to review progress and anticipate future developments in his career—what he called his "annual report." He uses it to gain insight and to tee up issues he might otherwise put off or avoid.

## Jackson's Annual Report

Jackson was a first-class management consultant. He cared both about his clients and about his institution. There were ups and downs, but most of the time he liked what he was doing. One reason for Jackson's success throughout his career is his natural listening skills. His annual reports are a productive way to listen to himself and to act on what he learns.

Jackson takes vacation each year in late December, usually skiing combined with family activities. In a low-key way, he also takes an hour or maybe half a day to review what he's accomplished that year and what he hopes to do the next year. It's a way for him to gain perspective. He gets the big picture clearly in mind and then usually can decide with confidence what he should do.

He starts where he was at the same time the year before. He updates that with feelings about colleagues, the substance of his work, and what he's learning and accomplishing. Sometimes he takes notes; other times he simply does this accounting in his head.

Time and time again, Jackson's annual report led him to conclude that he was doing what was right for him. He conceptually re-upped. But one year, he recognized that he was getting bored. He then engineered a transfer to another location and with that came a shift in clientele. He returned to a productive and enjoyable period.

Six years later, however, Jackson saw himself standing on a plateau. He'd stopped growing and no longer felt the excitement he'd had after the move. Here's how he described his annual report process:

> I almost always had two weeks off, or close to it. It was also family time. Being with family forced me to deal with feelings about the lifestyle. Early on, I had a pretty simple way of gauging where I stood—a good day/not-so-good day tally. Sometimes I kept written track of it; often I simply reflected on it once a week or while on planes. My view was pretty simple: if the good days—defined as a feeling of accomplishment and growth, mainly, but also including strength of personal relationships—outnumbered the not-so-good days. Immediately prior to getting elected a partner, that ratio was two-thirds or three-quarters positive.
>
> Later, I tended to think through my program. That led me shortly after election to realize I no longer wanted to work in the same commodity industries. I wanted to work with clients who sold differentiated products. Six months later, we moved to another office where there were more of these opportunities.
>
> My decision to leave consulting occurred as I was headed off to Christmas break. While there were a number of reasons why it was time for me to leave, the main reason was that I simply did not have the desire or energy to continue. I knew it was the right decision when I felt a profound sense of relief over the holidays.

Jackson had had a calling or was close to it, but he lost it. The discipline of creating his annual report helped him realize what he was thinking and feeling. It encouraged him to decide and to act. Without that discipline, he might have stayed another year or perhaps several more years. If he'd waited to leave until then, he'd certainly have been frustrated and maybe a bit angry at himself. Annual reports can do a lot of good for most everyone.

## Creating Your Annual Report

Here's how to put together your personal annual report:

## What to Cover

If you've already done serious career thinking, your annual report won't require much preparation. It will be more about reflection than fact gathering and analysis—though that reflection can raise issues that you may decide to assess in depth.

Your aspirations and PVP are the baseline, but the inquiry shifts, as you'll see here.

- Ask: What's different from the last time I thought about my career direction?
- Instead of asking yourself, What are my aspirations? ask: How well am I meeting near-term objectives? Where am I on the road to reaching my long-term aspirations? Are those aspirations still the right ones?
- Instead of asking yourself, What's my PVP? ask: How is my PVP changing? Are my capabilities growing as much as I need them to?
- Instead of asking yourself, What should be my long-term initiatives? ask: Am I executing my long-term initiatives well? Are they working? Am I putting the right effort behind them? Should I take other initiatives?
- Instead of drafting the article, ask: How might I edit that article?

Reviewing past recorded decisions and their rationale can stimulate your thinking. Revisit your reasons for those decisions and consider how they're working out.

A last stimulus can come from your strategic road map. Where you are on that plan and what you'd intended from this point forward are natural inputs into your review of progress.

Collectively, these activities will allow you to update past conclusions and objectives, check on progress, and think about the implications.

## What Form to Use

Prepare a single page that covers two topics. First, list the big things that are happening or that might happen—for example, progress toward aspirations, your level of happiness or satisfaction, changes in your PVP, your view of your institution and role, the outlook for your institution and your field, and what's next on your long-term plan. Second, list any decisions you see on the horizon. For the most part, these decisions will relate to the events mentioned at the top of the page.

This page will trigger insights about your strategic situation at the time. If you keep these pages over the years, they'll also serve as a written record of your career. Looking back, you may notice patterns you'd otherwise miss. This can be a gold mine of information and insight about yourself.

## When to Do It

I suggest working on your annual report at the same time each year, perhaps around holidays at the end of the year, near your birthday, or after receiving an annual performance appraisal. There's ample precedent for picking the same time each year—the president's State of the Union address, an annual checkup with your physician, and a corporation's annual report. A personal annual report directs your attention to strategy once a year. When you've completed it, put it aside and focus on being successful in your work the rest of the year.

Alternatively, you can create a report when you need it. It's natural to revisit strategy when something's changing or when you're restless. Maybe you expect to be asked to change positions in your organization a year from now. Maybe it will soon be time to decide whether to obtain a certification in your field or a graduate degree. Perhaps there's a conflict with a supervisor.

Steve, the corporate CEO whose three-person network routinely presented new opportunities to him, used a limited version of this approach. He didn't write out an annual report, but he was prompted to do a quick recheck like this at least once a year when people called him about a job he found intriguing.

One unusual self-assessment approach is minister Alan's. It's not annual, but from time to time he writes a sermon about his calling. As he told me, "I try to confront that original call to come home and serve people. What that means. If it comes up blank, I'm done. I have to find meaning in that." This sermon guides him, and it connects him to his congregation.

Creating a personal annual report is good practice in careers—stepping back, noticing what's happening, and thinking through the implications. A second aspect of staying on track is developing the personal resilience required to deal with disappointment, the subject I'll cover next.

## Chapter 15

# PERSONAL RESILIENCE

**EVEN THE STRONGEST CAREER STRATEGY** and excellent performance at work can't guarantee that everything will go as you wish. Everyone needs resilience to respond when setbacks appear. Resilience contributes significantly to a strategic career.

Resilience comes from several sources. A sound career strategy that leads to accomplishments and expertise builds resilience. People want to work with craftsmen, and high performance makes it easier to land on your feet. Financial resources create space and time to handle whatever comes along. Follow the suggestions in this book, and you'll be on your way to this kind of toughness.

There's another aspect of resilience: cultivating the ability to maintain perspective and stay productive when things are going badly.

Imagine someone looking for a job. He has a solid track record. His job search strategy reflects aspirations he trusts, a winning PVP, and a strong professional network. He's putting good effort into executing that strategy. But what if no good opportunities have surfaced after three months? Maybe it's been hard to set up network discussions, or perhaps the network is coming up dry. Or maybe there've been possibilities, but the interviews haven't led anywhere. The anticipation of landing a position may have created energy to prepare thoroughly. With a lot riding on the interviews, however, maybe he didn't sleep well the night before, his handshakes were moist with perspiration, he looked nervous, he didn't really listen to the interviewer, and he stumbled when asked questions. Or perhaps he felt good about the interviews, but then the hot conversation went cold, and follow-up calls weren't returned. Maybe there was only a single job opening rather than several. Or management may have promised the position to an internal candidate and viewed outside interviews as necessary to complete a required process. He can't find out what's going on.

People can be crushed when things like this happen. They feel that they've failed. They learn little. They're immobilized. Where can you find strength and courage when you need it?

## Two People Facing Tough Challenges

Two people who sprung back from disappointment were graduate student Erika, whose job search was failing, and financial adviser Edward, who'd just been laid off. For me, their stories never get old.

### Inventing Erika's job

Twenty-six-year-old Erika was nearing graduation with a master's degree in public health. And she didn't have a job.

Her summer intern position had been with a health care company near school. Those two months had gone well, and she was asked to return full-time after graduation. Although she liked the people and the role, she turned it down. This job was ideal except for location. She had a relationship with a man who worked in a different part of the country. She hoped to find the right position in his city or close to it.

In February, her school's placement office identified a position in that city with just the kind of work she sought. A first meeting on campus went well, and she was invited to travel for an interview. She had three weeks to prepare.

With the PVP concept in mind, Erika positioned herself with strong quantitative skills, knowledge of different parts of the field, and the ability to create and maintain relationships. She felt she was distinctive—not a geek, though good with technology, but also someone who could link technology to markets.

She wanted to do more than just talk about herself. She hoped to bring some interesting content to the visit, maybe give the people whom she'd meet something they hadn't thought about, and in that way let them see what it would be like to work with her. Fine idea, but what was that content? Erika researched the two products the company was developing and what they'd need to accomplish to be a hit. One of her courses gave her a perspective on a challenge they faced, and that's what she took on the trip. The presentation went well. She knew she'd made a good impression.

There was another good possibility. Erika had contacted her cousin attending another university. His career office listed an attractive position in her target region. She applied and was invited to visit for an intense day and a half of interviews. Three days after returning to school, she was asked to return the next week for a second visit. She felt that went well.

So in early April six weeks before graduation, Erika had done everything right: clear objective, smart PVP, networking, and solid interview preparation. She had two strong possibilities and was confident at least one would come through.

By the end of the week, however, Erika learned that neither company had selected her. A PhD with ten years of industry experience got the offer at the first company. The people she'd met there told her she did well, but that he was a stronger candidate. The second company had had 250 applicants; they interviewed 100 on the phone, interviewed 50 in the first round, and met a smaller number in round two. They hired three people, and Erika wasn't one of the them.

Not a good place to be. Erika could continue job search after graduation, but there was no guarantee that summer recruiting would be more successful than her last few months had been. She wanted to settle things sooner than that.

She could have been devastated. Here's what she said about her reaction at the time:

> It was really hard. School ends in a month. It felt like a deadline. I was stressed out. But you can't do that. It's really important to remain confident to be ready for future interviews. I was well prepared. Doing the presentation at the first company showed me I could add real value. The interview experience prepared me for almost anything. I did twenty interviews across these two companies in a single week in late March. Before, I was confident in my ability, but not in my ability to articulate it. After the interviews, I felt I'd be fine in any interview. There was no point in getting upset. I knew I was capable at getting a job. There are a lot of jobs out there. I had to be proactive. So I started over.

Her interviewing skill was no surprise to me. I'd seen her engage in class discussion in a way that wasn't exactly funny but that left many in class with smiles on their faces. I'd also seen how she could disagree by using questions rather than arguing. She was a natural at standing in the other person's shoes.

One of Erika's courses had included a short project with people in other university departments, and she'd met one member of that PhD class. Recalling his plan to found a health care company, she contacted him to learn how things were developing. The company was up and running and soon would locate in her target region. A nice coincidence!

The new company had good technical talent, but over several conversations it became clear both to her and to him that the organization lacked relationship management know-how. That was one of Erika's core strengths. She conceived a business development role to try to speed customer trial. The founder hadn't envisioned needing to do this so soon, but after talking with her he realized the potential to accelerate. That's the job she began in July.

Erika's amazing. Not getting either of the two offers didn't mean she was a failure. She knew that she was competitive in her target field. She knew her job search skills were growing. She approached the continued search with energy and optimism. The surprising possibility with the man she knew casually from school was a position that didn't exist until after she spoke to him. She didn't fill an opening she found at her career office. She identified the company. She created the job.

Let's shift from school to finance. Not long after Lehman Brothers went bankrupt in 2008, Wall Street firms looked at their cost structures and made big cuts. One of the people terminated was Edward.

## Edward's Comeback

Edward left the Marine Corps at twenty-eight, joined a private wealth management group, went through their training program, and began finding clients. According to the records the company shared with staff, he had more assets under management than any other member of the class of sixteen people who joined his group that year. At the three-year point, Edward assumed he was in a strong position.

When he was called in by his boss, he expected to be congratulated for bringing in a new client the day before. New clients were especially valued at a time when financial markets were reeling. But no, he was one of the 20 percent terminated. This highly impersonal process included an immediate trip with people from the compliance department to clean out his office. No one, certainly not his management, seemed sympathetic or at all interested in him.

No one told Edward why he'd been selected. He's not sure, but believes it was because his accounts didn't emphasize the investment products that earned higher fees for the bank. He also was slow to introduce his clients to more senior people at the firm. Many were personal connections, and he saw no reason why he couldn't handle them on his own.

This was not a good time for anyone to lose a job, certainly not for people in finance. Edward faced special challenges. He and his wife had just bought their first house and had their third child. He was open about his feelings: "The hardest thing was telling my wife that evening. She fell down on the couch and cried for most of an hour. For two days I didn't sleep. The firm brings you in, they transform your life, and then there's no loyalty to the people or to the clients."

Edward had no interest in the two large investment companies that called him about jobs. They were more of the same. Then he learned he could become an independent financial adviser while contracting to a service firm to handle administration and legal requirements. He wouldn't be selling any particular firm's investment products. He could pit those firms against each other in the interest of his clients. He'd have no compensation unless he had clients, but finding clients had never been Edward's problem, and several had told him they'd move with him. So he took the plunge and went into business for himself. Within twenty-four hours of signing on, he was up and running.

Edward's been quite a success. He transitioned 80 percent of his client list to his new business, and now his time is spent more on serving his clients than on prospecting for new ones. Most new clients are referrals. He's spending more time with his children. Compensation is three times what it had been at his old firm.

Being terminated turned out to be a blessing in disguise.

Events could have taken a different course. Edward might have slid into depression and self-doubt. He might have shut down. I asked him why that didn't happen. His view was this: "It's not about me. It's about my clients. It's about my wife and kids. It's not why this happened to me. It's get better or get bitter."

His client focus helped. If he was right about why he'd been selected for termination, it was because he had put clients' interests before the firm's. That was nothing to feel bad about; it was behavior to be proud of.

Edward also put things in perspective: "I'm not on a train to Auschwitz. I'm not in a combat zone. This is peanuts. How dare I get hurt by this?" This former Marine recalled one of the premises of Officer Candidate School: "adapt and improvise." That's what he did over the six weeks he took to reassess his situation, his interests, and what he could do about them. He concluded, "I have all the skills and all the education. It's about what I'm going to do with it." At the end of that period, he had a blueprint to set up an independent business, to add more value to his clients, and to move clients to his new shop.

Edward knew that being terminated didn't reflect badly on him; he detached himself from the bad experience and put his attention on what to do about it. After a brief period that was something like mourning, he played the cards he'd been dealt rather than worrying about why his luck was so bad. That attitude gave him courage. And it was courage that led him to take the risk to start his own business, to be successful there, and now to enjoy the benefits of a calling. Edward's resilient, that's for sure.

You've seen two models of resilience—Erika's job search and Edward's response to being fired. How to build your personal resilience is where we go next.

## Finding Resilience

The topic of personal resilience is huge. It's embedded in many philosophical and religious traditions.[1] That broad and important topic is far beyond the scope of this book. But in the context of career strategy, there are several ways to seek resilience.

## 1. Prepare a First-Class Plan and Follow It

If you're well prepared and you're aggressively following a sound plan, you'll be in a strong position to deal with whatever happens. Your strategy may not have worked yet, but confidence comes from doing what creates the prospect of success. You have permission to be frustrated about the results so far, but there's no reason to blame yourself. It's your fault only if you don't prepare or if you don't execute.

If you're emphasizing values that we know can lead to a calling, then you start with an advantage. Working for service, craftsmanship, or institution can be a high purpose, and that high purpose can provide the energy needed to bounce back from a bad outcome.

## 2. Detach

Maintain a healthy distance from the result.

No matter how sound your plan or how well you execute it, some things won't work. There's randomness. Recognize the inherent uncertainty in your endeavor. Recognize that a lack of success may have nothing to do with you.

Take a look at the Alcoholics Anonymous program's Serenity Prayer. It has advice for job seekers just as it does for people needing help with addiction: "Give me the serenity to accept the things I cannot change, the courage to change the things I can, and the wisdom to know the difference."

I'll illustrate this concept of detachment with a sometimes stressful aspect of career strategy: the job interview. Who conducts the interview, how skilled she is at it, and what kind of day she's having can affect the interview and the hiring decision. All of that is outside your control.

To prepare for the interview, follow the suggestions in Part III to think through your winning PVP and how to make your case. Don't spend time imagining how happy you'd be if you got an offer or how your friends would react if you didn't. Thoughts like those can create pressure and distract your attention from what's required to have great interviews. They can increase your disappointment if things don't develop as you hope they will.

In the interview, focus on the substance of the discussion. Listen to what the interviewer is saying or asking. Think about your response. Do your best at that, and don't let anything else get in your way (or in your head). Your best shot is to center on the content of the work you're seeking and a full execution of your search strategy. Think of it this way: "If I prepare and emphasize the substance of the interview, I'll do my best and give myself the best possible odds."

### 3. Notice Small Victories

No matter how sound your search plan or your more general networking, many successful activities—for example, setting up a meeting with someone who can provide important insight or having a great meeting with an executive at a company that has no job openings—won't lead anywhere. These things weren't easy to do, but you did them well, and even though they have no immediate result, you can recognize those achievements and take some pride in them. That will help keep your energy up.

### 4. Work with Others

At the outset, I suggested reading this book with someone else to test your thinking and learn from each other. Whether they're reading the book or not, you'll do well to compare notes with other job seekers or with others who are serious about long-term strategy initiatives. They can push you to follow a sensible plan. They can provide support if you get discouraged, and you can do the same for them.

### 5. Learn and Adjust

Pay attention to what's happening.

If what you're doing isn't working the way you expected, slow down and reassess. Maybe the preparation you're doing isn't enough. Maybe you're reaching too high for now and aren't yet competitive for the jobs you're targeting. Perhaps the culture's not right for you. Maybe you're not approaching people in your network in the right way. Or maybe you need to pause for a while and reconstruct that network or get some additional education or a certification.

Disappointments can be positive if they lead to a strong career strategy. That's exactly what happened to Erika and Edward, and they aren't the only ones. For example, remember Pallab, who shifted his PVP to empathy when he was terminated, and then found a new position. Or take Dr. George, whose growing unhappiness with his practice and his health issue led him to a position he loved. And recall how Nina's discomfort with her institution's culture led her to commit to art. I hope you won't experience big disappointments, but if you do, I hope you'll learn from them and refashion your strategy.

Don't shut down. Learn from what's happening and adjust. That will keep you targeted on success and productive. It will improve the odds of a good result in the inherently uncertain world of careers.

I don't know anyone who's seen everything go exactly as he or she wished it would in their work lives. You'll face challenging situations. Don't let events take their course. Consciously cultivate personal resilience. Maintaining perspective will not only enable you to feel better in a tough situation but also help you respond to that situation in a productive way.

# CONCLUSIONS

**I'LL MAKE THREE BROAD POINTS** to conclude the book. I'll first present a short summary of the book's principal takeaways. Then I'll describe the benefits you can realize if you not only develop a winning career strategy now but also build career strategy skill. Finally, I'll reflect on the potential benefit to our broader society if more and more people develop and follow winning career strategies over their work lives.

## This Book's Elevator Speech

An elevator speech that explains how you meet a target employer's needs is a critical ingredient in opportunity search. I covered that topic in Chapter 10, but I raise it again now to suggest this question: What is the elevator speech for this book? Here's the three-minute version.

The foundation of this book is business strategy. Business strategy principles are conceptually identical to the principles that can guide careers, and people who use them to plot their career will benefit greatly. Those people certainly can be in business, but the principles apply just as well in other fields of work.

The book shows how to deploy these principles in addressing the five big career challenges: determining aspirations for the long term, building the strengths and presence needed to realize those aspirations, finding good opportunities in the near term, deciding which opportunity to accept, and building staying power. Out of all that, the book's seven most important takeaways are these.

## Calling

Seek a calling in work that emphasizes service, craft, and institution and that capitalizes on your strengths. Put these fundamentals of work first, not the rewards from work. When you do that, you're giving yourself an excellent prospect for accomplishment, happiness, and satisfaction.

## Personal Value Proposition

The PVP is the heart of career strategy. It's your target field or role, what's required to succeed there, how you meet that requirement, and what you expect in return. Everything then flows from your PVP. Your aspirational PVP guides long-term strategy. Your current PVP guides near-term opportunity search.

## Long-Term Strategy

Build your aspirational PVP by following a strategic road map of initiatives to strengthen your product through the positions you hold and the educational experiences you have. Also take initiatives to build marketing muscle by creating reputation and network. Do that, and you'll be competitive for the positions you want and well equipped to find them.

## Opportunity Search

To identify opportunities that match your current PVP, reach out aggressively to your professional network and to others you can meet. Make your best case as it's summarized in that PVP.

### Decisions

Thorough assessments will give you a strong basis for the big decisions. Evaluate how well different alternatives meet your objectives. Forecast scenarios of what may happen if you pick one alternative or another, and evaluate how well your alternatives manage the uncertainty.

### Rigor

Strategy principles are just principles. Although they can lead to deep insight, they have little meaning until they're interpreted in actual situations with facts and judgments. What separates the better strategists from the also-rans is the quality of understanding of those situations. Rigor wins.

### Staying Power

Even with the best career strategy, you will experience surprises and disappointments. Routinely check on your progress and learn from what's happening. You may be on the path to your calling, or you may need to shift direction. Cultivate personal resilience to deal with those disappointments. That's how to stay on track.

Let these principles guide your career, and you'll be in a good position to find the calling you want and to enjoy the results.

## The Benefits from Career Strategy Skill

If you become proficient at applying career strategy principles, you'll have developed career strategy skill, a skill that people don't normally consider a part of their arsenal. Why develop career strategy skill? Here's another lesson from the business world.

Many companies follow the same strategy year after year. That simplifies everything. Organization processes, structures, and systems are set with that strategy in mind. People cultivate the skills needed for their role in executing that strategy.

Good for them—or, I should say, good for them until something important changes, and that strategy no longer works. Maybe a new technology causes the old strategy to fail. Or perhaps it's new regulations, market shifts, or new competitors. When these sorts of changes occur, the company's leaders may need a very different strategy and not know how to get one. Or if they recognize the strategic shift required, their fossilized organization may not support that new strategy, and their people may not have the skills needed.

Other companies, in contrast, get ahead of the curve. They cultivate nimble organizations with skills in strategy development and change management. That's essential in fast-changing industries and new ventures. What might this suggest about careers?

Decades back, careers were simpler. People were more likely to accept what the work world served up. Today, people expect more from their work life—not only achievements and financial rewards but also personal fulfillment and meaning. And job satisfaction has declined. A 2010 report by the Conference Board found that only 45 percent of people in the United States were satisfied with their jobs, down from 61 percent in 1981.[1]

It wasn't that long ago when people could commit to a single employer with a good chance that they would stay with that company until it was time to retire. Or at least they could commit to a single field and expect to remain in that field over the course of their work life. They may have had less freedom and less opportunity, but they also had more stability and security. That world's a distant memory. I doubt it exists for anyone in management or in the professions today. Situations change. Challenges appear. Opportunities knock.

I hope you'll use this book now to establish an unbeatable career strategy. I hope the strategy leads you to a calling, with the happiness and satisfaction that callings can provide, not the uncertain prospects that can come with a career mentality and certainly not the unhappiness or disconnectedness that can come with a job. When you do that, you'll find you're also growing career strategy skill.

Repeat this process when you reach the next juncture. Your assessment should be more instinctive the second time around, and you'll augment your career strategy skill. If a friend is facing a tough career choice, draw on these concepts to help him or her while multiplying your skills. Follow the model provided by successful companies that continuously prepare for change. Your career strategy skill will equip you to deal with changes throughout your work life. It will be an important asset year after year.

## The Broader Benefits of Winning Career Strategies

Winning career strategies will be good for everyone who has them, but they won't only be good for individuals. They'll also be good for employers. Or at least they'll be good for those enlightened employers who can attract, develop, motivate, and retain the people who have winning strategies. They're the people who will make big things happen.

Gallup surveyed people on their levels of engagement at work.[2] Using 2012 data from the United States, the study team concluded that 30 percent were "engaged" (defined, for example, as working with passion), 52 percent were "unengaged" (referred to as checked out and sleepwalking), and 18 percent were "actively disengaged" (undermining others at work). These differences in engagement correlated with differences in profitability, quality, safety, and several other goals most enterprises share. These engaged people sound very much like the calling people I've known.

Highly engaged employees are very good for employers. Companies that attract and retain highly committed people will benefit greatly. Their organizations will be more capable, and accomplishments will expand. Companies that fail to attract and retain these people will decline.

Imagine how different our world would be if a good number of people shifted from casual career choices to purposeful strategic plans. If you and others do that, many will find callings that will lead to greater accomplishment, personal satisfaction, and happiness. They will have found The Strategic Career that works for them. Ultimately, they will build a better society. That's my aspiration for this book.

# NOTES

## Chapter 1

1. Amy Wrzesniewski, "Finding Positive Meaning in Work," in *Positive Organizational Scholarship: Foundation of a New Discipline* (San Francisco: Berrett-Koehler, 2003), 296–308.

2. For example, see Martin E. P. Seligman, *Authentic Happiness: Using the New Positive Psychology to Realize Your Potential for Lasting Fulfillment* (New York: Free Press, 2002); and Robert Frank, *Luxury Fever: Weighing the Cost of Excess* (Princeton: Princeton University Press, 1999).

3. Daniel Kahneman and Angus Deaton, "High Income Improves Evaluation of Life but Not Emotional Well-Being," *Proceedings of the National Academy of Sciences,* August 4, 2010, http://www.pnas.org/content/107/38/16489.full.

4. Bryan J. Dik and Ryan D. Duffy, *Make Your Job a Calling: How the Psychology of Vocation Can Change Your Life at Work* (West Conshohoken, PA: Templeton Press, 2012).

## Chapter 2

1. For a deeper perspective on how using strengths can lead to happiness, I suggest: Martin E. P. Seligman, *Authentic Happiness: Using the New Positive Psychology to Realize Your Potential for Lasting Fulfillment* (New York: Free Press, 2002).

2. See, for example, the surveys at authentichappiness.sas.upenn.edu and StrengthsFinder.

3. Laura Morgan Roberts, Gretchen Spreitzer, Jane E. Dutton, Robert E. Quinn, Emily Heaphy, and Brianna Barker, "How to Play to Your Strengths," *Harvard Business Review,* January 2005, https://hbr.org/2005/01/how-to-play-to-your-strengths.

## Chapter 3

1. Barbara Sher's book describes a wide range of brainstorming techniques, including these extreme exercises and the perfect/horrible job exercise. Barbara

Sher, *I Could Do Anything If I Only Knew What It Was: How to Discover What You Really Want and How to Get It* (New York: Dell, 1994), 33–38.

## Chapter 4

1. These publications are at bls.gov/ooh/ and at onetonline.org.

2. Michael Porter, *Competitive Strategy: Techniques for Analyzing Industries and Competitors* (New York: Simon & Schuster, 1980).

3. Herminia Ibarra, *Working Identity: Unconventional Strategies for Reinventing Your Career* (Boston: Harvard Business Publishing, 2004).

## Chapter 5

1. Ed Michaels, Helen Handfield-Jones, and Beth Axelrod, *The War for Talent* (Boston: Harvard Business Publishing, 2001).

## Chapter 6

1. Sheryl Sandberg, *Lean In: Women, Work, and the Will to Lead* (New York: Knopf, 2013), 53–60.

2. Amy Wrzesniewski, Justin Berg, and Jane Dutton, "Managing Yourself: Turn the Job You Have into the Job You Want," *Harvard Business Review*, June 2010, https://hbr.org/2010/06/managing-yourself-turn-the-job-you-have-into-the-job-you-want.

3. Mark S. Granovetter, "The Strength of Weak Ties," *American Journal of Sociology* 78, no. 6 (May 1973), 1360–1380.

4. Adam Grant, *Give and Take: A Revolutionary Approach to Success* (New York: Viking, 2013).

## Chapter 7

1. A good discussion of highly adaptive career strategies and their similarities to start-ups is found in Reid Hoffman and Ben Casnocha, *The Start-Up of You: Adapt to the Future, Invest in Yourself, and Transform Your Career* (New York: Random House, 2012).

## Chapter 8

1. Barry Schwartz, *The Paradox of Choice: Why More Is Less* (New York: HarperCollins Publishers, 2004).

## Chapter 10

1. If you'd like to read more about how to craft your story, I suggest: Herminia Ibarra and Kent Lineback, "What's Your Story," *Harvard Business Review*, January 2005, https://hbr.org/2005/01/whats-your-story.

2. How leaders interview is one of the topics in the Corner Office column by Adam Bryant in the *New York Times*; that's a good ongoing source of ideas for career strategists.

3. Although there's no perfect guide to prepare for case interviews, one book to consider is: Marc P. Cosentino, *Case in Point* (Needham, MA: Burgee Press, 2001).

## Chapter 13

1. If you'd like to learn more about the business side, I recommend: Hugh Courtney, Jane Kirkland, and Patrick Viguerie, "Strategy Under Uncertainty," *Harvard Business Review,* November-December 1997, https://hbr.org/1997/11/strategy-under-uncertainty/ar/1; and Hugh Courtney, *20/20 Foresight: Crafting Strategy in an Uncertain World* (Boston: Harvard Business Publishing, 2001).

2. The book Sean read was Po Bronson, *What Should I Do with My Life? The True Story of People Who Answered the Ultimate Question* (New York: Random House Books, 2002).

## Chapter 15

1. People have written about this topic through the ages. One book I like on this is: Jonathan Haidt, *The Happiness Hypothesis: Finding Modern Truth in Ancient Wisdom* (New York: Basic Books, 2006).

## Conclusions

1. John M Gibbons, "I Can't Get No . . . Job Satisfaction, That Is," The Conference Board Research Report #1459-09-RR, January 5, 2010.

2. Gallup, "State of the American Workplace: Employee Engagement Insights for U.S. Business Leaders," 2013, http://www.gallup.com/strategicconsulting/163007/state-american-workplace.aspx. The sample in this survey is broader than the professionals, managers, and executives who are this book's main target audience.

# INDEX

CPSIA information can be obtained
at www.ICGtesting.com
Printed in the USA
BVHW030655220820
587069BV00005B/58